COLD WAR CASUALTY

Major General Robert W. Grow (1949).
Courtesy of the U.S. Army, National Archives

COLD WAR CASUALTY

The Court-Martial of

Major General Robert W. Grow

GEORGE F. HOFMANN

THE KENT STATE UNIVERSITY PRESS
Kent, Ohio, and London, England

© 1993 by *The Kent State University Press,* Kent, Ohio 44242
All rights reserved
Library of Congress Catalog Card Number 92-30839
ISBN 0-87338-462-8
Manufactured in the United States of America

Library of Congress Cataloging-in-Publication Data

Hofmann, George F.
    Cold war casualty : the court-martial of Major General Robert W.
Grow / George F. Hofmann.
       p.   cm.
    Includes bibliographical references and index.
    ISBN 0-87338-462-8 (cloth : alk. paper) ∞
    1. Grow, Robert W.—Trials, litigation, etc. 2. Grow, Robert W.—
Diaries. 3. Trials (Military offenses)—Maryland—Fort George G.
Meade. 4. Courts-martial and courts of inquiry—United States.
I. Title.
KF7642.G76H6 1993
343.752'55'0143—dc20
[347.525503143]   92-30839

British Library Cataloging-in-Publication data are available.

To my mother
Helene Stoppelkamp Hofmann

The accused is entitled to a fair and impartial trial; that none of the demands of discipline require that he be deprived of the safeguards provided for an accused by the Constitution; that provision should be made for conducting the trial according to law; and that the question whether the accused has been given a fair and impartial trial is one of law, which should be decided by a judicial tribunal and not by a military officer claiming to act by right of command without respect to or regard for law.

Colonel Edmund H. Morgan
Yale University

CONTENTS

ABBREVIATIONS

AR	Army Regulation
CIA	Central Intelligence Agency
CIC	Counter Intelligence Corps
CINCEUR	Commander in Chief, U.S. European Command
CIS	Criminal Investigation Service
CPO	Chief Petty Officer
DC of S, OA	Deputy Chief of Staff for Operations and Administration
DDR	German Democratic Republic
EUCOM	European Command
G-1	Personnel
G-2	Intelligence
G-3	Plans and Operations
HICOG	High Commissioner for Germany
IDC	Individual Defense Counsel
IG	Inspector General
IO	Investigation Officer
JAGC	Judge Advocates General Corps
JCS	Joint Chiefs of Staff
MCM	*Manual for Courts-Martial*
MGB	Ministry for State Security
SED	Socialische Einheitspartei Deutschlands
TDY	Temporary Duty
USCMA	United States Court of Military Appeals

PREFACE

THIS BOOK IS about the general court-martial of Major General Robert W. Grow, senior United States military attaché in Moscow from July 1950 to January 1952. General Grow commanded the 6th Armored Division during World War II and was a major participant in implementing the postwar containment policy in Iran. His court-martial occurred during a period of international and domestic tensions, an era of fear generated by the residual effects of the world war, Soviet expansion abroad, and alleged communist subversion in the United States. The court-martial was the first in which a general officer was accused of using questionable judgment in keeping a personal diary that contained sensitive information, portions of which fell into communist hands. Media in communist countries and the United States paid considerable attention to Grow's diary, embarrassing the army staff in the Pentagon, who decided to prosecute the unfortunate attaché rather than refute the charges. The court-martial was a national and international cause célèbre in 1952.

The erosion of civil liberties, media pressures and propaganda, paranoia about spies, and bureaucratic intrigues provided the political context that resulted in Grow's court-martial. Grow was afforded the usual option for fallen generals—voluntary retirement rather than public disgrace—but he decided to withdraw his retirement request and take a chance with the military justice system.

Disciplinary actions against generals are usually handled outside the military justice system. An example was President Harry S. Truman's unceremonious relief of General Douglas MacArthur because of their fundamental disagreement over the nature and scope of the

Korean War. During the Kennedy administration, Major General Edwin Walker, commanding general of the 24th Infantry Division in West Germany, distributed right-wing propaganda to his troops and publicly criticized the administration's foreign policy. He resigned his commission. Years later, Major General John Singlaub, chief of staff of the U.S.-South Korean Combined Forces Command, twice publicly condemned policies of the Carter administration. He took an early retirement.

The key relationships in the Grow episode involved the army staff and the media; the army staff, command influence, and the Uniform Code of Military Justice; the army staff and managerial careerism; bureaucratic intrigues between and within the army staff, the State Department, and the Central Intelligence Agency (CIA); and the question of a military ethos of service and self-interest. The key event was the decision by an army staff management group in the Pentagon to prosecute rather than counter the charges against Grow. The military justice system became a tool for command influence.

The reader may conclude at times that I am pleading a defense for General Grow. I must emphasize that my position is based entirely on extensive evaluation of primary sources and supported by secondary sources and oral interviews. General Grow should be viewed as a lens so as to understand the internal and external forces that interacted during the foreign and domestic turbulence of the early 1950s and their effects on military management.

In 1974, I was introduced to General Grow's son Colonel Robert Grow, who commented in passing that his father's court-martial was worth a historian's investigation. My curiosity was aroused. Preliminary research showed inconsistencies in the records. Documents were lost or misplaced, and several of the participants were not entirely truthful about their involvement or declined to discuss the incident. General Grow was also reluctant to discuss the case. He had accepted the decision of the army and the court as an order to be obeyed. Time spent in readdressing the army's decision in 1952 also took a toll on the general. Eventually, he consented to release documents and made available his diaries for the post–World War II era. For this I am grateful. Finally, I promised the general not to publish anything about the episode until at least two years after his death. He passed away in November 1985. Nevertheless, I was able to share part of my research with the general before his death. He was not aware of many events surrounding his trial, especially the degree of command influence staged by the army staff in the Pentagon. Although suspicious of Pentagon intrigues, he sincerely believed in the honor and justice of the military legal system.

Special appreciation is extended to the Department of the Army for support during my research and for photographs made available through Public Affairs and the Intelligence and Security Command. Without the army's cooperation, this book would have been impossible. I must emphasize, however, that all opinions based on analysis of primary sources are mine and do not reflect official views of the Department of the Army or any other government agency. I appreciate the cooperation of the National Archives, National Defense University Library, Department of State, and Central Intelligence Agency. Though responsive, the CIA withheld clues identifying some of the participants in the Grow case. These people were known, and their actions were conspicuous. Analysis of their activity was important because one aspect of this historical discourse was to measure the link between the army staff in the Pentagon and the CIA regarding an episode that became a public issue because of extensive and mismanaged media coverage. Another problem was the consistent vagueness and frequent "no recall" in responses from some army staff members actively involved in the incident. Because of the conspicuous actions of certain army staff members who maintained a "no recall" and the pruning of CIA documents and excessive use of cryptonyms, I offer a disclaimer regarding the actions of particular individuals mentioned in this book. Because of these deletions, I was not made privy to the exact bureaucratic actions of CIA participants who interacted with the army staff. Other than this, I assume full responsibility for analysis and interpretation of sources.

I was fortunate to receive a grant from the University Research Council, University of Cincinnati, which was supplemented by the Veterans Assistance Program. Their financial assistance and support made the research possible. Special thanks go to Ben H. Schleider, Jr., of Schleider, Ewing and Frances, Houston, Texas, who not only offered valuable advice but carried the civil action against the Central Intelligence Agency (CA 80-1792, *George F. Hofmann* v. *United States*

Central Intelligence Agency, et al.). Unfortunately, financial considerations prevented an appeal.

I wish to extend sincere thanks to my mentors and peers at the University of Cincinnati, Department of History, especially Professors William D. Aeschbacker, Daniel R. Beaver, Otis C. Mitchell, and David V. Sterling, and Professor of Military Science Lieutenant Colonel Spencer V. Carey, U.S. Army, for guidance and constructive criticism. To a past president of the 6th Armored Division Association, Forrest C. Herbert, who also read the manuscript, special thanks is in order. He was a close friend of General Grow and described the anguish the general experienced years after the trial. In spite of the disgrace, Grow maintained a strong sense of loyalty to the army, the armor branch, and the members of his division. Eventually, this attitude prevailed, and the general was given due credit by his peers for his many years of honorable service to his country. Other members of the 6th Armored Division Association who need to be acknowledged are Charles W. Barbour, Embry D. Lagrew, James S. Moncrief, Jr., Edward Reed, and former United States Senator J. Caleb Boggs.

I am grateful to certain individuals who graciously provided reinforcement and guidance. The late Joseph D. Heard, unofficial mayor of Fort Knox, provided invaluable direction and views on protocol. The concepts of late Colonel Robert J. Icks, U.S. Army, Retired, on military ethics provided the substance for my thesis. Our numerous discussions and his reassurance proved invaluable. Perhaps the key catalyst in offering the manuscript for publication is General Donn A. Starry, U.S. Army, Retired. His numerous comments, suggestions, advice, and encouragement gave me the incentive to complete the manuscript at a time when I had reservations concerning the past actions of certain army personnel of high military rank. Two associates from the Society for Military History, Professors Allan R. Millett of Ohio State University and Russell F. Weigley of Temple University, offered constructive criticism that helped me to reconsider many points in the manuscript. In particular I wish to thank Professor Christo Lassiter from the University of Cincinnati College of Law for his valuable constructive critiques from the position of a military lawyer. Last, Clara Speer, a dear friend from the Texas A&M University, was kind enough to correct the manuscript and offer unbiased comments on its organization and structure.

In writing a book, it is essential to learn from the numerous articles and books pertinent to the study. With this in mind, I offer my sincere appreciation to all those authors listed in the Bibliography and their contribution to the historiography of the subject. Finally, I owe very special thanks to Jeannie Wilson, who not only processed the draft on a word processor but was always gracious in tolerating my last-minute changes.

COLD WAR CASUALTY

INTRODUCTION

LATE IN JULY, 1945, the commanding general of the 101st Airborne Division, Maxwell D. Taylor, recorded in his war diary information about America's new weapon, the atomic bomb. During the war, Taylor habitually kept the names of promising young officers in a little black book for future consideration. He was an aspiring officer with a strong driving ego and would become army chief of staff, assistant for military affairs under President John F. Kennedy, chairman of the Joint Chiefs of Staff, and ambassador to South Vietnam. On 28 July 1945, at Berchtesgaden in southern Bavaria, Taylor acquired highly sensitive information about the A-bomb from Generals George C. Marshall and George S. Patton and recorded it before the weapon was used against Japan. At about the same time, Major General Robert W. Grow, wartime commander of the 6th Armored Division, was recording in his personal diary the problems of rapid demobilization after the German surrender. Taylor's 101st Airborne Division and Grow's 6th Armored Division had fought in the Battle of the Bulge. Serious friction occurred between the two divisions when, on 31 December 1944, the 6th attacked out of the Bastogne pocket and was counterattacked and severely bruised by the Germans. Grow claimed that the hard-pressed 101st, on the left flank of the 6th, failed to support the salient created by the armored division. Years later Taylor and Grow were again antagonists but this time over differences in military ethos and the institutional employment of military justice. The immediate issue was not a combat situation but the question of maintaining a diary, and it would lead to a general court-martial.

It is not unusual for an American military commander to keep a diary. Unfortunately, portions of General Grow's diary for the year 1951 were photocopied in Frankfurt, Germany, by a reputed Soviet "mole" and used in a communist propaganda vehicle. At the time, Grow was the senior American military attaché in Moscow and Taylor the deputy chief of staff for operations and administration in the Pentagon. It was Grow's misfortune to be the only general officer brought to trial for falling victim to a Cold War propaganda effort, and it happened because his diary was exploited by the communists and then by the Western press, especially the *Washington Post*. Grow's court-martial foreshadowed the growing power of the American press, its limitations, biases, and journalistic techniques. It also invites a comparison of how various elements of the media handled the general's indiscretion and how their reports influenced not only the readership but, more important, the Pentagon and Congress during an era of extreme fear for American security. An analogy can also be drawn to the Oliver North case, for, as with Grow, the essential problem was an embarrassing disclosure of official government concern and activities about the position of power structure and its interests. However, unlike Grow, in North's case the power politicians, military, and contractors went on the offensive, not so much to verify the true facts, as Grow attempted to do, but to expose the political nature of the attack and the weakness in the opposing political view. The points of similarity remain due to the use and power of the media, effective propaganda, and the expansive role of politics that grew to impeach the viability of the judicial process.

A reporter from the *Saturday Evening Post* wrote after the trial, "This is the first time since Civil War days that an officer of General Grow's rank has been court-martialed." Ten years later, a Pulitzer Prize winner from the *New York Herald Tribune*, Sanche de Gramont, wrote in a book on international espionage that the 1952 court-martial was the first time since the Civil War that an officer of Grow's stature had undergone the "indignity" of a military trial by his peers. General Dwight D. Eisenhower's judge advocate in North Africa during the war, Brigadier General Adam Richmond, Retired, commented that Grow's court-martial was the only case in the history of military jurisprudence "upon which eight senior major generals have sat, not only behind closed doors but on a Top Secret level." Prominent military historian Alfred Vagts in *The Military Attaché* (1967) noted that it was the first court-martial for "poor services" rendered by an American attaché.

The Grow affair became a cause célèbre because of the intolerance, political extremism, and uncertainty produced by the Cold War. Mc-Carthyism—a term derived from the actions of Senator Joseph R. McCarthy during the early 1950s—fed upon real or imaginary threats to American security, and McCarthy more than any other public figure represented the political extremism of the time. He delivered scathing attacks on Truman's foreign policy and probed alleged subversion in the army. The latter had proved to be his undoing, and by the end of 1954 the Senate censured him for abuse of legislative investigatory power. The communist conspiracy—McCarthy's provocation—was the focal force. The far-ranging communist debate touched every American institution in 1952. No less than two Senate and two House committees that year searched for possible subversive influences.

This period also saw changes in military management. As a result of World War II, the military began to emphasize business management techniques for administering the demands created by globalism. This new trend compromised traditional military values as managerial careerism replaced ethical responsibilities based on service and sacrifice. Furthermore, military cooperation in the conduct of foreign policy had prodigiously increased as a result of the Cold War. Military occupation of Germany, Austria, Korea, and Japan; the sale of armaments and foreign military assistance; and participation in international organizations added considerable stress to military management.

The Grow court-martial symbolized the inherent tension between a military profession that tried to police its own ranks during an era of political turbulence. Questions of conduct among senior army officers, as in most professions, are usually handled outside the judicial system. In the Grow case, the army staff in the Pentagon did not choose that option in spite of recommendations by certain members of the State Department and the Central Intelligence Agency to take the initiative and refute communist charges rather than court-martial the former attaché. The result was an exercise in army staff incompetence. There also exists a lack of interest in a history of the

U.S. Army Counter Intelligence Corps (CIC), especially during the Cold War period. The investigative role the CIC performed in the European Command (EUCOM) is amply described in chapter 4 because of the critical impact of its reports on molding the decision by the army staff to court-martial Grow. This decision also demonstrated the problems the army staff encountered by placing self-interest over service.

The Grow episode provides an example of managerial careerism exercised by the army staff in the Pentagon using the military justice system as a tool for unlawful command influence, causing political interests to usurp the judicial process. The pioneer work of Richard A. Gabriel and Paul L. Savage, *Crisis in Command: Mismanagement in the Army* (1978), stands out as one of the most provocative studies of the changing ethos from service to self-interest or exaggerated careerism that was evident during the Vietnam period. Another pertinent study is William L. Hauser, *America's Army in Crisis: A Study in Civil-Military Relations* (1973). Hauser argues that the army was having difficulties adjusting to the social, political, economic, and intellectual changes brought about by America's industrial society. Earlier during the Vietnam conflict, General David M. Shoup, writing in the *Atlantic* in April 1969, and James A. Donovan in his book, *Militarism, U.S.A.* (1970), trace the roots of modern careerism to the experience of World War II and the burgeoning military establishment. More recently, the editor of *Parameters*, Lloyd J. Matthews, writing in *Army* in July 1988, noted the positive value of the legitimate desire for personal advancement, but he stressed the need for a distinction between legitimate ambition and careerism.

American jurisprudence existed before the Articles of Confederation and the Constitution and developed independent of the civilian judiciary. I refer to this dichotomy as the "agency theory of separatism," in that courts-martial were established under executive Article II of the Constitution, which made the President the commander-in-chief of the armed forces, and legislative Article I, which authorized Congress to make rules for the government of the military. Courts-martial were not established under Article III, thus denying appellate review by the Supreme Court. Once institutionalized, the agency theory provided the substance that evolved into military formalism that provided procedural controls, protection, and immunities for the military structure outside of civilian courts and influence. The system sustained this status throughout the nineteenth century. The experiences of two world wars, however, subjected military legal institutions to numerous challenges, most noticeably objections to control by commanding officers over all aspects of trial procedures and the decisions of those who administered military justice under their command. For example, the commanding officer decided on the charges, created the court, selected the court members from his command, controlled the evidence and permissibility of documents and witnesses, and executed the power to judge the fitness reports. Unlawful command influence became a major issue because of the inability in many cases, especially in the Grow case, to sever political command interest from the judicial process. Thus the judicial process was made unreliable by unlawful command influence. It was always difficult to balance justice with discipline; historically the tilt was for discipline, because political considerations many times usurped the judicial process.

In the recent, award-winning study at the Air Command and Staff College, Major Martha Huntley Bower wrote that the issue of unlawful command influence is an elusive problem. Furthermore, she noted the accused may be denied a fair trial and access to beneficial witnesses. Moreover, when courts are made unreliable by command influence, public and military confidence in the military justice system becomes questionable. A 1977 report to Congress by the Comptroller General of the United States acknowledged the prohibition of unlawful command influence. However, the study conceded that it could be exercised in many subtle ways not readily susceptible to detection and that military courts have had considerable difficulty in identifying unlawful command influence.

Military legal institutions remained unchanged until the much-heralded Uniform Code of 1950. In May 1950, a Department of Defense press release claimed that the new Code provided the accused a fair trial and prevented undue command influence over the administration of military justice. For example, Article 37 of the code forbade the exercise of unlawful command influence in any form. An article in the *Vanderbilt Law Review* in February 1953, stated that unlawful command influence had been abolished under the new Uniform Code. The case of General Grow demonstrates otherwise. Although unlawful command influence was prohibited by Article 37, it was exercised in the Grow case. Military justice as a formalized institution remained intact, but it was modified in such a way as to accommodate the new managerial style of military management.

According to Donald G. Nieman ("Military Law, Martial Law, and Military Government," in Robin Higham and Donald J. Mrozek, eds., *A Guide to Sources of United States Military History: Supplement I,* 1981), insufficient attention has been given to the military justice system. Nieman's comment is still valid today. Most material on the military justice system can be found in law journals, occasional books, and government publications authored by members of the legal profession. The most notable and extensive studies are by Edward F. Sherman ("The Civilization of Military Law," *Maine Law Review,* 1970) and Luther C. West ("A History of Command Influence on the Military Judicial System," *UCLA Law Review,* 1970, and *They Call It Justice: Command Influence and the Court-Martial System,* 1977). Though command influence has been widely discussed, the Grow court-martial as an example of blatant or subtle command influence is not discussed by either author. In his excellent dissertation, "The Evolution of the Court-Martial System and the Role of the United States Court of Military Appeals in Military Law" (George Washington University Law School, 1954), Frank Fedele comments briefly on the Grow case, noting the influence of public opinion and political considerations on the decision. He maintains that these influences cannot be dismissed, but he leaves the answers to be reconciled by "the searching mind of the student." American military historians have shown little interest in dealing with military justice, its institutional history, and its actual implementation.

This book describes the failure to sever political, command interests from the judicial process made unreliable by unlawful command influence, the use of the military justice system as a tool for managerial careerism and its operation under the reformed Uniform Code, bureaucratic intrigue, the influence of the media, the conflict between service and self-interest, and, most important, the inherent tensions caused by the temper of the times, resulting in the decision to prosecute General Grow.

★ ★ 1

The Man, the Times,
and the Cold War

THURSDAY, 6 MARCH 1952, was a sunny, cool day in Washington, D.C. The temperature was expected to reach a high of around 40 degrees before evening. Political life on that beautiful winter day in the nation's capital during the Cold War was momentarily directed toward a sensational headline in the *Washington Post:* "Red Agents Reveal U.S. General's Diary. Secret Writings of Moscow Attaché Tell of Search for Bomb Targets."

The article, written by John G. Norris, an experienced, enterprising reporter assigned to the Pentagon, contained extracts from Major General Robert W. Grow's personal diary. The diary, reportedly stolen by Soviet spies, alleged that the United States was seeking to provoke a third world war. Norris's source was a book written by a British defector named Richard Squires, entitled *Auf dem Kriegspfad* (On the warpath) and published in East Germany late in 1951. Chapter 6 of Squires's book contained ten facsimiles from Grow's 1951 diary, which in essence called for "war now" and "hit below the belt." An unidentified top army spokesman verified the authenticity of the diary extracts and noted: "It was an inside job. Two employees with German names, obviously agents, have since disappeared." Later, the high-ranking spokesman would be identified as belonging to the office of Major General Floyd L. Parks, army chief of information.

Norris's scoop and subsequent articles spread over the entire Western world. It was a sensational item capable of gripping the reading public. Moreover, at the time America's foreign policy was being challenged by an unprecedented limited war in Korea and a policy of containment designed to halt Soviet expansion. Domestically, a new

The Weather
Today—Sunny and cool with the high-est around 40 Friday—Fair and con-tinued cool. Yesterday—High, 44 at 3:25 p m.; low, 34 at 7 a. m. (Details on Page B-2.)

The Washington Post   FINAL

Seventy-fifth Year in the Nation's Capital

NO.   27,657   Phone NA. 4200   THURSDAY, MARCH 6, 1952   WTOP AM (1500) FM (96.3) TV (Ch. 9)   FIVE CENTS

Red Agents Reveal U.S. General's Diary

Hearing Told U. S. Tankers Carried Oil To Red China

Craft Were Bought By Chinese Interests Represented by Morris Law Firm

By Edward F Ryan

Investigating Senators were told yesterday two American-flag tankers owned by a Chinese-financed com-pany represented by the New-bold Morris law firm hauled Soviet oil to Communist China in the period before the Ko-rean war.

Surplus Metal Going To Civilian Products

By Sam Stavisky

The Government yesterday disclosed that a considerable amount of aluminum and cop-per declared "surplus" by the military, will be pumped into civilian production, including autos, during the second quarter of this year.

In a second gesture towards balancing the Nation's "butter" economy as against the "guns" mobilization program, the Gov-ernment directed that special consideration on military con-tracts be given four areas suf-fering from severe unemploy-ment.

Tax Reform Voted Down In Committee

By John G. Norris

McClellan Group Approves George Resolution to Kill Truman Proposal

President Truman's at-tempt to corruption in the In-ternal Revenue Bureau by replacing politically-appoint-ed collectors with Civil Serv-ice career officials was voted down, 7 to 3, by the Senate Executive Expenditures Com-mittee yesterday.

Secret Writing of Moscow Attache Tell of Search for Bomb Targets

By John G. Norris

The stolen diary of Ameri-ca's military attache to Rus-sia is being circulated behind the Iron Curtain as part of a propaganda effort to show that the United States is seek-ing a third world war.

Army counter-intelligence is investigating the surreptitious photo-graphing of the indiscreet docu-ment. The author, Maj. Gen. Robert W. Grow—has been re-lieved of his command and may be temporarily on duty at the Pentagon awaiting the outcome of the investigation.

House Call For Justice Data Refused By McGrath

Powers Exceeded, Letter Tells Chelf; Probers May Resort To Use of Subpenas

Attorney General Mc-Grath yesterday refused to turn over a huge stack of records to a House committee investi-gating Attorney General Mc-Grath's conduct of his office.

Eisenhower's Creed

The Formative Years; 6 With MacArthur

By Kevin McCann
President, the Defiance College

President Approves D. C. Redevelopment

By Chalmers M. Roberts

Non-Gun Held At Belvoir in Safe Robbery

Floor Leader Pays Marshall Tribute For Kin's Benefit

McCarran Would Cut Off Pension

Acheson Admits Reversing Security Decision And Clearing Clubb; Senators Demand Probe

By Alfred Friendly

The Telephone Kept Ringing!

Laskie, Former Washingtonian

Victim's Widow, Bible Help Free Hit-and-Run Death Driver

BALTIMORE, March 5

Truce Hopes Hinge On High-Level Talks

noun had emerged: McCarthyism. This term was associated with the actions of Senator Joseph R. McCarthy of Wisconsin (1947–57), who traded on distrust, suspicion, and guilt by association. McCarthyism fed on fears generated by the Cold War and was marked by unsubstantiated accusations of disloyalty and abuse of legislative investigatory power. McCarthy's actions during the early 1950s engendered fear over real or imagined threats to the security of the United States.[1] President Harry S. Truman described it as a period when corruption of the truth was the norm rather than an exception.

The Grow episode, when brought to public attention by the *Washington Post,* also raised the question of media responsibility. Walter Lippmann wrote after World War I: "True opinions can prevail only if the facts to which they refer are known; if they are not known, false ideas are just as effective as true ones, if not a little more effective." This is exactly what happened when the *Washington Post* exploited the compromise of Grow's diary. Freedom of the press is an Anglo-American tradition, and rightly so in a democracy structured on popular sovereignty. This right is expressed in the First Amendment to the Constitution. Historically, however, criticism of the press has flourished. For example, Lippmann, after experiencing the propaganda and censorship of World War I, criticized reporters for their generally sloppy work. In his view, "The work of reporters has thus become confused with the work of preachers, revivalists, prophets, and agitators." He added: "The current theory of American newspaperdom is that an abstraction like the truth and a grace like fairness must be sacrificed whenever anyone thinks the necessities of civilization require the sacrifice."[2] Lippmann was arguing for media reform, and his comments would have relevance thirty-two years later when the *Post*'s disparaging journalism dramatized the Grow incident. Norris and the *Post* would be guilty of what Lippmann had called a lack of truth and fairness in newspaperdom. In the months to follow, the Norris article would contribute to one of the most bizarre general courts-martial of the twentieth century. The resulting investigation and trial would defame the reputation of one of America's highly regarded general officers and make a mockery of the military justice system, which had undergone its first major reform since its inception.

Robert W. Grow was born on 14 February 1895 in Sibley, Iowa. On 17 November 1915, he was appointed a second lieutenant of field artillery in the Minnesota National Guard. The following year, he graduated from the University of Minnesota with a Bachelor of Science degree and then mustered into the federal service as a second lieutenant. During World War I he attended Army Service School at Fort Leavenworth, Kansas, and the School of Fire at Fort Sill, Oklahoma. In 1919 he spent five months in Germany. In 1923 Grow enrolled in the Cavalry School and six years later graduated from the Command and General Staff School. The following year he joined the 12th Cavalry at Fort Brown, Texas. From November 1931 to January 1933, he was the plans and training officer of the newly created Mechanized Force at Fort Eustis, Virginia. Grow then moved to Fort Knox, Kentucky, in a similar capacity with the detachment, which was combined with the 1st Cavalry at Fort Knox. This consolidation formed the first mechanized cavalry regiment. During this period Grow became a pioneer in the mechanization of the U.S. Army. In the mid-1930s he became an instructor at the Command and General Staff School, then enrolled in the Army War College, graduating in 1936.

In the 1930s Grow met George S. Patton, Jr., and was impressed by the flamboyant cavalryman's wide knowledge. But it was not until early in the 1940s, when Grow, as a G-3 (Plans and Operations), came in working contact with Patton, who commanded the 2d Armored Division, that the two struck up a professional and personal friendship that lasted throughout the war. Grow considered Patton an outstanding tactician and "the greatest fighting leader of World War II."[3] Patton, as commander of the famous Third Army, said that the "Super Sixth" and its commanding general were among his best. Patton's chief of staff, Brigadier General Hobart R. Gay, added that the 6th Armored Division was "the most dependable division which ever served in the Third Army during World War Two."[4]

Grow took command of the 6th Armored Division in May 1943. After extensive training, the division was sent to England, where it was assigned to Patton's Third Army. The two cavalrymen thought very much alike about the employment of armor tactics, but their personalities were very different. Grow, whose stiff jaw and stone-faced look showed his determination, possessed a businesslike demeanor and tended to avoid public dramatization, whereas Patton was a flamboyant, dramatic warrior who entered combat with flair.

A year after the war ended—after a short tour in the United States—Grow joined the U.S. Military Mission to Iran. By 1949, when he returned to Fort Devens, he had an impressive military career behind him. In July 1950, he became the army attaché in Moscow. He was considered an outstanding combat commander and a progressive in the deployment of armor. During his career he had shown consistent professional growth and a strong sense of loyalty to the army and the American system of pluralistic democracy. But his distinguished record was soon to be forgotten.

Grow had maintained a personal diary since the 1930s. This was not unusual; numerous ranking general officers kept diaries, and they provided the material for many books. As he was finishing a successful military career, Grow thought of writing a book. While visiting Frankfurt some time in 1951, however, he did not secure his diary in his residence, the Victory Guest House, and it was photographed on a desk by a communist agent. His carelessness provided an opportunity for Soviet-sponsored propagandists and set in motion the events that led to a general court-martial. Communist and Western newspapers in turn made considerable use of the incident, and the Pentagon launched an extensive investigation. Grow was marked as a security risk and a disloyal officer.

On 14 January 1952, General Grow arrived in Berlin from Frankfurt-am-Main en route to Moscow. He was returning to his post in Russia after a brief leave in West Germany. At Tempelhof Airport he was intercepted by Michael B. Lustgarten, an intelligence officer from the Office of the United States High Commissioner for Germany (HICOG), who informed the general that an important cable had just arrived from the U.S. embassy in Moscow. It stated that Grow's personal diary had been stolen by Soviet operatives and advised him, for reasons of personal safety, not to return to Moscow.

The cable also referred to articles in the East Berlin *Berliner Zeitung* of 3 January 1952 and *Neues Deutschland* of 6 January 1952.[5] The articles were based on a book written by Richard Squires, *Auf dem Kriegspfad, Aufzeichnungen eines englischen Offiziers* (On the warpath: Notes by an English officer).[6] Squires's work was a pro-Soviet polemic against the United States and the West and provided a rationale for the Soviet presence in Eastern Europe. But it was also probable that the Soviets used it to discredit Grow and embarrass the United States government. In the characteristic fashion of Soviet propagandists, they accused Grow of being a "warmonger."[7] "Hit below the belt . . . RR is good target . . . total war with all weapons . . . it seems to me the time is ripe for a blow this year" were a few of the comments from Grow's diary that were reported by the newspapers.

General Grow had initially come in conflict with the Soviet government shortly after World War II while heading the U.S. Military Mission to Iran, where he gained the confidence of the shah of Iran and General Ali Razmara, the Iranian chief of staff. At the time, Grow's function was to determine the applicability of U.S. military methods to the needs of the Iranian army in the areas of organization, administration, and training. In addition, he was responsible for assisting the U.S. ambassador to Iran in securing Iran's territorial integrity and domestic order to avoid Soviet influence.

In the fall of 1945, President Harry S. Truman made a statement designed to guide future foreign policy. The traditional "Open Door" concept was affirmed: that "all states which are accepted in the society of nations should have access on equal terms to the trade and the raw materials of the world." Truman also affirmed that the United States would not seek territorial expansion or selfish advantage but would "encourage return of sovereign rights and self-government to all peoples who have been deprived of them by force."[8] This statement was no more than an attestation of the Atlantic Charter of 1941, the Declaration of the United Nations in 1942, and the Moscow Conference in 1943 in the Wilsonian tradition of internationalism or universalism. This idealistic concept of a concert of nations in foreign relations was rooted in America's perception of history and its legal-moral tradition. Truman's policy statement obviously was designed to blunt the sphere-of-influence notion applied for centuries by the European powers, which most American policy makers sincerely believed was the cause of the two major world wars of the twentieth century.[9]

One of the first postwar conflicts that would test U.S. foreign policy goals began late in 1945 when Stalin attempted to establish separatist Azerbaijani and Kurdish regimes in northern Iran. Soviet troops, in violation of the tripartite alliance of January 1942, the declaration at Tehran in December 1943, and the reaffirmation of Iranian territorial integrity at the London Conference of Foreign Ministers in September 1945, were determined to stay on Iranian soil and support the communist Tudeh party. Stalin argued that the Iranians were hostile to the USSR and a threat to the strategic Baku oil fields. In addition, under the 1921 Treaty of Friendship, Soviet military forces claimed that they had a right to stay on Iranian territory to protect against possible hostilities.[10]

Stalin's argument masked the real Soviet intention, which was to extend pressure in Iran, Turkey, and Greece so as to gain access to the Persian Gulf and its vast oil reserves and to acquire control of the Dardanelles. For centuries Russia had been preoccupied with the desire to secure warm water ports, especially near or on Turkish and Iranian territory. Iranian oil simply added to the desire to move south and southwest. The noted British military historian and theoretician J. F. C. Fuller wrote in 1945 that Stalin understood very well the maxim "he who has the petrol has the Empire." He also reported that the Soviets were more interested in obtaining oil concessions in neighboring countries than in developing and exploiting their own oil fields. This action was part of Stalin's strategy to preserve Soviet oil and deny petroleum to the USSR's potential enemies. Oil was power. Thus Stalin's goal was to establish a sphere of influence from the Curzon line to the Carpathian Mountains to control the Galacian oil fields and the Ploesti oil fields in Romania, then turn to Iran.[11]

Stalin's foreign policy toward Iran was relatively uncomplicated; he knew what he wanted. But there were problems. The Soviet Union was experiencing a pronounced economic dislocation as a result of the war, and there was also instability in the Soviet-controlled Eastern European countries. Finally, Stalin's paranoia led him to be concerned that the United States and England would increase their military presence in the area.[12] This was especially probable because the United States had emerged from the war with superior technology and military power.

On 9 May 1946, twelve months after Germany's unconditional surrender, Soviet forces left northern Iran under considerable international pressure. As part of the pullout agreement, the Soviets expected Iranian oil concessions and the formation of a joint-stock Iran-Soviet oil company, plus a degree of autonomy for the Soviet-sponsored province of Azerbaijan. Such an arrangement was not unusual; England and then American oil interests had been active for years in exploring and exploiting oil-producing territories along the Persian Gulf. The Department of State supported the efforts of the Standard-Vacuum Oil Company and Sinclair Oil Company in vying for concessions along with the British Royal Dutch Shell Company.[13]

But much to Stalin's displeasure, the Iranian parliament, the Majlis, with dramatic suddenness in October 1947 refused to ratify Soviet oil concessions. While the United States government found the decision highly gratifying, the Soviets were repelled by the idea of defeat in an area that, since Peter the Great, had been a sphere of Russian influence.[14] The decision of the Majlis indicated that the Tehran government had aligned itself on the side of the Western powers. The Soviet ambassador to Iran called the decision "an act of categoric discrimination against the USSR," especially since British oil concessions along the Persian Gulf were maintained.[15]

Early in 1946 the United States began implementing a "get tough" policy toward the USSR.[16] This reorientation from the wartime Grand Alliance was in part a result of the notion of universalism exhibited in Soviet intransigence in Iran and pressure against Turkey and Greece. The United States increasingly moved to embrace the sphere-of-influence notion that it had rejected in 1945 as a cause of conflict.[17]

American leaders, exasperated at Soviet moves in Eastern Europe, the Middle East, and Asia, decided to contain what they considered overt and covert communist expansion. The United States adopted the firm policy of aiding Iran so that political independence and a reasonable degree of stability could be maintained. Iran was gradually becoming a sphere of influence for the United States.

As soon as he arrived in Iran, General Grow became a key implementor of U.S. foreign policy. Almost immediately he became indirectly involved in the recovery of the rebellious provinces in northern Iran. Grow did not accompany the Iranian army late in 1946 when it moved north, but he did offer some advice to the shah and the chief of staff, General Razmara.[18] By the end of December, the communist-inspired Azerbaijani insurrection was extinguished in spite of vehement threats by the Soviets to intervene. Shortly thereafter, the Kurds also sued for peace.

For the next two years Grow was heavily engaged with problems of organization, administration, and training the Iranian army. In addition, as head of the small U.S. Military Mission, he was responsible for integrating the air force and navy to meet the security needs of the country. It was imperative that the country become stabilized, determine its own destiny, and free itself from Soviet territorial aggrandizement.[19]

As chief of mission, Grow worked closely with the shah and his chief of staff. The shah believed the giant from the north to be a greater threat to his country than British imperialism. Thus he emphasized military security as most important in implementing postwar Iranian foreign policy. The Americans conveniently fitted into the scheme because it was Iran's policy to use a third power to negate Soviet and British endeavors. This foreign policy was very similar to that followed by the shah's father during the interwar period.

On 6 October 1947, Ambassador George V. Allen and Minister of War Mahmoud Djam signed an agreement to renew the engagement of the U.S. Military Mission with the Iranian army.[20] Grow and his small contingent of military advisers were well aware of Iran's strategic importance to the United States, and Grow felt it was essential to furnish military supplies to Iran free or on favorable terms. Accordingly, he recommended that high military delegations come to Iran promptly to evaluate the importance of Iranian security by strengthening the army. There was some fear in the Military Mission that the War Department might limit military supplies because of problems in Greece and Turkey.[21]

At first, the State Department raised questions regarding Iranian arms purchases. Some Iranians feared that the shah would use such arms to suppress domestic political opposition. In addition, could the Iranians pay? And if so, how much would it strain their economy? In the meantime, Ambassador Allen advised the State Department to consider an immediate $50 million grant to Iran. He based his request on the advice of Grow, whom the Ambassador rated "most highly and whom I regard as one of the most effective Americans I have seen in action abroad."[22] It was Grow's contention that Iran could build up a stable government and maintain its territorial integrity only if it had internal security.

American policy makers began to view security in Iran as "substantially as important to the United States as is security in Greece and Turkey." Though Washington recognized the inherent weakness of the Tehran government, its goals were Iran's independence, stability, and friendship and especially its protection from Soviet expansion.[23] In other words, the objective was to deny the Soviets a foothold in the area, to develop oil resources, and, if necessary, to use American military forces upon threat of war. Although the Iranian army could not offer substantial defense against the USSR, it was expected to discourage aggression from the north and slow enemy progress in case of an invasion.

Though many Iranians would have welcomed a withdrawal of influence by the major powers, it became evident that no major power could afford to abandon Iran. "Stakes here are too important," Allen advised the State Department. Yet in implementing its policy, the United States government was cautious. It would have been improper to appear to be forcing a loan or gift on the Iranians, which might make them feel financially obligated to a foreign government. Also, the United States was concerned that such action might precipitate Soviet-inspired charges of U.S. imperialism. Secretary of State George C. Marshall advised Allen to discuss with Grow and Brigadier General H. Norman Schwarzkopf (chief of the American Military Mission with the gendarmerie) the possibility of suspending activities in the event of abnormal internal conditions.[24]

By 1948 U.S. attitude regarding the purchase of military equipment had changed through the efforts of the Military Mission and the ambassador. On 29 July 1948, the Iranians were extended credit for $10 million worth of American surplus military equipment. Though the situation in Iran seemed precarious at times, Grow continued to work actively with the Iranian military. His mission was stationed in Tehran, but its duties required that the twenty-some members travel extensively. On several occasions, Grow flew close to the Soviet border to take photographs and make military investigations.

The Soviet ambassador, Ivan Vasilyevich Sadchikov, wrote the Iranian prime minister, Ibrahim Hakimi, calling attention to Grow's role in advising Iran's armed forces and of the reconnaissance flights along the Iran-Soviet border. The Soviet government believed that such activities were transforming Iran into a strategic base for the

United States. The Soviets vigorously opposed foreign military assistance to Iran. They were well aware that the United States's presence in the oil-rich Middle Eastern country bordering the USSR and so close to the Caucasian oil fields was a security threat and part of an attempt to contain Soviet interests militarily, politically, and economically.[25]

On one occasion, Sadchikov implied to the Iranian prime minister that the "USSR could not stomach" the decision of the Majlis to deny the Soviets an oil concession. On another occasion, he talked about the bad relations between the United States and the Soviet Union and the possibility of war, adding, "Yet Iran, the neighbor of the Soviet Union, was permitting the army and Gendarmerie to be taken over by the American Army." Later the Soviet military attaché said that the Soviet Union was not afraid of Iran's army but feared a U.S. attack on Baku through Iran. He stated forcefully that the Moscow government would not permit the Iranian army to be integrated with the United States Army. Moreover, Moscow wanted the arms credit program to be canceled and American military advisers to leave the country.[26] Throughout this period the Soviet government threatened to invade Iran because of the U.S. military presence. The basis for such contemplated action was the 1921 Treaty of Friendship, which gave Soviet troops the right to enter Iranian territory if a third power should threaten the Soviet Union through Iran.

By the end of 1948, Grow was on his way back to the United States after two years of duty in Iran. He had upgraded the Iranian military organization and was instrumental in promoting arms credits to the Iranian government. Iran had become allied with the West.

Shortly after Grow left Iran for reassignment, Walter Bedell Smith, the American ambassador in Moscow, wrote to Secretary of State Marshall, "I consider Iran the most sensitive point on the Soviet periphery requiring our most continuous and careful attention." The lack of oil in sufficient quantities for mechanized warfare "is probably the most serious weakness in Soviet war potential." In addition, Stalin wanted to increase the strength and influence of the Soviet navy in the Black Sea and the Middle East area. Iranian petroleum and simultaneous denial of Middle Eastern oil to the Western powers were critical to these Soviet moves. An unstable and ineffective Iranian government would encourage the Soviets to enter Iran.[27]

In October 1948, Grow took command at Fort Devens, but the new assignment was to be short-lived; soon he would again be a Cold War participant, but in a different role. In February 1950 he reported to the Strategic Intelligence School for a sixteen-week course. The school was operated by the Office of the Assistant Chief of Staff, G-2, Intelligence, Department of the Army. The student body was composed of designated army and air force attachés. All replacement personnel for the army's Office of the G-2 were required to attend the school.

The course was divided into three phases. The first dealt with strategic intelligence. The second was concerned with the application of strategic intelligence to the country to which the student would be assigned. In Grow's case, the country was to be the Soviet Union. The final phase dealt with such matters as finance, administration, supply, cryptography, and security. When Grow reported to the school he requested the same treatment as any other student, specifically that prerogative of rank, since he was a general officer, not be considered. The school staff observed that Grow pursued the course with above-average vigor, commonly putting in extra hours. His performance was excellent, and he was highly regarded by the school faculty and his peers. He was rated in the top third of his class with respect to security standards.[28]

After completing the intelligence course, Grow prepared for his new assignment in Russia. From the time he arrived in Moscow in the summer of 1950, internal security "tails," as was the common practice, covered his movements whenever he ventured forth from the American embassy. As military attaché to the Soviet Union, Grow was to gather military intelligence and submit it to the Office of the G-2. There was nothing unusual about this assignment. It was common knowledge in the international community that military attachés report on military activity and related matters.[29]

The Ministry for State Security (MGB) soon decided that Grow's intelligence-gathering methods were overly aggressive.[30] He was seeing too much of intelligence value. Major General Alexander R. Bolling, the U.S. Army's assistant chief of staff for intelligence, G-2, considered Grow's performance as a military attaché in Moscow "superior." The G-2 revealed that Grow's "reports were second to none received from any station in our Attaché System." His character was "unquestionable," and "his memory for detail is outstanding due to the fine reports he submitted."[31]

Grow demonstrated his gift for gathering intelligence one day in January 1951. He and an aide had hired a Russian taxicab in Vladimir. The owner claimed to be a mechanic on leave and was permitted to use his private car as a taxi. The Americans suspected the driver had been ordered by Soviet counterintelligence agents to accommodate and observe the visitors. As the two toured the area, they were followed as usual but not disturbed. The primary purpose of the trip was to identify troop units in the vicinity of Vladimir. Though they could not identify specific Soviet troops, they saw enough to prove the presence of a tank or mechanized division, an artillery division, and probably an officer candidate school. Grow and the aide also observed tanks being used to train crews and firing on a tank range in zero weather with deep snow, at times under blizzard conditions. In his report to the G-2 in Washington, Grow noted that Soviet training continued regardless of winter conditions. He also commented on Soviet propaganda: "There is an increasing feeling among us that the Russian 'man in the street' is becoming convinced that war is inevitable. Propaganda has implanted in the citizen's mind the firm idea that the warmongers are going to attack." Grow surmised that "every activity and the lives of all individuals are controlled and directed in such a way that the nation could pass from its present state to that of active military operations overnight."[32]

In June 1952 the recently arrived ambassador to the Soviet Union, George F. Kennan, observed that the activities of the American staff over the past two or three years had "been intensively and somewhat recklessly exploited by the military intelligence-gathering agencies of the Government for their particular purposes." He was highly critical of the military attachés, including Grow, for impairing the usefulness of the American diplomatic mission. Kennan argued that these activities "are self-defeating in that they lead to a steady and gradual curtailment of the very facilities which they exploit." Furthermore, he maintained, they "have a deleterious effect on the actual diplomatic potential of the mission" and place in jeopardy "the physical security of the members of the mission and their families." Kennan mentioned Soviet awareness and sensitivity to the "Grew diary." Kennan presumed that this reference was to the former under secretary of state

Joseph G. Grew's *Turbulent Era: A Diplomatic Record of Forty Years, 1904–1945,* in two volumes, based in part on his personal diaries and published in 1952. The ambassador made several references to Soviet sensitivity to Grew's diary, but in all probability it was Grow's diary to which Kennan referred because Grew had retired from foreign service in August 1945. Only one of his forty-one chapters dealt with the Soviet Union and the United States.[33]

Apparently, the MGB became aware of Grow's diary through Colonel Stig Erick Constans Wennerström, a debonair Swedish air force officer who was a member of the Soviet intelligence system from 1948 until 1963, when he was arrested by his country's security police. The Wennerström affair was one of the most spectacular espionage cases to unfold during the early Cold War period, and it prompted a United States Senate subcommittee of the Committee on the Judiciary to investigate the degree to which Wennerström had penetrated U.S. strategic planning activities and the North Atlantic Treaty Organization.

During his tour as Swedish air attaché in Moscow, Wennerström met Grow, although not by accident. Pyotr Pavlovich Lemenov, who was identified as an MGB general of the American section of Soviet intelligence, ordered Wennerström to cultivate Grow at the U.S. embassy in Moscow for the purpose of acquiring information. The Ministry for State Security needed to embarrass Grow and the U.S. government for a possible propaganda attack during the Cold War. Early in 1951, Wennerström was asked by Soviet intelligence to establish whether Grow had the habit of taking notes and if he was accustomed to maintaining a notebook. According to Wennerström, he had observed Grow on several occasions taking notes and passed this information on to his Soviet superior.[34] Little did Soviet intelligence realize how successful these efforts were to be.

$$\star \quad \star \quad 2$$

The Book and the Diary

THE KREMLIN'S DESIRE to continue to propagandize the East-West conflict was fueled when in 1951 General Grow became careless with his personal diary. It was photocopied by a Soviet agent at the Victory Guest House in Frankfurt. The two East German newspapers that published excerpts from the diary were organs of the Sozialistische Einheitspartei Deutschlands or the SED (Communist Socialist Unity party of Germany), conceived in 1946 by Soviet occupation authorities. The papers presented reviews of Squires's *Auf dem Kriegspfad*. Of particular interest was chapter 6, "Worte und Taten: Das Tagebuch eines Diplomaten" (Words and deeds: The diary of a diplomat). The reviews, like the book, constituted propaganda aimed at the East Germans. Richard Squires was the ideal person to lend credence to the propaganda effort. A former British army major who defected in 1947, Squires was reported to be living in the Soviet zone in East Germany. His book was published as part of an ongoing Soviet bloc propaganda effort to prove American aggression. In a brief preface, Squires contended that he wrote the book because of "a desire to fight through reason against the fanatics who are striving to incite a world conflagration."[1]

The work was nearly completed when unexpected events prompted him again to take pen in hand. In August 1951, Squires had been in a cafe in the Soviet sector of Berlin, where he occasionally met with acquaintances from Western Europe. There he conversed with an old friend, the Berlin correspondent of a London paper. The discussion centered around the reported weakening of United States aggressive tendencies toward the Soviet Union. Squires was under the impression that the Cold War was moderating. His friend, however, expressed surprise and became visibly disturbed. Finally, he remarked that America's efforts to lessen tensions were misleading, and to prove his point, he opened his briefcase and handed Squires a fairly large sealed package. Squires wanted to open the package immediately, but his contact preferred to wait until they were outside. Squires was told: "This is a copy of the diary of an American general. I acquired it from an American officer in Frankfurt and had an opportunity to read it. I was so shaken up that I decided to have a photostat made." Squires was then asked to find a way to publicize the contents of the diary.[2]

Squires's reaction to the diary was dramatic: "As long as I live I shall never forget the impact it made upon me. I was horrified at the thought that the fate of a great land and a great people rests today in the hand of brutal inhuman beings such as the man who wrote this diary. And these people have atom bombs, poison gas, napalm, bacteriological and other weapons with which they are preparing to convert the old cities of Europe into rubble and ashes and sweep our civilization from the face of the earth." Chapter 6 of Squires's book contained entries and facsimiles intended to demonstrate that an American general officer was part of an international conspiracy to unleash a new world war. Squires wrote emotionally, "no one who hates war from the bottom of his soul can read this work without feeling profoundly disturbed." He then quoted from Grow's diary:[3]

> Our attack should be directed at enemy weakness. Although the military services are primarily concerned with military weapons and methods, we must understand that this war is total war and is fought with all weapons.
> We must learn that in this war it is fair to hit below the belt.
> Got a letter from Geo. King who has been showing my letters to Smith, who is interested. I am urging action on preparation for the time after the next war. . . . He says Smith is interested. . . . He also feels that this is a very critical year.

Squires interpreted the entry to be the views of an officer sent to Moscow by Washington, which were shared by Walter Bedell Smith, director of the Central Intelligence Agency and former U.S. ambassador in Moscow.

After quoting a few brief diary entries, Squires stated: "Obviously it is Major General Grow's task in Moscow to use every effort to prepare for a repetition of present events in Korea, where Yankee bombers systematically make targets of peaceful cities and of the civilian population." He then stated Soviet concern about encirclement: "Grow's entries indicated Americans are establishing their bases as close as possible to the Soviet border, converting England into an American air base, with only one purpose in view—to prepare for aggressive warfare against the Soviet Union, thus starting a new world war." He linked other diplomats who were helping "the American warmongers" to this effort. A British military attaché, a Canadian diplomat, a Greek diplomat, and a Turkish attaché in Moscow were singled out as assisting American intelligence.

Squires went on to explain Grow's intelligence activities as sketched in the diary:

> Big power plant at Shatura . . . Good target.
> The bridge here is best target in S. Russia. This, together with bridges over Kuban R. at Kavkazskaya, would cut off all the Caucasus except for power lines to Astrakan which could easily be cut.

Squires portrayed Grow as being elated when he found potential targets that could be destroyed and profoundly disappointed when unable to discover a suitable target. As he put it, Grow "knows nothing but gratification of his insatiable craving for blood and destruction." Regarding the personality conflicts between various members of the embassy staff and Grow, he wrote: "We learn from the diary that Grow takes his revenge by never missing a single occasion to offer cynical remarks about the Ambassador." Yet, paradoxically, Squires goes on to explain that the ambassador appreciated Grow's reports, using an example from the diary:

> Threw a minor bombshell by reading our paper which definitely estimated action this year or before July 1952 by all forms of warfare including Europe. It was backed up by capabilities and reason. Amb. accepted our paper as sound and worthy of serious consideration.

"I believe there is no need for comment," Squires wrote, for a "reader can see from these lines that Grow is building up his egotistical plans . . . for another world war." Then the capitalist element was introduced: "Anyone who reads Grow's diary will no longer feel surprised at hearing of U.S.A. generals who hope for another war just as the stock market speculators do." Squires then describes the war plans of American generals by using the analogy of a medical report: "One of the leading principles of this war maniac, in whom the disease has reached the acute stage, is expressed in his [Grow's] own words":

> War! As soon as possible! Now!
> This is the year!

The British defector linked the notion of Grow as a maniac to an American intelligence conference in Frankfurt in June 1951, intimating that the conferees concurred with Grow that "Communism must be destroyed . . . the necessity of better work at Washington, and a great expansion of CIA espionage." According to Squires, the conference dealt with the use of atomic weapons and chemical and bacteriological warfare. Finally, he said, the conferees discussed how to fill the vacuum after the Soviet regime was destroyed: "So the thing that Grow and his chiefs desire is a puppet regime formed by men who are entirely dependent upon them and are hated by the Soviet population." Just how was this to be done? Squires had the answer, again quoting from the diary:

> We must start by hitting below the belt. This war cannot be conducted according to Marquis of Queensbury rules.
> Our intelligence agencies must strive ceaselessly to find and report points of strength and points of weakness as well. We must employ every subversive device to undermine the confidence and loyalty of Soviet subjects in their regime. We must cause them to lose faith in communist leadership . . . anything, truth or falsehood, to poison the thoughts of the population.

Finally, Squires chastised world leaders such as Truman, Dean Acheson, Winston Churchill, Herbert Morrison, Eisenhower, and Viscount Bernard Montgomery for allowing men like Grow to assume responsible government positions "where they can employ every means to precipitate mankind into a third world war."

Squires claimed that his mysterious friend at the East Berlin cafe gave him notes for Grow's speeches at the Frankfurt intelligence conference. In addition to photostats of the diary, the notes were mentioned in support of Squires's conclusions. He offered no proof of the authenticity of the copied notes other than a brief unsupported reference and took considerable pains to avoid identifying the source of the photostats. In fact, the mysterious friend from the West was a fabrication.

Some of the purported quotes were not from Grow's diary, and the remainder of the material cited was taken out of context so as to convey an entirely different meaning. Squires's exposé was in large part a fabrication designed to enhance communist propaganda efforts. Unfortunately, certain ranking army officers did not realize the material was fabricated. The American military community mishandled the episode, thereby providing a propaganda coup for the Soviet government and wreaking havoc on the career and personal life of a major general in the United States Army.

When the book reviews appeared in East Berlin newspapers, American intelligence authorities in Berlin displayed little interest. They judged Squires's exposé an unimportant bit of Soviet propaganda and did not add the reviews to files on the East Berlin newspapers, which contained half a dozen clipped political items deemed more interesting. Nor was Squires's book noted in the daily digest of Soviet press items published by the Berlin intelligence office. Elmer Cox, chief of the Information Branch, Public Affairs Division, HICOG, Berlin Element, first heard of the reviews on or about 12 or 13 January, less than two weeks after they appeared. According to Cox, there was no indication that anyone regarded the quotes from the diary as anything unusual or out of the ordinary because editorials or cartoons presented in the communist press, especially that of East Berlin, were not considered wholly reliable. By 14 January Cox noted that Michael Lustgarten, the intelligence officer from HICOG, had informed Grow that he did not remember the reviews and a search of the files was required.[4]

Auf dem Kriegspfad was not known to Berlin intelligence nor did they seek it until 14 January. It was not until a HICOG clerk stationed in West Berlin mailed a copy of the reviews to a friend, Hugh Smith Cumming, Jr., chargé d'affaires in Moscow, that action was initiated. Cumming claimed that the review in the *Berliner Zeitung* was called to his attention on 3 January, yet it was not until

14 January that he advised the secretary of state that he had learned of the newspaper publication "for the first time." According to Cumming, the diary's contents as depicted in Squires's exposé might have affected Grow's personal safety. He believed that Soviet state security might arrest Grow on charges of espionage as a direct result of the incriminating information in the diary.[5]

Grow and fellow attachés characterized Cumming as a "jittery ass." The foreign service had reason enough to be nervous during this era, for it was experiencing a morale problem as a result of Senator Joseph McCarthy's attack on so-called communist subversives in the government. McCarthy's attacks, often directed at "pinkos" in the State Department, caused consternation and apprehension in many American embassies. Thus moved to action, Cumming sent a top secret coded telegram to Secretary of State Dean Acheson. He wrote: "Published facsimiles are definitely in Grow's handwriting." He also listed "typical extracts":

> January 8, 1951. This is year of the war.
> February 23, 1951. Letter from Bolling [Assistant Chief of Staff, G-2, Intelligence] makes clear that my letters go to all leading quarters even to the President.
> April 16, 1951. Tolstoy's place closed today for which we were not sorry since we had not gone there at all for purpose of seeing it . . . many military vehicles numbers noted. Saw some anti-aircraft installations.
> May 1951. Only bridge is railroad and is good target. Big power plant . . . good target.[6]

Cumming suggested that the publication "seriously jeopardizes not only Grow's personal security, but also security of this mission." Accordingly, a cable was also sent to Grow in West Berlin advising him to defer his return to Moscow pending further notice.

Cumming soon acquired a copy of Squires's book. He believed that the diary should be scrutinized by qualified personnel in the State Department to evaluate the damage "content." He feared that it gave the Soviets a gold mine for propaganda purposes and that they might use more quotes from it. Unfortunately, Cumming did not consult with Grow about the diary. Little did Cumming realize, nor did the Soviets at the time, that indirectly he would be a party to Soviet propaganda efforts.

26

Meanwhile, Grow, perplexed by the developments, had cabled Acheson with a message pass-through to the assistant chief of staff, G-2 (Intelligence). Grow's surprise was evident: "Have diary which never left my possession. German newspaper article not seen here. Fail to understand circumstances or significance."[7] The same day Grow telegraphed Acheson, State Department personnel in Washington consulted top army officials regarding the incident. Lieutenant General Maxwell D. Taylor, deputy chief of staff for operations and administration, and Major General Alexander R. Bolling, assistant chief of staff, intelligence, agreed that Grow should not return to Moscow. Accordingly, a cable was sent to Brigadier General Mark McClure, director of intelligence, European Command, asking that he secure details of the incident. Immediately, EUCOM counter-intelligence began an investigation in West Germany that in the following months would reveal a lapse of intelligence and security procedures, embarrassing not only European Command and the army but also HICOG.

While Grow was anxiously waiting for new instructions from Washington, Warrant Officer Junior Grade George A. Henri, an agent of the 66th Counter Intelligence Corps (CIC) Detachment in West Berlin, was directed on 16 January by his commanding officer to purchase Squires's book. Henri had visited seven or eight bookstores in the western sector but failed to locate a copy. As far as he could ascertain, the book was distributed only in East Berlin. Henri then visited the railroad station in the British sector of Berlin, where he met Joachim Meier, a German national. On instructions from Henri, Meier crossed into the Soviet sector and purchased two copies of *Auf dem Kriegspfad* from Hannemann Buchhandlung. These books were turned over to Henri and eventually made their way to General McClure.[8]

While Henri was securing Squires's book, a conference took place between Grow, McClure, and representatives from HICOG. A detailed comparison of the diary entries with the facsimiles depicted in the East Berlin newspapers was not made at the time. Although their assessment was only suggestive, it did indicate that Squires's version was highly distorted. On 18 January, Grow had the opportunity to go over the recently acquired book with McClure. Grow was convinced that the diary had been stolen and photostated in July 1951 at the Victory Guest House in Frankfurt, where he was staying while attending a top secret conference of attachés. He believed the "German job" was Soviet-controlled and thought the diary would not have been published if it had had intelligence value because publication would have dried up the sources. Grow conjectured that the photostating was "done in Germany when my security was lax" at the Victory Guest House and possibly throughout EUCOM.[9] Little did he realize how serious the situation was in West Germany and how the "lax" statement he recorded in his diary would figure in his conviction.

The next day Grow received orders relieving him of his assignment in Moscow and ordering him to return to Fort Meade, Maryland. Within four days, he arrived in Washington and reported to the office of the G-2 in the Pentagon. His military future appeared in doubt and his outstanding army career jeopardized.

Meanwhile, a copy of *Auf dem Kriegspfad* and the two reviews had arrived at the Pentagon. Major General Bolling, like Cumming, did not have access to Grow's diary to make comparisons and verify the authenticity of the published quotations. And like Cumming, he made a hasty judgment. The G-2 summary sheet prepared for General J. Lawton Collins, army chief of staff, concluded that the material contained in the diary and the facsimiles published in the book were a compromise of classified security information. The G-2 further explained that the quotations in Squires's book contained a vast amount of classified security information of both a personal and official nature. A number of examples were listed:

> A quote from a letter of Bolling that was classified TOP SECRET
> A statement of proposals and suggestions made at the 1951 Frankfurt Attaché Conference by other representatives of the American Intelligence Service—"The necessity of better work at Washington and a great expansion of CIA espionage."[10]
> A statement from a Memorandum that General Grow presented to Ambassador Kirk in which General Grow predicted "the attack is with certainty estimated to happen this year or before July 1952, with all forms of warfare, including Europe."
> An expression of General Grow's "War! As soon as possible! Now!" and twenty pages of similar material.

General Bolling acknowledged that Squires's "book is obviously communistic propaganda" and "the publication of the material contained in the diary is extremely embarrassing to both the Army and the Government."[11] Very shortly, however, Bolling would discover that the published diary entries were not accurate.

Early on 28 January 1952, the acting inspector general, Brigadier General Fay Prickett, was summoned to Maxwell D. Taylor's office. Also present was the G-2, General Bolling, who promptly declared that his office must acquire Grow's diary for the year 1951 to determine whether it contained mention of security matters. Taylor directed Prickett to obtain the diary from Grow for Bolling as soon as possible. Prickett hesitated because he thought it unusual for the Inspector General's Office to obtain the diary without a proper request for an investigation. Following this unusual oral directive, a concerned Prickett went immediately to the office of Major General Ernest M. Brannon, the judge advocate general, for advice and to discuss the best method of obtaining the diary. Because he too believed it unusual to request the diary before a formal request for an investigation, Brannon advised Prickett to write a letter to Grow in the form of a request from the chief of staff.[12]

After resolving Taylor's order with Brannon, Prickett returned to his office and drafted a letter to Grow; he signed it and turned it over to Colonel Edward J. Maloney, head of the IG Investigation Division. Maloney in turn passed it to another officer, Colonel John E. Ray, who was given the job of procuring the diary, ending a circuitous execution of Taylor's order by the Inspector General's Office. Normally, the IG made such investigations as directed by the secretary of the army or the chief of staff. On occasion, the IG would make preliminary inquiries and examine documents when information came into its possession suggesting need for an investigation. But in the Grow incident, the request for procurement of the diary, unaccompanied by a formal directive for an investigation, was unusual, as Prickett and Ray readily admitted.[13]

Early in the afternoon of the twenty-eighth, Ray—by now showing considerable agitation over the prospect of executing his unusual mission—went to the office of the G-2 and interrupted a conference Grow was conducting on intelligence matters. Grow asked that he be permitted to finish the lecture, but Ray nervously replied that he had been instructed to complete his mission immediately. Grow countered that the chief of staff had no right to demand the diary, prompting

Ray to point out that the wording in the letter was "a request." Grow responded that "a request from the Chief of Staff was tantamount to an order." The class was abruptly terminated, and both officers left the Pentagon and drove to Grow's quarters in the guest house at Fort Meyer. The perplexed Grow asked Ray, "What would you do if you were in my situation?" The IG representative responded, "Comply and turn over the diary without any difficulty." With hesitation, Grow turned the diary, "Date Book 1951," over to Ray, who, in his haste, issued an unsigned receipt. It is significant that Ray signed the receipt for the diary the next day.[14] A sense of urgency was evident. Colonel Ray, like his superior, General Prickett, felt the request to obtain the diary was unusual because no investigation was pending in the Inspector General's Office. For this reason, Ray did not advise Grow of his legal rights. Thus the seizure of Grow's diary initiated the question of legal consent.

As soon as he returned to the Pentagon, Ray rushed into General Prickett's office and informed him that he had the diary. Prickett told Ray to take it immediately to General Bolling.

While Ray was performing his unpleasant mission, the secretary of the general staff rapidly cut orders for an investigation "to determine whether in connection with the publication of a book with English title, *On the Warpath,* the author of which was Richard Squires, there has been a compromise of classified information or evidence of misconduct on the part of Army personnel." Enclosed with the memorandum were newspaper articles from the *Berliner Zeitung* and *Neues Deutschland,* with translations, and a copy of *Auf dem Kriegspfad* and a translation of chapter 6. The IG file regarding the compromise of the diary was listed under IG 333.9—Squires, Richard. For overt purposed, Squires was being investigated rather than Grow.[15]

By now Grow had settled nervously into his assignment in the Pentagon in the Office of the G-2. With his role of military attaché abruptly terminated, he had to think seriously about his future in the army. General Collins, the army chief of staff, was friendly but cautious. "Pretty sad situation after long and faithful service and superior record. The Soviets won, but with a United States assist," he recorded.[16]

Shortly after two o'clock on the afternoon of 30 January, Colonel Harold R. Booth, a determined investigator from the Investigation

Colonel Harold R. Booth (1950).
Courtesy of the U.S. Army, National Archives

Branch, Office of the Inspector General, walked into Grow's office and reported in the customary manner. Early in the day Booth had spent several hours reading Grow's diary for 1951 and chapter 6 of

31

Squires's book. Unfortunately, like Cumming and Bolling, he did not identify the errors in Squires's book. Apparently, Booth's approach to the investigation was at least partly flavored by a preconceived notion that security had been compromised.[17]

Booth handed Grow a photostatic copy of a directive from the chief of staff and explained the need to take testimony under oath. After Grow was sworn in, Booth asked him if he fully understood his rights as a witness under the Uniform Code of Military Justice, Article 31, which dealt with prohibiting compulsory self-incrimination and compelling "any person to make a statement or produce evidence before any military tribunal if the statement or evidence is not material to the issue and may tend to degrade him."[18] After a short discussion during which Grow expressed some confusion regarding his rights, he asked Booth about the allegations. Booth responded: "General, the allegations are that you . . . were responsible for the compromise of classified security information . . . that the compromise of classified security information was the result of misconduct by you . . . in failing to provide adequate security for the protection of the contents of a personal diary and other papers written by you while on duty as Military Attaché in Moscow, USSR. Do you fully understand the allegations? Grow replied that he did not understand the accusation. He wanted to know if Booth's allegations were a specification for a possible court-martial charge. Booth replied: "Sir, that I cannot answer. This is an Inspector General investigation to determine the facts in connection with these allegations." Grow, now quite concerned, inquired about the origins of the charge. "They are based on our directive from the Chief of Staff to investigate the allegations. They are not charges and specifications; they are allegations only," Booth declared.

Grow felt that the allegations were, in fact, an indication by the chief of staff of possible legal action which the IG intended to set in motion as a result of the interview. But Booth contended that the IG was endeavoring to find the facts concerning the diary episode. Meanwhile, Grow proceeded extemporaneously and without written sources at his disposal to answer the allegations in the form of a sworn statement, being specific as to names, dates, places, and circumstances contained in the compromised diary.

For two decades Grow had maintained a personal diary. He had a wide range of friends going back to his horse cavalry days and the controversial time in the 1930s when he was actively involved in mechanizing the cavalry. In his Army War College days he had been in close contact with many of the successful combat leaders of World War II. His diaries portrayed him as an outspoken proponent of armor, and they offer valuable insight into the makings of a division commander. Moreover, his postwar diaries describe the army's newfound role in the international scene. Thus for years Grow included in his diaries comments concerning contacts with friends and events of the day as they appeared to him. The diaries were kept in book form, one book for each year, beginning in 1931. Because Grow frequently referred to his diaries in responding to letters from friends and official army agencies, he had copies of past diaries in his Moscow apartment. The diary for 1951 was kept in a locked desk drawer but not sufficiently secured to hinder a determined effort to force entry. This did not concern Grow at the time. He believed that the diary never included comments which he objected to having anyone read, including the Russians.

Grow took his diary along on his various visits to West Germany. During one trip to Frankfurt, which included the first two weeks of July, the period he suspected the diary had been compromised, Grow stayed at the Victory Guest House, an impressed German establishment under the charge of a United States Army officer. While staying in the Guest House, Grow took no special security precautions, and the diary frequently laid on the desk where it could be seen by the German domestic staff who had access to the suite.

Grow next recalled the situation as it appeared to him on that day in January 1952 when he was approached by Lustgarten. The representative from HICOG had advised the attaché to remain in Berlin until further notice, presumably because of the East German newspaper articles containing extracts from Grow's diary, which also presumably had been lost. Lustgarten also advised Grow not to return to Moscow for reasons of personal safety. An inquiry in Berlin regarding the East German exposé at that time produced no one who knew anything about the articles in question. Grow concluded that there had been no threat to his personal safety and advised the embassy in Moscow that he planned to return unless ordered otherwise. Suddenly a rash of cables followed in rapid succession between Washington and Moscow, terminating in a directive from the Department of the Army stating that Grow would not return to Moscow but instead await orders for return to the United States.

Meanwhile, according to Grow, a search was conducted for the article that appeared in the *Berliner Zeitung* on 3 January 1952. Eventually it was found in the intelligence files in West Berlin. A number of news items had been clipped from the East Berlin newspapers, but the article regarding Squires's exposé was not recorded by the political intelligence officers because they had found it to be of little importance. In fact, it had been forgotten. Because the article referred to Squires's book, an effort was then made to secure copies of the book in East Berlin. Finally, a few were secured. In the meantime, Grow, who had returned to Heidelberg, received orders to return to the United States, arriving on 21 January.

Grow then recounted what he had recalled about Squires's book. He knew Squires was a British defector and the book was a denunciation of the Western powers for their actions regarding West Germany. Chapter 6 was an afterthought added to the book by communist propagandists. He challenged Squires's story that a package of photostats of the diary had been secured from an American officer. Grow claimed that he had never shown the diary to anyone. On occasion he read extracts to individuals to answer queries that arose in the course of a conversation. He then told the IG officer that "the facsimiles contained in Squires' book are authentic. The quotations contained in the book in addition to the facsimiles were substantially correct, but contained errors, and in many cases, short quotations have been taken from the context and given an entirely different meaning than that contained in the original, in order to support the author's contentions as to my warmongering thoughts."

In the same conversation Grow noted, though he could not prove it, that the theft of the diary may have occurred on 14 July 1951. At that time ample opportunity existed for a communist operative or members of the household staff to examine the diary during the absence of the general and his wife. According to Grow, the headwaiter or manager at the Guest House always asked how long the couple would be gone for the ostensible reason of determining whether the

Grows would return for the next meal because meals were served at odd hours. As far as he could ascertain, no extracts were made from the diary except for the period from January 1951 to mid-July of the same year. No extracts were made from the 1950 diary, which had remained in Moscow.

Grow emphasized that it was apparent "the contents of the diary were of no intelligence value whatsoever to the Soviets. The Soviets knew that my tour of duty in Moscow would extend to mid-1952." He then forcefully told Booth, "It is inconceivable that they would have eliminated the source of intelligence information by permitting this publication had the information been of any value to them for other than the purposes of propaganda."

During the interrogation, both officers discussed the question of continuity. The subject matter of the diary bore no relation to the balance of the book other than to give "evidence of the fact that Grow was another warmonger." To Grow, this indicated that chapter 6 was "planted" and that the communists had directed the British defector to include that chapter as a propaganda medium. There was no doubt in Grow's mind that the Soviet government was anxious to get rid of him because of his success in making intelligence observations and analysis as desired by the assistant chief of staff, G-2. While in Moscow, he had adhered to all local regulations and restrictions so that the Soviet government had no legitimate grounds on which to declare him "persona non grata." It appeared to him that Squires's book was selected by communist propagandists because it provided an opportunity to disgrace him, thus producing a reaction from the American government. Grow then contended that "no one in Berlin had given any serious consideration to this propaganda blast." It was only when Cumming, the charge d'affaires in Moscow, was made aware of Squires's book by a former clerk in the Berlin office that action was initiated.

In concluding his sworn statement, Grow again reflected on the specific quotations and facsimiles in Squires's book. The passages that contained references to his travels and observations did not reveal anything not already known to Soviet state security. Soviet security personnel not only watched Grow on his trips but also saw everyone with whom he spoke. The comments he recorded on personal events were in no case different from similar comments that appeared regularly in the Western press. Grow emphasized that "the Russians cannot be considered to be so stupid as not to realize the nature of my business since they are past masters at the same." At the end of the sworn statement, Grow admitted that the incident was unfortunate, and it might be construed as evidence of undue carelessness on his part. But in his own defense, he reasoned that the diary exposé had no intelligence value nor was it of sufficient importance to require security classification.

Following Grow's sworn statement and his observations about the episode to date, Booth began his interrogation of the former attaché. First, he asked about the "American officer in Frankfurt" from whom Squires had claimed to have acquired the diary. As far as Grow could determine, his name was Captain Radigan. He was not sure of this connection. After some thought, he noted: "My suspicion is that no such officer existed, in that I have never showed the diary to anyone during the time I was in Frankfurt, nor did I ever read or copy any extract from it to anyone during that time. Therefore, I can only believe that the statement in the book is a complete fabrication." Booth then asked the name of the manager of Victory Guest House, which Grow could not recall but whom he described as "a rather surly-looking individual who impressed me unfavorably." During his last but brief visit to the Guest House in early January 1952, he had noticed that the officer in charge had been reassigned and did not know whether the manager had left. Booth continued to probe: "Was it [the diary] always in your possession?" Grow replied in the affirmative and added that it was either in his briefcase or in his desk. Concluding his interrogation, Booth asked, "In your opinion and judgment, there was nothing contained in the matters published herein [the diary] that in any way affected classified security matters—is that correct?" "That's correct," Grow replied.

It was late in the afternoon when Booth finally completed his inquiry, and by the time Grow arrived at his quarters at Fort Meyer he was tired and apprehensive. Late that evening he recorded the allegations as presented by Booth: that as military attaché, he had failed to secure classified material. "I denied that material was classified and that I failed to take reasonable precautions," he wrote.[19]

In the meantime, Colonel Gordon E. Dawson, chief of the Security Division, made a page-by-page analysis for Bolling to determine whether the diary contained classified security information. It was then concluded that the contents of the diary as depicted in Squires's book were either falsified or taken out of context. A number of items recorded should have carried military security classification, however, either "Secret" or "Top Secret." Examples of subjects were listed: the movement of the 1st Armored Division to Germany; status of the tank program in relation to the 1st Armored Division; information received from discussions with friendly attachés and diplomatic personnel; mentioning the attaché conference in Frankfurt; and recording the views of the American ambassador to the Soviet Union and Grow's comments and opinions.[20]

On 4 February Booth completed his report and forwarded it to the assistant chief of staff, G-2. In general Booth outlined Grow's statement fairly and accurately, but, as required, he also added his own opinion. He suggested a further inquiry to determine the identity of personnel responsible for the photostating of the diary and the means employed to place the photostats in the hands of Squires. Booth contended that the investigation should be aggressively and determinedly pursued to establish the facts. In addition, he wrote, "It is all too evident that Gen. Grow's actions were not in accord with the provisions of . . . *Army Regulations* . . . which provides that the responsibility for military security and the safeguarding of military information is a command responsibility." In concluding, the IG investigating officer stated that "there had been a compromise of classified security" and Grow "is responsible for the compromise of classified security information through his failure to properly classify, store and safeguard classified security information contained in his personal diary."[21] He recommended that appropriate disciplinary action be taken against Grow and that the investigation continue so as to determine how Squires had obtained access to the diary.

After studying Booth's report, Bolling immediately prepared a memorandum for the chief of staff. For the first time, a court-martial was mentioned. "The Inspector General may recommend that General Grow be tried by court-martial for this act. From the viewpoint of the Inspector General, there is every valid reason for such a recommendation." The idea of a court-martial was not specifically mentioned in the "Report of investigation of alleged compromise of classified security information" that Booth prepared.

Rather, Booth recommended "appropriate disciplinary action" without elaborating.[22] After carefully considering national and international implications of the Grow episode and consulting with Walworth Barbour of the Eastern European Division, Department of State, Bolling recommended "that court-martial charges *not* be preferred against General Grow."[23]

Bolling was concerned that Grow would protest a trial "behind closed doors," and an open trial would be aired in the press and all documentation associated with the compromise of the diary would be made public. The G-2 noted that "this could only result in extreme international embarrassment to this Government" and added, "publication and press comment on such breaches of confidence would only tend to diminish the effectiveness of our diplomatic personnel throughout the world." Bolling had undoubtedly realized that the army would be severely criticized for not taking punitive action against General Grow, "but our interests will be served better by accepting this criticism and not further reviewing the entire matter in a court-martial proceeding."[24] Thus Bolling, on 5 February 1952, decided against a court-martial, a decision that was later to be reversed by Taylor. When that happened, Bolling supported Taylor.

The next day Bolling wrote the United States Army attaché in Canada referring to an excerpt from Squires's book which mentioned activities on a trip to Tbilisi in the Georgian SSR by American and Canadian military attachés. The G-2 requested that an apology be passed on to the Canadian chief of the general staff. Similar letters were sent to American attachés in England, Greece, and Turkey regarding references in the diary to specific individuals. Bolling also tendered to the concerned foreign attachés and their governments the apologies of the chief of staff of the United States Army "for the carelessness and the irresponsible act of a United States Army officer." Bolling then requested that the matter be treated as confidential. He did not mention that the diary quotes had been falsified or taken out of context so as to benefit Soviet propaganda efforts. Even though names of foreign attachés had been mentioned in the diary, it would not surprise or be of intelligence value to the Soviets, who tailed all foreigners, especially attachés.[25]

It was now apparent that Bolling was in a quandary as to how to handle the matter. Somehow Grow's diary had been compromised.

At the least it could be an embarrassment to the United States and the army. The affair had to be handled prudently.

Meanwhile, Grow became more and more concerned about what he perceived as Bolling's reluctance to deal aggressively with Squires's propaganda effort. He was beginning to fear a "stab in the back." Finally, early on 25 February, he made an effort to see the G-2 and discuss the possibility of getting out a press release to "beat the Soviets to the punch." Grow knew the diary quotes were false and taken out of context. So did Bolling. But why were those who knew the facts not doing anything to stop the Soviet propaganda exposé before it reached the Western press? According to Bolling, he did recommend some action to General Taylor, who had demurred. A frustrated Grow went to see Taylor, who agreed to a press release providing it could be worked out with Bolling. Taylor promised Grow he would then try to get Collins, the chief of staff, to release it. Grow immediately drafted a proposed answer to Squires's book and gave it to Bolling. But the attempt died. That night Grow recorded in his diary, "I doubt very much that Collins will do it—our top brass is too afraid to take the offensive although this offers a great opportunity. They always wait for the Soviets and then have to go on the defensive."[26]

Grow was not aware at the time of the CIC investigation in EUCOM and that General Taylor, an opportunist, was taking a more active role in managing the incident for General Collins. For Grow, there was little future left. On 29 January he requested retirement, effective 1 May 1952.

Media Reaction

O N WEDNESDAY, 5 MARCH 1952, the Central Intelligence
Agency moved to increase its involvement in the Grow
case. The agency hoped that a counteraction would reduce the psychological value of the diary to the Soviet government, although before that day, the only mention of the diary had been in the East
German press. After the initial newspaper reviews in January, propagandists dropped their campaign against Grow only to have the
charges revived by the *Washington Post* in a 6 March exclusive.[1] General Bolling claimed that John G. Norris, the Pentagon reporter for
the *Post*, "had in effect forced him to release the incident to the press."
What he gave Norris was a copy of chapter 6 of *Auf dem Kriegspfad*,
without comment, thus implying an army stamp of authenticity to
Squires's book.[2] Unfortunately, Norris did not question the quotes
in Squires's book. The *Post* virtually reprinted chapter 6 and included
some of the extracts from the diary as they appeared in the book.
Norris in effect substantiated the communist version of the incident
with Bolling's approval.[3] The G-2 in turn tacitly approved Squires's
version for public consumption even though he knew the book was a
communist propaganda ploy. Even so, Bolling made no effort to
counteract the article.[4] Little did Norris realize when he accepted the
army's version and sensationalized it that he would be serving the army's and the Kremlin's purposes.

The *Post* article portrayed Grow as an aggressor who believed that
the United States "must fight Russia." This effect was not lessened by
Norris's admission that counterintelligence was investigating the incident nor by his refutation of Squires's story about the American of-

ficer who wanted to bring the contents of the diary to the attention of the public. The army did concede, according to the *Post* reporter, that a communist agent had secretly photographed the diary at a VIP hotel in Frankfurt sometime between 6 and 13 July 1951. After quoting generously from chapter 6, Norris identified Grow as a pioneer in the development of armored warfare and an outstanding division commander. But nowhere in the lengthy article did Norris challenge the validity of the quotes. Why Norris did not question Squires's version or the role of the Soviet government is perplexing because the Kremlin frequently and extensively engaged in propaganda based on distortions. Perhaps it was a reflection of the mood of the Cold War period. The *Post* editors had accepted Norris's story without a challenge. Moreover, when composing his exclusive, Norris made no attempt to contact Grow to gain his perspective on the diary episode. It was also possible that Bolling would not have approved of any contact with Grow because the chief of staff had ordered Grow not to talk to reporters.

After Norris's article appeared, the CIA attempted to acquire Grow's diary for 1951, which, at that time, was in the office of the G-2. If the CIA could get the diary, it no doubt would "lick this situation," noted Grow optimistically. Two agents drove to the Pentagon office of the chief of information to discuss the situation with Major General Floyd L. Parks, who reported to the army chief of staff. But Parks was out of the country. They discussed the propaganda incident with his deputy, Brigadier General Frank Dorn, who initially agreed to assist in any way possible but advised against exposing Grow to cross-examination at a press conference. Later, with the army's reluctant approval, the agents visited Grow. Dorn declined to accompany the agents because he wished to avoid any complications. For an hour Grow and the CIA agents talked about compiling a more accurate story using the diary and listing true extracts instead of those falsified or taken out of context by Squires and repeated in the *Washington Post* article. Grow agreed to help, but the agents still had the task of acquiring his diary.[5]

The agents next went to Bolling's office for a further discussion of the incident. Also present was Brigadier General James H. Phillips, deputy assistant chief of staff, G-2. Bolling was perturbed over what he perceived to be the CIA's improper entry into the case. He

Major General Floyd L. Parks (1945).
Courtesy of the U.S. Army, National Archives

42

Major General Frank Dorn (1944).
Courtesy of the U.S. Army, National Archives

emphasized that under no circumstances would he give consent to a press conference. Bolling insisted that all statements originate within or through the Department of the Army. The G-2 gave the agents, as he had given Norris, a photostatic copy of chapter 6 of *Auf dem Kriegspfad* and suggested that it be used "to salvage the Army and the United States from its extremely embarrassing position." The agents were not made aware of how the diary had been distorted.[6]

That evening Grow recorded in his diary that the *Post* had virtually copied the East German release verbatim. He believed the article to be "distinctly antagonistic" and took little comfort from the conviction that it "played completely into Soviet hands. [The] Soviets got a terrific propaganda buildup in their favor—gratis." Grow's fears in January and February began to be realized. Meanwhile, the two CIA agents who had interviewed Dorn, Grow, and Bolling drafted plans for a counteroffensive by attempting to capitalize on the disparities in the published version of the diary.[7] To be effective, however, they needed the diary and the G-2's cooperation.

The next day the *Washington Post* editorially supported Norris's exclusive story, stating that compromise of the diary was extremely damaging to the United States and "it is exactly the sort of thing that General Grow's monumental ineptitude invited." The editorial went on to say that Grow fit the Soviet picture of a "warmonger" and he "stooped to the Kremlin's level in advocating 'anything, truth or falsehood, to poison the thoughts of the population.'" The *Post,* along with its Pentagon reporter, repeated and endorsed the validity of the quotes from the diary. In fact, Grow had never used the term *warmonger* in his diary, and by associating the term with him, the *Post* gave substance to the manufactured portions authorized by communist propagandists.[8] Grow's diary for 1951 contained no entries reflecting his or the United States's intentions to engage in military action against the Soviet Union. What he did record was his estimate of Soviet intentions against the United States. The communist propagandists simply reversed the theme of the diary entries. Grow was not a warmonger, but rather a person who was anticipating the Soviet threat for propaganda purposes.[9]

On the same day the *Post* editorial appeared, Norris wrote a follow-up article. He quoted an unidentified army spokesman who claimed that the investigation of the circumstances surrounding the diary compromise was not complete, therefore, no decision as to possible charges could be made. Norris emphasized that the facts of the diary compromise were printed in the *Post* on the sixth after "wide publication behind the Iron Curtain and confirmation of their authenticity by an Army spokesman."[10] But the CIC investigation in EUCOM, of which Bolling was well aware, indicated the opposite. There had been no wide publication, only a few selected newspaper clips and Squires's book, which was distributed only in East Germany. Norris did admit that army officials were perplexed as to why major Soviet propaganda outlets such as the telegraphic agency of the Soviet Union, TASS, and other Soviet media had not exploited the diary quotes. In Grow's sworn statement to the IG on 30 January, he mentioned that publication of the diary facsimiles in Squires's book in the East German press proved the diary was of no intelligence value to the Soviet government other than for propaganda purposes. The *Post* reporter tried to collapse this theory by suggesting that the communists were saving the rest of the diary for a well-timed exploitation of the episode. Perhaps in some respects Norris's guess was correct.

The opportunity to deal with Soviet-directed propaganda by exposing Squires's book would have been available to concerned top army officials in the Pentagon for almost two months. During this period Grow vainly tried to convince Bolling and Taylor to consider a counterpropaganda effort. He was silenced and no steps to offset Soviet propaganda or to neutralize it were taken until the CIA attempted to enter the picture. Meanwhile, the story of the "warmonger" theme spread throughout the Western world. The *New York Times,* whose news policy was predominantly conservative, printed a condensed version of Norris's article mentioning army endorsement of Squires's exposé.[11] Soon the Western press corps recycled Norris's copy. The common practice of reprinting copy without question if it came from an authoritative wire service assured that accusations against Grow would be spread. The press had a hot news item that would sell during the period when McCarthyism and the red scare were flourishing in the United States. The communist conspiracy and related topics, until they had run their course, were marketable. Indeed, even insignificant elements of any Cold War incident could develop into a news story. The Grow case was no exception, largely because of Norris's exclusive.

The official American Communist party newspaper, the *Daily Worker,* quickly responded to the *Post* article, calling the news "sensational" because it "exposed" a top United States Army officer on a spy mission plotting an atomic war against the Soviet Union. After quoting from Squires's book as it had appeared in the *Post,* the *Daily Worker* divulged that "Defense Department officials made no attempt to deny" the validity of the excerpts. The Moscow correspondent for the *Daily Worker* called the former attaché a "loud-speaking regular army officer . . . who rarely misses a cocktail party." "Capitalist press correspondents" were aware of Squires's book earlier, it claimed, but failed to file one word about its existence. On the ninth the *Daily Worker* quoted from the "Dere Diary" editorial in the *Post.* The communist paper alleged that the Pentagon and the Department of State were "violently upset," not over the aggressive war plans Grow supposedly recorded, but over his carelessness in keeping a diary that revealed the plot for "War! As soon as possible! Now!"[12]

Also on the seventh, the *London Times* reported on the episode, copying the Norris version. Grow was portrayed as promoting a world war in his diary entries, which were authenticated by an army spokesman from the Pentagon.[13] Though the *Times* periodically carried accounts of the Grow story, its treatment did not display the sensationalism exhibited in America.

The news released understandably caused Grow considerable frustration and anger. "The 'loyal' army never lifted a finger either to correct the error or to put out the counter-propaganda," he recorded. He believed top army officials had either abandoned him or were about to "set him up." But for what? He was in a dilemma. Regarding the G-2, Grow wrote, "for the record—I am satisfied that Bolling is both stupid and weak." As for Taylor, he "is smart enough to see it but is too politically-minded," and Chief of Staff Collins does not "know the whole story and is concerned about security and politics." Floyd Parks, chief of information, was referred to as "dumb as well as malicious." Furthermore, the Department of State's reaction to counteract the newspaper articles was viewed by the former attaché as "hopeless."[14]

The only immediate response by the State Department to Norris's revelation was through the Voice of America, which beamed a broadcast into Eastern Europe and Russia, telling the listeners the United States did not endorse Grow's call for an attack on the Soviet Union. The Voice quoted liberally from the *Washington Post* and did not dispute the authenticity of the excerpts from the photostated diary. Finally, it emphasized that Grow's opinions "bear no resemblances to official American foreign policy."[15] The broadcast actually supported Squires's version. At the time, it was not known in State Department circles that the quotes were falsified or had been taken out of context. Only select top army officials knew, but they remained silent.

Throughout the United States the news media continued to feed its readers developments regarding the compromise of the diary. Army authorities were quoted as saying that additional "top secret" military information may have fallen into communist hands during the annual intelligence conference in Frankfurt in June 1951 as a result of the compromised diary. The *New York Times* reported, "The Army emphasized that strict security measures had been carried out during the meeting."[16] Certain G-2 personnel knew this was not true, especially those who had read the reports from the 66th CIC Detachment.[17] Information that could have been kept in-house was now, it seemed, being leaked to the public, particularly details of a possible breakdown of security in EUCOM, which was a reflection of the G-2 function in the Pentagon. If explored further and the truth made known, it could ruin, or at least adversely affect, the careers of Bolling and Taylor and perhaps Collins. Top army officials in the Pentagon remained silent, thus giving tacit approval to distorted newspaper accounts of the affair. Perhaps they were waiting for the final CIC report from EUCOM. The prevailing attitude was to wait and see. In this way, the major thrust would be centered on Grow. And if Bolling and Taylor managed the episode in EUCOM, it could be kept in the background, or, even better, isolated from the heated political atmosphere in the nation's capital.

Congressional reaction to the Grow disclosure was anger. Representative Robert L. F. Sikes, a Democrat from Florida and a member of the House Military Appropriations Subcommittee, demanded an investigation. Sikes said, "It was not at all smart of the general to keep a diary, and I think Congress should ask some questions about why he did." Another representative, James Patrick Sutton, a Democrat from Tennessee, called for a court-martial. Both representatives believed that the former American military attaché in Moscow should be investigated by Congress.[18] The army's chief of legislative liaison, Major General Miles Reber, was responsible for making sure Congress did not enter the case. General Reber was under the general supervision of General Parks, chief of information. He was cautioned to avoid a public airing of the incident because no decision had been made to prefer charges. Later, when the decision was made to draw up charges against Grow, Taylor advised Collins that it would be in the best interests of the army "to avoid stimulating discussion in Congress and elsewhere."[19]

Meanwhile, the *Daily Worker*, ecstatic over its newly discovered propaganda opportunity, told its readers that top Pentagon leaders were hungry for war with the Soviet Union, and "they cannot wait for the day when they unleash . . . a rain of A-bombs." The editorial referred to "Grow's clamor for a Hitler-style blitz attack on the Soviet Union." Using the diary incident as a springboard, the *Daily Worker* began attacking the "German question" and America's involvement in the Korean War. An editorial accused the United States of moving to "re-arm the German Nazis" and stalling the truce efforts in Korea. In addition, the editorial tied Grow's comments to germ warfare. It reported: "When Grow urged the use of every savagery of 'hitting below the belt' he was, in fact, casting a full light on the Chinese-Korean charges of germ warfare in Korea." Concluding, the editorial accused the former attaché of premeditating a hideous crime against humanity and of suggesting that President Truman held similar views. The next day, Rob Hall of the *Daily Worker* wrote that news-paper editorial writers, congressmen, and high Pentagon officials were not critical enough of Grow's views or of his activities while serving in Moscow.[20]

While the news media was playing out the drama of the diary com-promise, a CIA agent outlined a counterpropaganda plan. Two alter-natives were available to the Department of the Army. It could give the diary affair the "silent treatment," thus tacitly admitting to "loss of face" as well as "loss of secrets." To punish Grow for breach of security would only accentuate the army's "embarrassed position." Or the army could bypass Grow's derelictions by making as much counterpropaganda capital as possible out of the incident. The agent favored the second alternative only if bold strokes could be taken such as making public the true contents of the diary through a press interview. He was concerned that a weak and hesitant counter-offensive would serve no constructive purpose. The agent strongly believed "it would be something less than brilliant for the United States military establishment to take the whole episode in red-faced silence" or to accept the other extreme by officially taking punitive action against Grow. He preferred to take the initiative. Thus on 10 March, the "Plan for Propaganda Counter-Offensive, re: The Diary of General Grow" was submitted through CIA channels for recom-mendations and implementation.[21]

What Grow had feared materialized on 12 and 14 March when the *Literaturnaya gazeta* (Literary gazette)—published by the Union of the Soviet Writers—featured chapter 6 of Squires's book. For the first time, a part of *Auf dem Kriegspfad* was translated into Russian and circulated. Shortly thereafter, the Soviet monthly *Bolshevik* presented its first written review of Squires's book. The author gave the warmonger theme intensified treatment.[22]

On the evening of 12 March, the same day the *Literaturnaya gazeta* printed its first installment, the USSR Overseas and Far East Service began a series of broadcasts in English aimed at North America quoting excerpts from Grow's diary as they had appeared in *Auf dem Kriegspfad*. Two days later, a second series of talks on Squires's book was presented. The listeners were told that chapter 6 was appearing on the pages of the Soviet writers' newspaper, *Literaturnaya gazeta*. Again the basic theme was expressed "that war is the object of Grow's fondest dreams . . . war must be launched in 1951." Once more the diary excerpts were presented with special emphasis on the Frankfurt conference in June 1951.[23] Also on the fourteenth, the USSR European and Near East Service broadcasted diary excerpts from Squires's book in English to the United Kingdom linking British accomplices with the warmonger theme. For the first time, the Soviets stated that "the United States press has fully confirmed the authenticity of Grow's diaries."[24] Three days later, the Soviet Overseas and Far East Service told American listeners, "The American press has admitted the authenticity of Grow's diaries."[25]

It should be stressed that foreign communist news media had made no comment about the diary compromise since 6 January. Only after the *Washington Post* article on 6 March did the Soviets begin to capitalize on the incident, and then the Soviet government home and satellite propaganda machines increased the propaganda value of *Auf dem Kriegspfad*.[26] The American press was used as an example so as to verify Kremlin accusations, and Squires's book, which had temporarily been forgotten, was resurrected. Soviet propaganda consistently hammered away on the warmonger theme. Moreover, the diary excerpts served to verify Russian propagandists' image of the United States as an imperialistic threat to world peace.

Propaganda is self-serving, and the Soviet Union—as do all governments—engages in propaganda and disinformation to gain influence abroad, convince its own people, and win acceptance for its respective policies. The roots and lineage of the Soviet propaganda machine can be traced to I. V. Lenin. Lenin, as the party's organizer and theoretician, viewed propaganda as a vital and indispensable instrument of policy. As a result, Soviet propaganda directly reflects policy objectives. In the Grow case, the communist propagandists had manipulated the contents of the diary, presenting a one-sided, distorted picture of an American "warmonger" who was accused of planning a preventive war. Consequently, the Kremlin, more adept and aggressive than the Americans, was on its way to achieving a major propaganda victory.

During a discussion in October 1951 with President Truman on United States–Soviet affairs, Ambassador Alan G. Kirk commented that "the effect of propaganda machinery of the Communist Party, with its control over all media of mass communication, was disadvantageous for our point of view." The United States, Kirk continued, was "being pictured as warmongers, imperialists, encirclers of the Soviet Union, and preparing to launch an aggressive war." The following year, the ambassador-designate and noted diplomat, Russian-Soviet historian, and political scientist, George F. Kennan, commenting on recent Soviet propaganda, stated "I have never seen anything to equal its viciousness, shamelessness, mendacity and intensity what is now being done in this country to arouse hatred, revulsion and indignation with regard to Americans in general and our armed forces in particular." He noted that the volatile anti-American propaganda had no parallel in the history of international relations. He was disturbed because the United States government, including the military, would not take the trouble to refute Soviet propaganda. Decades later a conference report on Soviet propaganda and disinformation sponsored by the State Department and the Central Intelligence Agency noted that "forgeries, in particular, tend to be counterproductive to the credibility of Soviet propaganda when they are exposed."[27] The army staff, perhaps jolted by the acrimony of the era—McCarthyism and the communist controversy—was now considering a prosecution rather than exposing the communist line and the warmongering theme. Only a general court-martial remained, thus providing the Kremlin with a golden opportunity in the propaganda war.

Meanwhile, the *Daily Worker* claimed the "deep silence" maintained in the White House, the Department of State, and the Pentagon over the Grow exposé was being accepted throughout the world as an admission of U.S. intentions to unleash another world war. The

Daily Worker gave credit to the *Washington Post* for breaking the story to the American people. For the first time, the American communist newspaper produced photostatic excerpts from the falsified Grow diary, the same excerpts that had appeared in the *Washington Post*.[28]

Newsweek and *Time,* two popular and widely circulated American weekly magazines, repeated the Norris story in their weekly editions of 17 March. *Newsweek* called Grow a "rough tough soldier of the old school with some equally-old ideas like bringing back the horse cavalry." It printed Squires's facsimiles of Grow's diary. *Newsweek* claimed: "At first the Army couldn't believe the diary was authentic. Investigation proved that it was." The diary excerpts were a propaganda bonanza for the communists because they compromised every Western military attaché Grow came in contact with. Concluding, *Newsweek* announced that "the Army was loath to court-martial the general." *Time* also quoted facsimiles and gave credibility to Squires's book.[29]

The various articles in the Western press demonstrated an unfortunate fact of journalistic life: once something appeared in print, the press corps tended to repeat the first stories, thus compounding initial gaps in the truth. In the months to follow, the snowball effect generated by the Western press would continue and top army officials such as Taylor and Bolling, who were in a position to tell the truth, remained silent. Were they afraid of becoming targets of the press? Were they merely struggling with ways to manage the affair and avoid embarrassment? Soon these questions would be answered.

From the time Squires's book became known in Washington, Grow was silenced by order of the chief of staff, thus raising the question of legal due process if there was to be a hearing. He thus had no opportunity to acquaint anyone, especially other agencies such as the State Department and the CIA, with the facts. Though publicly chastised by the press as a warmonger, he was helpless to defend himself.[30] It was difficult for him mutely to witness the press exploitation of Squires's version of his diary. On 17 March he reacted, sending a detailed and angry memorandum to Bolling. Grow's outburst contained the following assertion: "The chief difference between *The Washington Post* and Red Fleet is that the former is written in English. Both carry the Soviet line without regard for facts." He emphasized that "nowhere in my diary did I advocate or imply that the United

States or western allies should initiate military action 'now' or at any future time." The former attaché continued: "Obviously the Soviets, in their desire to get rid of me and make propaganda favorable to themselves, liberally extracted quotes out of context to 'prove' that I was a warmonger." He criticized the *Washington Post* for gullibly swallowing the Soviet line. "No greater service could have been done to Moscow." He added, "To accept the Soviet statement that I advocated military action is not only stupid on the part of the press, but implies a stupidity in strategic thinking on my part . . . in view of the relative conventional military strength of the Soviet Union in Eastern Europe in 1951 as compared to the West." Concluding, Grow reproached the *Post* for being both stupid and malicious. Moreover, "it would appear in the best interests of the service, in spite of the late date, to distribute a press release primarily for the use of honest and patriotic" reporting. He recommended four points to be included and clarified in a press release:

> Soviet propaganda employs the familiar expedient of extracting from context and distorting statements to prove that "black is white."
> With my diary as an example, I am made to appear [as] an advocate of United States military aggression whereas in truth I was pointing to the danger of Soviet military aggression.
> Repetition of Soviet propaganda accusations by United States press is one of the objectives of the Soviets in which this case was admirably served. In other words, the press did exactly what the Soviets hoped they would do.
> The danger our nation faces is great and one of the most dangerous weapons is propaganda. The free press must guard itself against seizing a Soviet weapon and employing it to further Soviet ends.[31]

Bolling read Grow's memorandum and forwarded it to the chief of information, General Parks, for comment. Parks admitted that Grow's "complaint of quotations out of context and consequent distortions of his intent has merit." Nevertheless, he said that "no matter what newspaper may be guilty, it is my belief that we would accomplish no purpose by the issuance of a press release on the subject of his diary." Parks recommended that "the less we say the better off we will be" in view of the congressional, press, and public reaction to the publication of the diary episode.[32]

It would be expected that Grow would be highly critical of the *Washington Post*. He had reason to be. But he was not aware that Bolling had furnished Norris with a copy of chapter 6, then remained silent about its validity. Later, in reference to the *Post* articles, Bolling did admit "the entire case was poorly handled and played into the hands of the Soviets."[33]

On the nineteenth, Bolling was quoted by the *Daily Worker*, which reported that the G-2 was expected to tighten intelligence activities through control and censorship so as to prevent additional embarrassing leaks. The article reported further that "the war-bent militarists apparently are not prepared to repudiate the war plot indiscreetly tipped off by Grow."[34]

Harkening back to his reaction to Grow's memorandum, General Parks expressed concern about public reaction to the compromise of the diary. He, along with Taylor and Bolling, were right to be worried. On 20 March the Plainville Connecticut Council of Churches wrote the president about the entries from the diary which had appeared in the press. In their estimation, Grow was a serious security risk, who deserved to lose his rank because of the aggressive comments he made in his diary. They suggested as well that his words should be refuted by the president because "the integrity of the United States leaders should not be questionable and thereby forming an obstacle to world peace."[35]

The Plainville letter was circulated in the office of the chief of staff and the G-2, and comments were prepared for a reply by Major General Harry H. Vaughan, President Truman's military aide. The Plainville Council of Churches was subsequently told that "the President deems it advisable for the present to leave the matter in the hands of the Department primarily involved," the army. Vaughan frankly admitted that the episode had been "extremely embarrassing to all concerned," and the president did not wish to add to the problem by pressing the army for immediate action. Finally, the letter concluded, "Grow's indiscretion will not be lightly passed over, and whatever action is finally taken will be for the good of the nation."[36]

Taking a cue from the Plainville church group, the Great Neck Peace Forum from Great Neck, New York, called for Grow's quick removal from the army. If this were done, "the peoples and govern-

ments of the world know that the United States of America is truly and sincerely desirous of securing peace throughout the world." Vaughan advised the forum that "the decision reached will reflect sound judgment and will be in the best interest of our cause." Concluding, Vaughan stated that the president "believes it best for the present to leave the matter in the hands of the Department of the Army."[37]

The Grow incident was clearly achieving national, even international, attention. The liberal weekly opinion magazine the *Nation* took up the warmongering theme: "What is needed is proof that the words of General Grow do not in the smallest degree represent the policy of the American government." The *Nation* chastised the administration for the damage the incident had caused more than it blamed "the bellicose Grow" at a time when "government workers are being fired for talking to the wrong people or reading the wrong magazine. Grow should be fired as the most extreme security risk . . . as a warning to fellow warmongers."[38] In an ironic twist, before the year ended, the editor of the *Nation* was falsely accused of Communist party membership, and the weekly was removed from some school libraries in New York City and Newark, New Jersey.

The *Christian Century,* an ecumenical weekly, took its turn next by revealing a major point the newspapers had missed—the nature of the military mind. Grow, as a military attaché in a key post, reported to Washington information that had helped form American policy. Using the facsimiles of the diary quotes as examples, the weekly argued that his reports reflected "a mind which was eager for war." The ecumenical weekly criticized the Pentagon for its growing power in shaping the foreign policy of the United States, as indicated by the diary comments calling for an aggressive war against Russia "now."[39]

Toward the end of March, Grow again attempted to find a way to defend himself. Michael Galvin, who had served Grow as G-3 (Operations) of the 6th Armored Division during the war and eventually moved into the secretary of labor's office, knew Secretary of the Army Frank Pace, Jr. Grow thought Galvin would be in a position to intercede so he drafted a letter to Pace, which he first sent to Galvin for comment. Grow emphasized the importance of putting "out a propaganda punch now and forestall any other publishers." Galvin returned the proposed letter to his former commanding general stating he agreed with its contents, but Grow hesitated. It was not his style to use bureaucratic or political influence to achieve a favor—he preferred to work within the system. But it was difficult to do so in this instance. "It makes me sick and so depressed," Grow wrote, "to think that our leaders swallow this Soviet line. They just help the enemy when they could have delivered the punch."[40]

The Soviet propaganda campaign continued. The *Literaturnaya gazeta,* according to the *New York Times,* linked excerpts from the diary to germ warfare and accused the United States of employing bacteriological weapons in Korea and Manchuria.[41] *Pravda,* the Communist party newspaper, also began running commentaries on Grow's diary. The USSR European and Near East Service broadcasts to Western Germany stated that Grow's diary reflected the thoughts of "the United States ruling clique. Grow's notes are their own plans. . . . The United States rulers are preparing their aggressive war against the Soviet Union on German soil . . . with German soldiers."[42] This notion was tied to the proposed peace treaty the Soviets were striving to conclude with both German governments, to be followed by the merger of the Federal Republic of Germany and the German Democratic Republic and only then allowing general elections. Conversely, the United States, along with England and France, were calling for an all-free German election under international supervision, followed by the formation of a constituent national assembly that would install an all-German government, which in turn would conclude a peace treaty as a free sovereign state.[43]

By the end of March, Soviet propaganda and the American media had made much of the diary episode. The commentaries naturally bothered Grow, but not as much as the army's admission that the quotes were authentic. As before, he emphasized that Squires's quotes were "a pure and simple *lie,* as anyone who read the diary will note that the quoted remarks refer to the Soviets—not to us." He could not understand how the Pentagon, by remaining silent, would admit a defeat in the "cold war battle." On several occasions he pleaded with top army officials to fight back, "but, no, I was to be the goat, so anything I said must be wrong and the Soviets were right . . . so the Soviets again have a wide open field. What stupid oafs are running our Army."[44] Grow could only keep this to himself. He was, after all, an army officer and had been ordered to remain silent.

The press exposé took another turn when the noted American journalist and military analyst for the *New York Times,* Hanson W. Baldwin, attacked army intelligence management. Baldwin, a past recipient of the Pulitzer Prize for journalism, called Grow the "goat" but emphasized that a large share of the blame for the diary incident rested on the G-2 and the army. Baldwin referred to the former attaché as "a fire-eating type with very decided opinions that he is not slow to voice." He accused Grow of violating "a kindergarten principle of intelligence by keeping . . . a compromising diary, which . . . urged war against the Soviet Union" and recording observations and contacts with other attachés. Baldwin chastised Grow for "a nursery school violation of security," but he did quote from one of Grow's fellow officers who stated that "the diary, which displayed little erudition and less information 'might damn well confuse the Russians.' " Nevertheless, Baldwin emphasized the mismanagement theme. His argument was directed against "Army policies that permitted and encouraged the placing of a square peg in a round hole." Attachés were recognized for their intelligence service, but, more important, Baldwin claimed, "they are diplomatic representatives who should represent their country with tact, distinction, dignity and 'brains.' " He characterized many attachés as viewing the State Department and foreign service officers with "ill-disguised contempt" and displaying a tendency to work independent of the ambassadors. Also, "there have been times when the military, defying the tradition of civilian supremacy, have gotten too big for their boots and have virtually tried to run the show." Baldwin admitted that the criticisms did not apply universally, but the Grow case was an example of mismanagement.[45]

The next day Baldwin struck at the army personnel system for wrongly sending Grow to Moscow. Bolling was quoted as saying that "we were glad to have him [Grow]." But Baldwin noted that pressure was exerted on the G-1 (Personnel) or G-2 to find "plum" posts for deserving generals and senior officers with combat records. Baldwin did not think combat experience was a necessary prerequisite and argued for a separate intelligence career track for the army. He made his point by quoting at length from an unnamed "informed officer," who thought the intelligence function mediocre.[46]

Basically, Baldwin argued that the army had tended to "downgrade" the G-2 function and that G-1 had a major influence in the assignment of general officers to military attaché posts. Baldwin used the Grow case as the springboard for his analysis. It did not take long for the army to respond. For once, General Collins supported Grow and defended himself. He had selected Grow for the Moscow post because of his record in Iran and on the recommendation of the former American ambassador to Iran, George V. Allen.

General Bolling supported his G-2 function. He commented at length on Baldwin's two articles criticizing army intelligence policies. He advised Baldwin and his readers that there had been no deterioration in the intelligence service; in fact, intelligence in "the Army has improved greatly within the past few years." He called Baldwin's argument a display in "meager reasoning" because the G-2 function enjoyed "a very satisfactory reputation among the intelligence agencies in Washington" and contributed to the production of national intelligence. Bolling stressed that in spite of the diary incident, Grow's reporting was "outstanding." In response to the statement about misassignments in military attaché posts, Bolling asserted that every effort had been made to select officers with outstanding qualifications. Baldwin retorted that other letters he received disagreed with Bolling's view and were far more critical than the original *Times* articles about intelligence policies. Again he used unidentified sources to support his original argument. He resolved that the G-2 must "overcome the handicaps traditionally placed in its way."[47]

A few interesting observations can be made from Baldwin's articles. First, the perpetuation of Squires's quotes and condemnation of Grow continued and was used by a noted military analyst to attack the army's intelligence policies. Bolling went to great lengths to defend his institution and the job it was performing. Second, the media, typified by Baldwin's articles, provided evidence that reporting was far from immune to arbitrary and capricious exposés. There was no doubt that readers fearful of war would be receptive to unsupported facts and sensational journalism. An atmosphere was created which should have placed the credibility of the articles in question. Baldwin used unidentified sources, as did Norris in his exclusive of 6 March.

The sensationalistic exposés by the *Washington Post,* the *New York Times,* and *Auf dem Kriegspfad* not only appealed to readers but were accepted at face value by noted scholars. C. Wright Mills, a sociologist and a leading critic of modern American civilization, used Baldwin's article on Grow as an example of the disparity between the attachés and the ambassadors.[48] The media coverage was ample reason to criticize Grow and the embarrassment he created.

Alfred Vagts, a former professor at the Hamburg Institute of Foreign Affairs and Harvard University, as well as a member of the Institute for Advanced Study at Princeton, used Baldwin's articles and chapter 6 of Squires's book as the first case in which a military attaché was punished for poor performance. Vagts repeated Baldwin's mismanagement theme, including a few quotes from Squires's book, and noted Grow's quick recall in January and the damage done to America in the Cold War struggle. Another author, Sanche de Gramont, educated at the Sorbonne, Yale, and Columbia, a Pulitzer Prize winner and correspondent for the *New York Herald Tribune* in Paris, recorded in his book on modern espionage that the Grow case was the first since the Civil War in which a general officer underwent the indignity of an investigation and a trial. Gramont also followed the sensationalist theme and accepted Squires's and the communist propagandists' version of the diary compromise. He, too, used quotes which he claimed had appeared in the *Literaturnaya gazeta* shortly after Squires's book was published and concluded that Washington never disputed the authenticity of the diary contents as they appeared in the East German newspapers.[49]

While the American news media continued to cover the case, the communist media emitted further propaganda. The weekly journal of the Information Bureau of the Communist and Workers' Parties, *For a Lasting Peace, for a People's Democracy,* published in Bucharest, Romania, reviewed *Auf dem Kriegspfad.* The journal's long title in itself could have served as a propaganda slogan. The reviewer condemned the diary extracts as bearing "a striking resemblance to that of Hitler, Goebbels and other defeated fascist cannibals." The main theme that Grow was a warmonger was emphasized and related to Western desire for another world war. *Pravda*, published by the Communist party of the Soviet Union's Central Committee and the most widely distributed newspaper in the Soviet Union, as expected, capitalized on the diary as quoted in Squires's book. *Pravda* noted that the publication of the diary "caused a big uproar in America. Some American newspapers even reported that Grow's behavior caused no small 'indignation' in the United States." For the benefit of Soviet readers, *Pravda* declared that "the Pentagon—the United States war department—admitted the authenticity of the diary." The party newspaper even quoted Representative Sutton of Tennessee, who had called for a court-martial. The *New Times,* published weekly in English, French, German, and Russian by the newspaper *Trud,* the daily of the Central Council of Trade Workers, also became involved in the propaganda effort. The communist weekly dealt with foreign affairs and the foreign policy of the Soviet Union. It rehashed the quotes. The *New Times* recalled that the *Washington Post,* along with "the American monopoly press," disowned the "luckless general." Secretary of the Army Pace was quoted as admitting that Grow's call for an aggressive war was an official secret of the Department of the Army.[50]

Finally, the satirical magazine the *American Mercury* had a go at the defrocked attaché. His actions, according to the right-wing *Mercury,* "must come as a heartening reassurance to all those persons behind the Curtain who still aspire to freedom." The monthly took a shot at the Voice of America saying that it "would have done the cause of freedom a good turn if it had reassured the peoples of Eastern Europe that Grow's views are held by at least a vigorous minority of Americans—and that this minority may one day become a majority."[51]

The communist press perpetuated the warmonger theme and used the falsified and distorted version of Grow's diary to prove the point, placing its emphasis on the political theme of aggression. Since the 1947 May Day parade, one Kremlin strategy had been to use such exhortations as to charge the United States with warmongering to solidify military-political gains achieved as a result of World War II, the Great Patriot War.[52] More adept than the Americans in using the propaganda game, the Soviets took full advantage and won.

The Western press, led by the influential *Washington Post,* basically adhered to subjective journalism in the tradition of Joseph Pulitzer. The *Post*'s handling of the Grow incident was an example of hyped journalism that contributed to the negative culture brought about by America's new international role and McCarthyism. When Bolling, as a representative of the army staff, gave Norris a copy of chapter 6 from *Auf dem Kriegspfad* without qualification, he and the Pentagon authenticated Squires's propagandized version, even though they knew it was false. As a result, the Western press gave credit to the distorted communist version. Once the *Washington Post* initiated the exclusive, the story was repeated over and over again, and the Soviets were provided with a propaganda victory. Unfortunately, neither Norris nor the *Post* initially challenged the army's endorsement of the communist exposé. Perhaps they were more concerned with an exclusive and increased circulation than with verification of the facts. Moreover, Norris's and Baldwin's reports raise an interesting question about the editorial control that should accompany the preparation of a story. The media circulated a falsehood by printing the distorted version of the diary and then added unidentified sources to support their arguments. Such action can place in doubt the reliability of the press. But the sad situation was that readers, and even scholars such as Mills, Vagts, and Gramont, who should have known better, accepted these questionable procedures.

Many years later, after the dust had settled on the Grow case, a former diplomatic reporter for the *Washington Post,* Ferdinand Kuhn, Jr., commented that the *Post,* in its reporting during the period in question, was sloppy and stories were not completely checked for accuracy. The publisher and co-owner of the *Post,* Philip L. Graham, known for his keen mind, was not beyond being devious and malicious at times. He was noted for his anti-McCarthy stand, and during the early 1950s this attitude could very easily label a person or an institution as radical or communist-oriented. William Fulton of the *Chicago Tribune*—the parent firm of the conservative *Washington Times–Herald*—referred to the *Post* as the counterpart of the communist *Daily Worker.* A similar comment was made by the *Washington Times–Herald.* Though the charge was not true, the *Post* did develop a radical image, which Graham tried to offset. Another variable to be considered regarding Norris's scoop of the Grow incident was that since 1933, the *Post* had been losing money and needed to boost circulation. A sensational event like the Grow affair sold newspapers. It was not until 1954, when the liberal *Post* purchased its competitor, the conservative *Times–Herald,* that the *Post* began to make money.[53]

The Soviets succeeded in their propaganda ploy because Grow's diary was compromised. This, however, does not excuse Bolling from giving Norris and the *Washington Post* misinformation regarding the diary and its exploitation by Squires. The press in turn, by using the warmonger theme and negligence, inferred guilt upon Grow before a trial. Meanwhile, a Pentagon management group under Taylor's direction was gaining momentum and positioning itself for a decision. How to handle the international embarrassment would soon be resolved but not until the investigation in EUCOM was completed.

★ ★ 4

The Victory Guest House

To GROW, CONSIDERABLE inertia was impeding the disposition of the diary episode, but EUCOM was unearthing some embarrassing facts. Grow was not aware of the extensive investigation conducted by the Office of the Director of Intelligence, EUCOM, who reported directly to General Bolling. Nor did Grow realize that the evidence would be deliberately withheld from the proceedings in Washington. In fact, it would not be until 1978, twenty-six years after the court-martial, that Grow would become aware of the developments that took place in EUCOM. General Bolling, with General Taylor's support, went to considerable length to make sure the investigation in Germany was completely isolated from the disposition of the diary episode in the United States, even though it would have had a bearing on the proceedings and perhaps affect the future careers of certain aspiring general officers and a few colonels.

All reports from the investigating unit, the 66th Counter Intelligence Corps Detachment, would be channeled to Brigadier General Mark McClure, director of intelligence in EUCOM, who in turn would forward them to General Bolling's office. The reports, many of which were immediately sent in cryptographic form, were circulated and discussed only among a select few top army officials in the Pentagon.

The numerous discussions and conferences on the Grow case were usually held in Taylor's or Bolling's office because they were the two dominant figures in the management of the case. Other ranking army officials who sometimes attended included Bolling's deputy, Brigadier General James H. Phillips; the inspector general, Major General Louis A. Craig, and his deputy, Brigadier General Prickett; Lieutenant General Anthony C. McAuliffe, the assistant chief of staff, G-1 (Personnel); the judge advocate, Major General Brannon, and his assistants Brigadier General J. L. Harbaugh and Colonel C. Robert Bard, chief of the Military Justice Division; Major General Floyd L. Parks, chief of information, and his deputy, Brigadier General Frank Dorn; Brigadier General Robert A. McClure, chief of psychological warfare; and Major General Miles Reber, chief of the Legislative Liaison Division. The secretary of the army, Frank Pace, Jr., and army chief of staff, General Collins, were consulted on occasion. Collins tended to delegate management to Taylor and Bolling because he was occupied with the Korean War. Secretary Pace, however, showed more interest in the Grow episode than Collins because of its international implications. But only those in the inner circle of Taylor and Bolling's management group were completely aware of the developments in EUCOM. Since many of the discussions and conferences constituted oral airings of opinion between top army staff and administrative officers, documentation was considered privileged communication. No detailed records were available on any of the recommendations or decisions made on the oral airings, thus offering a convenient way to plant the seeds of suppression while monitoring the incident in-house.[1]

In mid-January, the 66th CIC Detachment in Europe began to unravel the details of how the diary was compromised. Initially, Warrant Officer George A. Henri, through the efforts of a German national, acquired copies of Squires's book in the Soviet sector of Berlin. In February the CIC began to center the investigation in Frankfurt-am-Main, the city in which access to the diary supposedly was obtained. It was expected that the investigation would require several weeks. Meanwhile, the inquiry regarding sale, distribution, and public comment on Squires's book continued.[2]

The directive issued by the Department of the Army requested that information regarding the sale of Squires's book "be obtained without disclosing official interest in this matter." In late January another CIC agent, Gustav Bard, acquired an additional copy of *Auf dem Kriegspfad*. Bard checked all SED and Soviet-sponsored newspapers circulated in the Soviet zone of Berlin and in the German

Democratic Republic (DDR). All of them had printed brief reviews of Squires's book during early January. Facsimiles of Grow's diary were published, and his espionage activities were emphasized. In addition, Bard made contact with several German journalists who were employed by the SED and Soviet-sponsored publications. The contacts revealed that Squires was an unknown figure, especially in East Berlin journalist circles. At the same time, another CIC agent, Eugene L. Maleady, checked leading bookstores in the Western sector of Berlin, Frankfurt, Nuremberg, and Munich to determine the extent of sales of *Auf dem Kriegspfad*. Sales were confined to the Soviet sector of Berlin, and there was no evidence of sales in the Western sector. A check in the cities of Frankfurt, Nuremberg, and Munich did not produce a trace of the book, nor did the book dealers know of its existence.

The following month a more extensive check of major bookstores in Frankfurt disclosed that the book was not sold in the area nor was Squires known to bookstore clerks in the city. Of the nineteen bookstores contacted, inquiries were negative with the exception of one store owned by Karl Poths, who claimed to have had a supply of Squires's book, all of which had been sold. Curiously, Poths could not recall the price and was vague about other details as well. The CIC agents surmised that Poths had lied because he wanted to leave the impression that if Squires's book had existed, it would have been obtainable only from him. A check of Poths at the 66th's Counter Subversive Section was negative.

Meanwhile, CIC agent Darrell C. Schroeder began an extensive investigation of the Victory Guest House in Köenigstein, a suburb of Frankfurt, where the diary had reportedly been photocopied. The Guest House was a large, two-story structure, under requisition by the United States Army as a billet for visiting dignitaries. On 1 April 1952, it was scheduled to be processed for return to private ownership. Schroeder soon discovered that no security regulations applied to the operation of the establishment housing the VIPs. Nor were there any guard details or a security fence to enclose the structure. Theoretically, the structure was made secure from surreptitious entry by metal shutters that could be lowered over all doors and windows on the first floor. Nevertheless, entry could easily be effected through basement windows located at ground level. The windows above the first floor were neither barred nor shuttered.

In 1951, Grow and his wife made four trips to Frankfurt and on three occasions had occupied Suite III of the Victory Guest House. The suite, located on the second floor, consisted of a living room, bedroom, bath, and one small room off the living room was a large terrace, which could be entered through a large, framed glass door with an outer lockable door made of steel bars. The terrace was so situated that surreptitious entry was no problem. In fact, this generally was true for the entire structure. Schroeder also discovered that the rooms or suites did not have safes or other accommodations for storing valuables. Instead, the military manager, Lieutenant David R. Peacock, had a military field-type safe in his office secured to a permanent heating fixture by a chain and padlock. The safe was used primarily to store valuables belonging to guests. Peacock could recall no arrangements to deposit documents in the safe, but he could speak only for the period beginning in early November 1951, when he was assigned as the military manager. There were two sets of keys to all suites and rooms. The guests, when they registered, received one set, while the other set was kept by the assistant manager, a German national named Gerhard Poss. He was the only alien employee of the Guest House who had access to keys and to all suites and rooms.

Schroeder was also interested in the security measures employed at the Sixth Annual Military Attaché Conference during the period from 6 to 14 June 1951. Squires had attacked the conference and Grow's participation as an example of America's aggressive attitude. In addition, Grow assumed that the diary had been compromised after the conference, in July. Schroeder needed to trace the attaché's steps to get some idea of his contacts and movements while in Frankfurt. With this in mind, he contacted Lieutenant Colonel James F. Hughes, chief of the Collection Section, Headquarters, EUCOM, to acquire information regarding the billeting of key personnel who attended the conference. The Victory Guest House was used to billet approximately thirteen persons, mostly military, and served as a temporary residence for high-ranking officers. Schroeder's interview with Hughes was very thorough. Virtually every move made by Grow and his family was accounted for. Nothing unusual emerged. Trips to a dry-cleaning shop, a visit from Grow's son, visits with army friends, and a physical checkup were some of his activities outside of the conference, Hughes recalled.

Although it was Hughes's responsibility to arrange quarters for personnel attending the conference, he had little to do with the actual quartering of personnel in the Victory Guest House. The conferees were instructed to report to the Guest House, and after they arrived all arrangements and accommodations were left to the army officer who managed the residence. The conferees were assigned vehicles and drivers by the Official Reception Bureau at the Frankfurt Military Post. To widen the probe, Schroeder centered his attention on Captain George P. Heald, chief of the Official Reception Bureau, who he suspected would have a record of the drivers assigned to the conferees. Heald's office would also have a file of the trip tickets outlining the movement of various official vehicles. The trip tickets would furnish information on the itineraries of individuals to whom the vehicles were assigned.

Captain Heald's Official Reception Bureau acted as an accommodation agency for visiting dignitaries, including military attachés from Eastern Europe. In his official position he met many important people. He told Schroeder that a chief petty officer from the United States Navy's Attaché Office in Moscow had recently passed through Frankfurt en route to Paris on leave. Heald could not recall his name, but while talking to him he learned of the unfortunate diary incident. This was early in February, and since then Heald had been expecting a visit from CIC personnel.

Heald was very cooperative with Schroeder and volunteered considerable information concerning his personal knowledge of Grow and his activities in Frankfurt. He had first met the general during the war but came to know him and his wife during the period from June 1951 to January 1952. On each of Grow's visits to Frankfurt, Heald's bureau made arrangements for accommodations, scheduled itineraries, furnished a vehicle and driver, and placed his office at the disposal of the attaché. It was natural that Heald would have many personal talks with the general. He sincerely believed he knew of Grow's activities in Frankfurt "better than anyone else." He described Grow "as a man of strong character, a career soldier and diplomat, dignified, diligent, and devoted to duty."

Heald furnished the CIC agent with a detailed report on Grow's itinerary while he and his wife were in the Frankfurt area. Special emphasis was placed on the period around the conference. When Grow

66

arrived in Frankfurt, all arrangements normally furnished VIPs by Heald's office were provided by EUCOM's Intelligence Division. Consequently, officers and drivers for the VIPs were assigned by the Intelligence Division on this occasion. After the conference, Heald's office would assume responsibility for accommodating attaché personnel who stayed over in the Frankfurt area.

The conference began on 6 June and extended to 14 June. Grow attended all lectures and briefings until 13 June. His wife spent most of the period shopping. Heald mentioned that Mrs. Grow purchased silverware and had visited the wife of Brigadier General George Read, Jr. Read had been the assistant divisional commander of the 6th Armored Division during the war and was a very good friend of the Grows. The Reads, Heald noted, had been dinner guests of the Grows at the Victory Guest House. The visit of Grow's son, a lieutenant in the regular army, was also mentioned. After the conference, the Grows took a two-week vacation through Western Europe, ending up on the island of Majorca. Returning to the Victory Guest House on 29 June, they spent several days shopping, taking short drives, and visiting acquaintances. On 5 July, Grow went to Vienna aboard the official courier plane from Rhine Main Air Base, returning to Frankfurt on 10 July. Three days later, the Grows left for Moscow, arriving early on 19 July. Grow initially had suspected that it was during this time, around 13 or 14 July, that the diary had been taken from him, perhaps at the Victory Guest House. The last quoted entry in Squires's book was dated 14 July 1951. The Grows returned to the Guest House late on 22 September for a medical check and stayed until the thirtieth, when they traveled to Berlin and then on to Moscow.

Schroeder was very interested in Heald's comments regarding the chief petty officer (CPO) from the United States Naval Attaché's Office in Moscow and reinterviewed Heald in an effort to obtain more information. Heald recalled that the CPO remained in Frankfurt approximately one week beginning 2 February. He had learned from the CPO that attaché personnel in Moscow believed Grow's diary was lost on the general's last trip to West Germany late in December 1951. The news of the compromise of the diary reached the United States attaché personnel in Moscow by the middle of January 1952. According to the CPO, word also reached Russian employees of the military attaché's office and many immediately resigned, at which time it became impossible to employ a Russian, even a cook. American personnel in Moscow openly discussed the diary compromise and expressed fear that the story would soon appear in *Pravda*. Furthermore, the Office of the Military Attaché in Moscow recognized the possible embarrassment and repercussions that might arise. Because of concern about the possible compromise of classified information, efforts were made to trace the diary. Heald received the impression from the CPO that all records and information of any nature maintained by the military attaché's office were stored in a large vault in the embassy. It was assumed that Grow's diary fell into this category. When a search of the vault proved negative, it was speculated that the diary had been stolen. Another possibility was that the diary was in Grow's possession when he left Moscow by train for Berlin in late December. According to the CPO, the diary may have been stolen during a routine inspection of luggage while Grow was en route. This opinion was shared by some attaché personnel in Moscow.

Schroeder described the second- and thirdhand comments on the diary compromise as hearsay, and evidence to support the CPO's story had been obtained. Earlier it was established that Squires's book had been published late in 1951, before Grow's visit to the West late in December. Schroeder considered Heald to be a responsible, mature individual. He was highly cooperative and was fully aware of the sensitivity of the investigation. He was cognizant of the necessity to avoid publicity regarding the Grow diary. To be sure, Schroeder reminded Heald not to discuss the incident at any time with anyone.

Schroeder next examined the Regional Registry of thirty-four alien employees of the Victory Guest House. Nothing unusual appeared at first except that one employee was identified as having been a member of the Nazi party from 1937 to 1939, and another had been involved in an incriminating investigation. After the check, the CIC agent had the opportunity to identify and interview the CPO Heald had spoken of. CPO Michael F. Cartmill, the chief hospital corpsman in the United States Embassy in Moscow, was exceptionally security-conscious. He carefully examined the CIC agent's credentials, wrote down his name, and told him that he must report having been interviewed upon his return to Moscow.

In general, Cartmill confirmed the story he gave Heald. He claimed that when he arrived in Frankfurt early in February, Heald asked, "How is General Grow?" This led Cartmill to believe Heald and Grow were friends, and he related the information concerning the diary. Regarding the Russian reaction to the incident, Cartmill mentioned that only one Russian employee, a female instructor of Russian, asked when Grow was returning. Later, the same Russian employee inquired why the attaché was not returning to Moscow. Contradicting Heald's statement to Schroeder, Cartmill recalled that there was no marked resignation of Russian employees at the American embassy. Cartmill believed they were not aware of the diary compromise. Moreover, it was common knowledge that all Russian employees of the embassy reported to Soviet intelligence. Cartmill did not consider the Russian language instructor's inquiry regarding Grow's status extraordinary though it was very unusual. Finally, Cartmill regarded Grow as a man of strong character and personal integrity and articulated a genuine affection and admiration for him.

Schroeder next contacted the driver from the VIP motor pool to establish Grow's itinerary and activities while he was in the Frankfurt area. His driver, Sergeant Owen M. Harris, had a detailed memory. He filled in some voids by referring to the daily dispatch report of military vehicles and the trip tickets. The driver substantiated in detail Heald's report on Grow's activities.

Hughes, Heald, and Harris revealed nothing unusual or irregular in Grow's movements. The investigation of reviews and disposition of Squires's book did not conclusively show where it was distributed, though it was only in East Germany, nor did the cursory security inspection of alien employees at the Victory Guest House produce anything unusual. Yet the interview with the military manager, Lieutenant Peacock, and an on-site inspection indicated a complete lack of security at the Guest House, which should have been the responsibility of G-2, EUCOM. The investigation also determined that at no time were any requests made to the CIC, Criminal Investigation Service (CIS), and military police for security coverage of the Guest House, even during the important attaché conference. In addition, it was confirmed that only one other person, the assistant manager, a German national, had an extra set of keys to all suites and rooms.

Four weeks had passed since Bolling recommended that no court-martial charges be brought against Grow. During that time, Grow attempted to make the episode public to combat the Soviet version. He visited General Walter Bedell Smith, director of the Central Intelligence Agency, but to no avail. Discussions with Bolling were also frustrating. At one point, Bolling mentioned that the IG would make no recommendations on the investigation, then hedged and said that Major General Louis A. Craig, the inspector general, would have to make some recommendation. This was after the IG, Colonel Booth, had, in fact, recommended disciplinary action on 4 February. Bolling was not candid with Grow.[3]

Earlier in February, General McClure, director of intelligence, EUCOM, advised Bolling that a complete investigation would require several weeks. This, as it turned out, would not be the case. Initially, the 66th CIC Detachment concerned itself with acquiring *Auf dem Kriegspfad,* determining its distribution, and outlining Grow's movements while residing at the Victory Guest House in Köenigstein. Nothing unusual emerged from Grow's activities. In March 1952 there were thirty-four German employees at the Guest House. An additional six employees had either been terminated or had resigned since 1 June 1951. The CIC agent concluded that any one of the forty employees could have obtained access to Grow's suite for the purpose of photographing his diary, especially any person with even an elementary talent for surreptitious entry.

The main reason the investigation exceeded several weeks was the time required for the CIC to screen and investigate the activities of the forty employees of the Guest House. In addition, suspicion was cast on Captain Bernard J. Rhatigan, the United States military manager of the Guest House until 5 November 1951. In chapter 6 of *Auf dem Kriegspfad,* Squires had claimed to have received a photostatic copy of the diary from a Berlin correspondent of a London newspaper, who in turn was alleged to have received it from an American officer in Frankfurt. Both Rhatigan and his wife would have had the opportunity to enter the Grow suite.

By February the prime suspect was Gerhard Poss, an employee at the Victory Guest House since 13 August 1947. Poss had served with the Wehrmacht in North Africa, where he was taken prisoner and sent to a prisoner of war camp in the United States. He was released in 1946 and transported to the Western zone, settling in Frankfurt. Lieutenant Peacock considered Poss the most likely suspect because he was the only employee who had ready access to all rooms and suites, and his movements were unrestricted. On 25 February 1952, CIC Agent Edwin R. Woods began a detailed investigation of Poss's background and activities.[4] Meanwhile, agents Darrell Schroeder and Don Witt screened the personnel records of present and past employees.

Agent Woods's first move was to interview Lieutenant Peacock, who had been Poss's superior. Poss and his wife, Helena, née Alter, occupied a rent-free three-room apartment in the servant quarters at the hotel. Since October 1948, Poss had functioned as an assistant manager. Peacock considered his work exemplary and rated him an efficient administrator. Some employees believed that Poss was implicated in embezzlement directed at the Guest House and the German employees. Although no concrete proof was attainable, suspicions against Poss were based on opinions and rumors from other employees at the Guest House. The only specific incident the military manager recalled occurred in early January 1952. Because the Victory Guest House was to be returned to its original owner on 1 April, Peacock began an inspection of the premises in preparation for the close-out inventory. In the basement he discovered approximately fifty odd pieces of sterling silverware hidden in a locked room under some unused machinery. Other than himself, Peacock discovered, only Poss and a handyman had keys to the locked room. Poss disclaimed any knowledge of the silverware, which was finally identified as the remainder of an eight-hundred-piece set that had disappeared in 1949.

Woods then asked if any unusual economic activity had been associated with Poss. A check of the personnel records of the Civilian Personnel Section, the German Payroll Section, and the Municipal Tax Bureau uncovered nothing noteworthy. Woods also contacted a German national named Adolph Liebmann, who was involved in the authorization for industrial or private construction in Köenigstein. Again, nothing curious emerged. Liebmann, however, knew the Alter family, who were well respected, financially independent, long-time residents of Köenigstein.

Next, Woods approached the storekeeper at the Guest House, Ludwig Christ. Christ had been employed at the hotel since March 1948 and had known Poss during that time. He disliked Poss for his overbearing manner and had been suspicious of his management of the Guest House's finances. Christ was aware of the silverware incident and Poss's involvement. He suspected Poss was involved in kickback payments from purchases made by kitchen personnel. Also, Poss's relationship with the head gardener supposedly produced a respectable profit from the sale to local merchants of vegetables that were supposed to be used at the hotel. Christ said Poss heartily disapproved of the Soviet occupation of Germany, which had caused his family in Erfurt considerable indignity. Because Poss had lost the right of access to property left him in Erfurt, he had moved to the American zone. His father had been a highly placed executive of the *Deutsche Post* but reportedly was forced into retirement by the Soviet authorities. Poss had one married sister in Erfurt and another who was employed in a clerical position for Glenn G. Wolfe, who was with the United States Office of the High Commissioner for Germany in Bonn. Christ believed that after the hotel was derequisitioned, Poss would attempt to secure employment with HICOG because his acquaintance with Wolfe was considered to be fairly intimate.

When Woods checked the personnel records of the Civilian Personnel Section of the Frankfurt Military Post, he noticed that Poss listed as a residence an apartment at Liebigstrasse, Frankfurt. This was unusual because he and his wife were also furnished quarters by the United States Army at the Victory Guest House. This raised the question whether the apartment was being used as a drop. The owner of the apartment told Woods that Poss had never lived in the room he rented, nor had he kept any personal property there. He was very prompt in his monthly rent of thirty-five Deutsche Marks, which he always paid by mail. This arrangement was against the policy of the Residence Agency, but the owner admitted it was to the mutual advantage of both her and Poss. She claimed that Poss was concerned about the discontinuance of his employment at the hotel, which would lead to the loss of his quarters.

The owner recalled that she had first met Poss when she was employed at the Guest House during 1948 and 1949. In 1949, she left her employment and assumed ownership of the building at Liebigstrasse, at which time Poss approached her about establishing residence in Frankfurt. This was the last time she had seen Poss even though he religiously made his monthly payments. She did remember that during her employment at the hotel he was considered entirely too severe with lesser employees, causing considerable ill feelings. To her, Poss had never expressed sympathy for the Communist party or the Soviet form of government, but he had spoken of his resentment over the treatment his family had received at the hands of the Soviet occupation authorities in Erfurt.

To learn more about Poss's employment at the Guest House, Woods interviewed Otto Seraphin, who had been employed in various capacities at the hotel since late 1946. In 1947, Seraphin was serving as a reception clerk when he decided to return to Romania to help his family move to the American zone. The military manager asked him to secure a capable replacement. Seraphin inquired around Köenigstein, and Poss, who was recommended by a former teacher, was hired. Soon Seraphin returned, but in the meantime Poss became assistant manager and gained considerable responsibility and authority.

Seraphin provided an extensive profile of Poss's activities. He told Woods of a slush fund established from tips and allowed to accrue until the Christmas season so a large party could be held for all the German employees. From 1947 through 1950, Poss was given unquestioned responsibility for the fund provided he maintained records on all expenditures. When Lieutenant Peacock replaced Rhatigan as military manager, he requested that Poss make a complete accounting of the party fund to Seraphin, who was then employed as the accountant. Seraphin, however, could make no sense out of Poss's records because few receipts were available and they were undated or without explanation. Seraphin refused to be responsible for further auditing of the fund. In fact, Poss met expenses for one year by the income from the following year. When questioned, Poss claimed he had paid money from his own pocket and was only collecting it back. Seraphin thought this was unusual because it was not in keeping with the nature of the employees' fund. Furthermore everyone knew that the Guest House would sooner or later be derequisitioned, leaving the employees' positions precarious.

Another matter regarding Poss's mismanagement of the hotel's finances involved the per diem allowance afforded the German employees. They received money for one meal each day. The purchasing of all rations for this meal was entrusted to Poss, who obtained the food from a grocery considered the most expensive establishment in Köenigstein. On one occasion Seraphin, who shared an office with Poss, noticed a credit to the personal account of the assistant manager for fifty-eight marks. The credit could not have any connection with the purchases of groceries, and Seraphin believed it was a kickback from the grocery. A check of the itemized accounts at the grocery for May 1951 to March 1952 indicated that the maximum authorized per diem rations allowances were expended each month.

Finally, Seraphin gave his version of the silverware incident. Poss and the American military manager at the time, Lieutenant John Alexander, were considered responsible. When Alexander was leaving the position and turning the managership over to Rhatigan, he and Poss began collecting and inventorying the various odd pieces of silverware for quartermaster accountability. They came up short and purchased a few pieces on the German market, but the quartermaster refused to accept the account until Alexander, through a political connection at the quartermaster, managed to have the replacement silverware accepted.

On 12 March, in a preliminary statement, the CIC determined that Gerhard Poss was the prime suspect, although there was still the question of the maids who had access to Grow's suite. In addition to perusal of the personnel files of the Guest House employees, a check of the guest list for 1951 was made. Guests who were persons of importance or held key positions with the military or the State Department were eliminated as suspects.

Meanwhile, agents Schroeder and Witt checked the background of hotel employees and found no questionable information or activities. Next, Schroeder talked to Lieutenant Colonel G. T. Stump, liaison officer to HICOG, and Captain Heald of the reception bureau regarding Rhatigan, who had been reassigned to the 9th Infantry Division at Fort Dix, New Jersey, in December 1951. It was established during the interview that the former military manager would not have compromised Grow's diary with the intent to damage the government, but according to Stump and Heald, might compromise it to impress someone that he knew behind-the-scenes information. In addition, some employees reported that Rhatigan delegated many of his duties to German employees, especially to Poss. Because some suspicion was cast on the activities, character, and integrity of Rhatigan, he remained a suspect in the compromise of the diary.

Agent Schroeder also checked with the officer in charge of the Adjutant General Section in Frankfurt, which was responsible for the final processing of all marriage applications, including those involving American soldiers and German nationals, during 1951. The reason the agent looked into the Adjutant General Section was that the controversial newscaster and journalist Walter Winchell had claimed Grow's diary was photographed by the German wife of a U.S. Army Signal Corps officer. Winchell's statement proved to be false; there was no record of any Signal Corps officer applying for permission to marry a German national.

On 27 March, Schroeder interviewed Poss, who claimed he first became aware of the diary compromise when he was shown an article by Lieutenant Peacock, who advised him not to discuss the incident with anyone. He also maintained that the maids assigned to the various floors of the Guest House had passkeys to the rooms, except for the suites. An extra set of keys for suites hung on a board in the manager's office, however; according to Poss, any of the employees could have had access to the suite keys. Between July and September 1951, when Grow and his wife used Suite III, seven employees, in addition to Poss, had potential access to the suite. They were Otto Seraphin, second in charge to Poss, two porters, Guenter Klemens and Gregor Rurainski; Ludwig Christ; Paulus Dagmar Collonia, an assistant receptionist and porter; and two maids, Hildegard Suessbrich and Johanna Dinges. A CIC background check on the two maids indicated their apparent trustworthiness, and the two porters were also eliminated as suspects.

During the interview, Poss left the impression that he was subtly trying to direct suspicion toward Collonia, whom he said was interested in journalism and often questioned guests concerning current and political developments. Collonia, who spoke in English, made an effort to interview VIPs and supposedly wrote articles on their activities. Yet Poss could not identify Collonia's political views or confirm the existence of his articles.

Toward the end of the interview, Poss claimed that he had never seen the diary or known of its existence. He also recalled that the employees had not discussed the diary incident. This last assertion hardly seemed credible because other employees had made statements about the diary. It appeared that if Poss knew more than he was telling, he had covered it very well. Finally, Poss signed a statement consenting to a polygraph examination.

Agents Woods and Schroeder decided to interview Collonia. He had had intelligence experience during the war, believed an employee at the Guest House photographed the diary, and suspected Poss. In his own mind, he had built up a case against the assistant manager, whom he considered untrustworthy. According to a story Collonia heard from the hotel gardener, sometime during the summer of 1951, Poss took a vacation and left the impression he was going to Bavaria. The gardener said that instead Poss visited Erfurt. Collonia wondered why he tried to cover up his movements. In addition, Collonia remembered Poss frequently making telephone calls to Erfurt. After placing the call, Poss would instruct Collonia to transfer it to an extension and enter his office and close the door. When answering the phone, he would say "Köenigstein" and avoid mentioning the Victory Guest House. When questioned by Collonia about this, Poss explained he did not wish anyone in the Soviet zone to know he worked at the hotel because he had many enemies in the Erfurt area. Collonia could not understand this because the telephone calls and visits to Erfurt would endanger members of his family who still lived there.

Poss frequently tried to give the impression that he did not understand photography. On one occasion when Poss was going on vacation, Collonia asked why he was not taking a camera. "No, I can't take pictures," he replied. Collonia did not believe Poss. Besides, one of the maids who had cleaned Poss's quarters had discovered pornographic studies of his wife, Helena. Collonia surmised that Poss would not likely have called in a professional photographer to take nude photos of his wife.

In the summation of the interview, Schroeder and Woods recorded that Collonia had planned to write an article setting forth his ideas on the Grow diary episode after receiving clearance from HICOG. Collonia, the agents noted, fancied himself a detective and was very verbose in outlining the way he had arrived at the assumption of Poss's guilt. Like Poss, Collonia signed a statement consenting to a polygraph examination.

Years later, Collonia contacted Grow in an effort to resolve the mystery surrounding the compromise of the diary. He boasted about an association with Hitler's famous clandestine SS commando Otto Skorzeny. Collonia's mastery of the English language brought him into Skorzeny's Einheit Greif. This unit operated behind American lines masquerading as American troops to cause confusion during the German offensive at the Battle of the Bulge in December 1944. Collonia extolled his involvement with the notorious Obersturm-bannfuhrer Joachim Peiper whose battle group spearheaded the 1st SS Panzer Division during the Ardennes counteroffensive. His correspondences were jumbled and lacked coherence, causing Grow to reject involvement. Collonia's background and his questionable character placed him along with Poss as a possible suspect in March 1952.[5]

The next day, 28 March, Schroeder and Woods interviewed Hildegard Suessbrich, one of the maids who had been assigned to Grow's suite. Suessbrich claimed to have no knowledge of the diary before the official news releases appeared in the media. It was not until the incident hit the newspapers that she recalled an episode that occurred during the Grows' residence in Suite III in September 1951. She did not remember the exact day but did recall the hours. She was working her usual schedule in the hallway on the second floor of the hotel between 1400 and 1600 hours near Suite III. Suessbrich was startled by Poss, whom she saw emerge from Grow's suite carrying a camera. He was surprised and seemed confused. "We have such nice weather today and I wanted to take some shots which I have just done." After that remark, he hurriedly turned and left the hallway. The maid remarked to the agents that she "was not impressed by this before, since its importance had never occurred to me prior to the news that the Grow diary had been copied." She agreed to testify concerning the information she had provided. Suessbrich then pleaded with the agents that her connection with the investigation be kept from Poss because she believed he had connections in the Soviet zone and might be able to have pressure put on her family, who still resided there.

Before the agents talked to another maid, Ludwig Christ was reinterviewed. Like Suessbrich, Christ had learned about the diary from the press. A week before he was reinterviewed, Christ remembered Suessbrich displaying considerable anxiety sometime in September 1951. After reading the press article about the diary episode, she had told him about an incident that might have some bearing on the case. Suessbrich told Christ about Poss coming out of Grow's suite with a camera in his hands.

The agents immediately interviewed another maid, Johanna Dinges, who had since married Christ. Suessbrich had told Christ's wife about Poss and the camera incident before the diary incident hit the press. Both Johanna Christ and Suessbrich thought Poss's presence in Grow's suite was strange, but they had attached no particular significance to it at the time. Suessbrich, Christ, and his wife signed a statement consenting to take an examination by polygraph.

Before preparing their report on the investigation, the CIC agents checked the Deutsch Post Telephone Exchange at Köenigstein and the Deutsche Post Central Exchange in Frankfurt to determine whether any calls had been placed from Köenigstein to Erfurt. Collonia claimed that Poss had made several such calls. The agents discovered that records were kept only until a call was paid for and then destroyed. No record of unpaid calls from the Victory Guest House to Erfurt existed.

On 3 April the agents' interim report was forwarded to McClure, G-2, EUCOM. The report recommended continuing the investigation, especially in regard to Poss. The agents believed Grow's diary had been compromised, not in July as originally thought, but perhaps in September. Arrangements were made for Suessbrich to take a polygraph test on 7 April. The agents decided not to question Poss again until all available background data had been compiled. The nature of the interview with Poss on the twenty-seventh led them to believe that he had no idea he was any more of a suspect then the other employees. The following questions and points, however, were raised regarding Poss and the need for continuing the investigation.

a. Poss's photographic ability and whether he does his own printing and developing,

b. The frequency of Poss's telephone calls to Erfurt, Soviet zone, and contacts located there,

c. The dates Poss visited Erfurt during 1951,

d. How much personal property Poss owns in Erfurt and whether he has made any exceptionally large deposits [money] since July 1951,

e. The nature of the relationship between Poss and relatives in Erfurt,

f. Comprehensive background history on Poss and his wife to include political beliefs,

g. Surveillance of Poss and his wife for possible leads regarding contacts and associates.[6]

Apparently, Suessbrich and the other employees at the Guest House had learned about the diary compromise from the West German media. One of the first to report the incident was the *Frankfurter Allgemeine,* which described the appearance of excerpts of Grow's diary in a book by a British deserter as an obvious propaganda ploy executed in the Soviet zone. The front-page article did mention that perhaps the diary fell in communist hands while Grow was in Frankfurt.[7]

In Württemberg, the old traditional newspaper the *Ludwigsburger Kreiszeitung* also reported on the Grow incident. The newspaper was noted for its nationalistic orientation and for taking an occasional anti-American stand. Taking a cue from the popular and influential French newspaper *Le Monde,* the *Kreiszeitung* compared Grow to former German generals who were still confined in prisons for the harsh measures they employed to counter partisan activity during the bitter fighting in Russia. Quoting generously from *Le Monde,* which also paraphrased Squires's book, it pictured Grow calling for "war as soon as possible; war immediately if possible" and repeated the much-publicized quote, "we must understand that in this war it is fair to hit below the belt." This aggressive talk, according to the newspaper, was too drastic. The newspaper made an interesting comment, again quoting from *Le Monde.* Squires's book "would have been regarded as Soviet propaganda forgeries if the Pentagon had not taken an official stand" by acknowledging its authenticity. The newspaper claimed the diary had been photocopied in Frankfurt by communist agents.[8]

In all probability, the hotel employees were made aware of the Grow incident by *Der Spiegel,* a widely distributed, influential, contemporary weekly magazine. *Der Spiegel* was something of a German counterpart to *Time* or *Newsweek* and tended to specialize in reporting revealing information and drawing attention to political abuses. On 19 March, *Der Spiegel* published a revealing article in regard to Grow's "intimate diary." It quoted Squires's book, thus creating an impression similar to that given by the *Washington Post* and the *New York Times.* Like the *Ludwigsburger Kreiszeitung,* it agreed that Grow's views were not shared by political leaders in the United States.

Both editorials deplored the assignment of an "outspoken militarist" to a sensitive position such as the American embassy in Moscow. A *Der Spiegel* editorial referred to Grow as "a half-grown school girl with an unresponded crush."[9]

Der Spiegel viewed Squires's book as a demonstration of "exaggerated nonsense" regarding the defector's comments on Churchill's dream of conquest and the rule of terror by the Western powers in West Germany. Even the so-called terrorized South German taxi drivers—and all the more, the readers in the Eastern zone—could laugh tiredly at Squires's book, *Der Spiegel* facetiously reported. What made the article interesting was a quote attributed to Squires's mother, who stated that her son had fallen from a motorcycle shortly before World War II and since suffered recurring lapses of consciousness. The magazine reported that Squires was presently in a Leipzig hospital undergoing treatment.

Der Spiegel likewise took a poke at Gerhard Eisler, the propaganda specialist for the East German regime who had gained the favor of Stalin for his ruthlessness as a communist agent and propagandist. Without supportive references, *Der Spiegel* claimed that Eisler finally found "a real dissolute character" in Grow's diary and had it published as a piece of propaganda carrying the indignant peace-loving "wail" of the communists.

Over the years Eisler had established an unsavory reputation. During the 1930s he was the top Comintern representative in America for five years. When France fell in 1940, he returned to the United States, claiming that he did not belong to a communist organization. He finally got in trouble with American authorities, left the country in 1949, and fled to Poland. He was elected a member of the People's Council of the Soviet zone of Germany and soon thereafter became head of the DDR Office of Information until it was disbanded by Walter Ulbricht shortly before Stalin's death in March 1953. Federal law authorities considered Eisler America's "number one Communist" during his stay in the United States. He was very persuasive in presenting the communist view, especially in his chastisement of the Americans. *Der Spiegel* left the impression that Eisler was behind the Grow diary incident. This was a very strong possibility. Nevertheless, before launching a propaganda blast, Eisler would have needed Kremlin approval.[10]

Die Tat, a progressive German-language newspaper published in Zurich, called the diary a full-fledged criminal novel depicting the incapability of a military attaché who called for a preventive war against Russia. The Grow affair, according to *Die Tat,* was a deserved Soviet propaganda victory. As long as the American government sent such "infantile persons" as Grow to foreign posts, the paper argued, it should not be surprised when the Kremlin exploited the situation.[11]

The German employees at the Victory Guest House no doubt read the local Frankfurt newspapers and *Der Spiegel.* The articles in *Le Monde,* the *Kreiszeitung,* and *Die Tat* were examples of how the Grow incident was handled by various newspapers in Western Europe. Like the American press, they depicted Grow as advocating immediate undeclared war against the USSR. The German press reaction was evaluated by the CIC and forwarded to Bolling's office in the Pentagon. Bolling, meanwhile, informed the G-2 in EUCOM that he preferred to continue the press coverage for everything regarding the Grow episode except for EUCOM and Berlin. In other words, the G-2 in the Pentagon had no objection to the continued press coverage in America, which continued to report the warmongering theme expressed in *Auf dem Kriegspfad.* It was imperative that the reaction in Europe be kept isolated from the proceedings in the Pentagon so as to lessen embarrassment to American intelligence operations in West Germany, which were beginning to come under scrutiny.[12]

During the initial stages of the investigation in February, CPO Michael F. Cartmill, the chief hospital corpsman from the American embassy in Moscow, suggested to a CIC agent that embassy personnel believed Grow's diary was compromised on the general's last trip to Germany late in December 1951. With this in mind and determined to be as thorough as possible, the CIC investigators continued the inquiry. Late in March, they moved the investigation to Berlin, where the Grows had stopped over on their way to Frankfurt or Moscow. Cecil B. Lyon, director of the Berlin Element of HICOG, was present at a conference on 16 January when Grow and McClure went over the diary facsimiles depicted in the East Berlin newspapers. Lyon recalled Grow mentioning that the diary in question was locked in his desk in his quarters in Moscow and he could not understand how the Soviets managed to copy it. Without having the diary at hand to make comparisons, Grow admitted that the photo reproductions of his handwriting appeared to be genuine. Then, said Lyon, he commented that in Moscow the Russian servants had access to the rooms in which he kept the diaries.

Michael B. Lustgarten, an administrative liaison officer and security officer from HICOG's Berlin Element, had been the first person to advise Grow that the contents of his personal diary had appeared in the East German press. On 7 April CIC agent Samuel G. Wingfield interviewed Lustgarten, who remembered receiving a cable from Moscow on 28 December indicating that Grow was on his way to Berlin. Two days later, Grow arrived and was met by Lieutenant Colonel Joel Lawson, chief of the visitor's bureau, and Lustgarten. Both were to continue on to Frankfurt with the attaché. Grow remarked that there was no need for his escorts to wait because he and his wife were planning to visit an old friend from his horse cavalry days, Colonel William W. Jervey, who was the post signal officer at the Berlin Military Post. During the short period Lustgarten had contact with Grow, he noticed nothing unusual in the attaché's activities.

The next day, 8 April, Wingfield interviewed Jervey, who recalled Grow's last visit in early January 1952. Naturally, they reminisced about their service in the cavalry before the war, but eventually the subject turned to the Soviet Union. Grow disclosed that freedom of movement was limited. As was the case with all other members of the United States Embassy in Moscow, Grow made the point that he, and even his wife, were followed whenever they left the embassy, whether in an automobile or on foot. Grow did not mention a diary or a package. The CIC agent was concerned not only about the diary but the four packages that Grow mailed to Illinois shortly after he arrived in Berlin from Moscow.

Jervey remembered Grow to be his usual affable, pleasant self. He also recalled that Grow had offered the opinion that the imminence of war between the Soviet government and the United States was not great and that the Soviet Union was ruled by fear. Jervey made it a point to explain that the attaché did not discuss the wisdom of a preventive war initiated by the United States against the Soviet Union and that he "was very surprised that the whole affair had happened."

As in Frankfurt, the CIC agents were determined to learn about Grow's movements in Berlin. When there, the Grows usually stayed at the Wannsee Guest House in the American sector. Interviews with the maids indicated nothing unusual. A check with the commissary personnel determined that the Grows did not behave strangely and did not discuss politics or the question of war with the USSR. They made several visits to the commissary because they had difficulty procuring certain foods in Moscow. One quartermaster officer, who was assigned to the commissary, recalled that sometime in the early fall of 1951 he had had a conversation with Grow. The attaché's manner was pleasant, and his demeanor failed to indicate any inner mental disturbance, according to the officer.

A check with the Army Post Office in Berlin also indicated nothing unusual in connection with packages sent by or to the Grows. One postal clerk recalled that the packages in question were fragile and it appeared to him that they contained no documents. None of the packages was sent to Frankfurt.

A detailed check on Grow's activities failed to produce any unusual activity indicating that his diary had been compromised in Berlin. The same was evident at the American embassy in Moscow. This was determined by 7 April. All evidence pointed to Frankfurt, the Victory Guest House, and Gerhard Poss.

In the meantime, the 66th CIC Detachment continued to pursue the investigation in Frankfurt. On 1 April, Otto Seraphin was re-interviewed by agent Schroeder. Recent newspaper articles concerning the compromised diary convinced Seraphin that Poss was the only person who was capable of executing the deed. Seraphin, who could not hide his dislike for Poss, recalled that the assistant manager owned an expensive Rolicord camera, which he had seen hanging in the duty room of the Guest House. The accountant, like Collonia, knew Poss was the only logical suspect because he had the intelligence, ability, and character needed to perform an espionage act.

Seraphin also commented on Collonia, who was considered a possible suspect by the CIC because of his relationship with German intelligence during the war and his excellent command of English. The accountant had never seen Collonia with a camera or heard him voicing an interest in photography. He considered Collonia to be an idealist and politically to the right with definite anticommunist beliefs. It was evident that Poss and Collonia were not friends because Poss, according to Seraphin, was largely responsible for Collonia's demotion from assistant receptionist to porter. Seraphin told Schroeder that he recently had heard through Ludwig Christ that the maid, Suessbrich, saw Poss emerging from Grow's suite with a camera. Poss's remark to the maid that the view from Grow's suite was most suitable for taking scenic snapshots appeared suspicious. According to Seraphin, a far better view could have been had from the third floor, where most of the rooms were unoccupied at the time. The accountant emphasized that most of the employees at the hotel had reason to dislike Poss. Suessbrich did not strike the CIC agent as a person who would create a story to get revenge.

Seraphin then presented some interesting, if not startling, information. Poss had a sister working for HICOG, and Seraphin recalled Poss mentioning that she formerly had worked for an important communist enterprise in the Soviet zone. Seraphin also considered Poss a "worshipper of money" who might have sold the copied diary for its monetary value. Another possibility was that Poss freely furnished the copied diary so as to retain ownership of property in Erfurt. Moreover, Seraphin speculated that if a Soviet invasion of the West materialized, Poss could always rely on Soviet favor because he had "cooperated."

Seraphin, who was scheduled to immigrate with his family to America in April under the Ethnic German Program, impressed Schroeder as very intelligent, honest, and sincere. The CIC agent believed Seraphin knew more about the incident but hesitated to say so for fear of delaying his departure. The information he provided was deemed valid and given with an eagerness to cooperate so as to afford himself and his family the opportunity to immigrate to America.

The next day Schroeder interviewed Johanna Dinges Christ. She concurred with the other employees regarding Poss's ownership of a camera and the telephone calls he made to Erfurt. Poss had made secret trips to the Soviet zone, including one in the fall of 1951, she noted. She recalled that Poss's sister from Erfurt had visited the hotel and was present at Poss's wedding in May 1951. In her opinion, there were only two people who could have copied Grow's diary. Poss was her main suspect; but she also suspected Collonia because she did not consider him trustworthy. Schroeder discounted her last assessment because Collonia, though in financial difficulty, was never seen with a camera and had no known contacts in the Soviet zone of Germany as Poss had. On the same day Schroeder questioned a seamstress, who also stated that Poss had visited relatives in the Soviet zone late in the summer of 1951. She noted that his only frequent visitor was his sister, who supposedly worked for HICOG in Bonn.

On 7 April 1952, the CIC report on the interviews with Poss, Colonia, Suessbrich, Christ, and his wife were forwarded to Bolling in the Pentagon. Poss was identified as the prime suspect because he had been caught leaving Grow's suite with a camera sometime in September 1951, not in June or July 1951 as originally suspected.[13] Meanwhile, a thorough background and agency check on Poss revealed that he did indeed make occasional telephone calls to Erfurt, where he had family and maintained property. Moreover, he had applied for an interzonal pass during September 1951, although it was not determined whether he had used it. In addition, it was evident that Poss had no friends among his fellow employees and had gone to great lengths to keep his movements secret.[14]

On 7 April, Hildegard Suessbrich was reinterviewed and subjected to a polygraph examination by CIC agents. This time she was much more explicit in relating her experiences regarding the incident because of the German press releases. She recalled that the Grows had left the suite at approximately 0800 or 0830 hours and did not return until about 1600 hours. A check with Grow's diary for 1951 puts the date at 27 September. Sometime after lunch, about 1400 hours, Suessbrich was cleaning the hallway when she saw Poss with a camera leaving Grow's suite. She did not know how long he had been in the rooms. After Poss had walked away, the maid entered the suite. She was curious. Had anything been disturbed? What would be of photographic interest? Suessbrich suspected that Poss's intimation that he had been taking scenic snapshots was not true. When she entered the bedroom, which she had cleaned earlier, she noticed nothing disturbed. Moving into the living room, she discovered that the glass plate on the desk was smudged and completely covered with fingerprints. She thought it highly improbable that she missed cleaning the desktop during the morning. Accordingly, Suessbrich took a cloth and wiped it clean. Then she noticed a book on the desk. Opening it, she found it contained writing in ink. This, apparently, was Grow's diary for 1951. Suessbrich was aware of the unsavory accusations made against Poss by other employees, in particular, that he had taken pornographic photos of his wife. She also remembered an incident that was well known to most of the former employees. Sometime in 1950, when Poss was engaged to his wife, he had tried to rape a maid. The polygraph examination of Suessbrich indicated that she had given truthful information.

The next day, Poss withdrew his agreement to submit to a polygraph examination. He appeared nervous and apprehensive. For these reasons and because close surveillance was not feasible, the 66th CIC Detachment urgently requested permission to detain Poss. A crypto-precaution priority message was immediately sent to the director of intelligence, EUCOM, for action. The message stated that the polygraph examination of Suessbrich indicated she was telling the truth and that Poss had withdrawn his consent to take the test, also refusing to submit to a direct interview. Moreover, Poss's wife was now in Erfurt, where he had a sister and numerous friends. He definitely possessed a camera suitable for copy work, and his recent attitude indicated a high degree of anxiety. McClure, the G-2, however, refused to permit Poss's detention. He instructed the agents to continue the investigation with a view to determining how the diary had been exploited. In spite of the information received, especially the reports on Suessbrich, Collonia, Seraphin, Christ, and his wife which had implicated Poss, McClure decided that close surveillance of Poss was not "considered essential." Instead, McClure suggested that an investigation of the former military manager, Captain Rhatigan, be initiated. McClure reasoned that the information concerning Poss was insufficient to warrant taking him into custody. The agents were advised by McClure that if Poss attempted to leave West Germany for Erfurt, no action was to be taken to prevent his departure. Any restraint on Poss, the G-2 added, must be based on evidence that he had violated a specific occupation statute.

Was McClure, who was responsible to Bolling, embarrassed at the deplorable condition of his organization which had provided the opportunity for a possible Soviet operative to function so freely? Such a revelation could damage the careers of aspiring general officers associated with the Grow case. As of 11 April, after extensive investigations by the CIC in Frankfurt and Berlin, only Poss stood out as a strong suspect capable of acting as a Soviet operative. The assistant chief of staff, G-2, in the Pentagon was aware of this development from the numerous correspondence between G-2, EUCOM, and Washington. Thus what made the situation more bizarre was McClure's desire to shift the thrust of the investigation from Europe to the United States.[15] If Grow had been irresponsible, so had McClure. The EUCOM G-2, furthermore, was condescending to Bolling to isolate the embarrassing discovery of lax security.

During the interviews with Christ on 26 February and Seraphin on 1 April, it came to light that Poss had a sister who was employed with HICOG and that Poss was on very friendly terms with the organization's executive director, Glenn G. Wolfe. Wolfe reportedly had acquired the position for Poss's sister Margaret in 1949 or 1950. Naturally, the agents were concerned that a connection existed between a possible Soviet operative and a HICOG official.

Because Glenn Wolfe was privy to secret policy information, the CIC approached him in regard to his relationship with Gerhard and Margaret Poss. On 11 April, Wolfe stated that he had met Poss for the first time at the Victory Guest House in 1949. At the time, Wolfe was in need of the services of a nursemaid for his granddaughter and Poss suggested his sister Margaret. During the ensuing months, a close association developed with the Poss family, including the father and mother, who on occasions visited their children. Wolfe found the parents "splendid people." The father was an anticommunist and had been just as much anti-Nazi during Hitler's regime. Wolfe contended that Poss's father furnished considerable intelligence information obtained in the Soviet zone, which in turn was passed on to the proper authorities. Margaret related many instances of their family life during the Nazi years when her father, through various schemes, was able to keep her as well as himself out of all Nazi party organizations and activities. After the need for a nursemaid ceased, Margaret obtained a position in the Property Unit at the American Housing Project in Bad Godesberg. Wolfe added that Margaret was still employed there and that the father and mother had since passed away.

Wolfe voluntarily revealed that he had already been advised of suspicions against Poss by the liaison officer to HICOG, Lieutenant Colonel G. T. Stump, who had been interviewed by the CIC. He had asked Stump to intercede for Poss, who on about 21 March had been asked by Lieutenant Peacock to move out of the Guest House because it was to be derequisitioned in ten days. Poss, who had made a lease agreement with the German owner to retain his quarters after the owner repossessed his property, had complained that it would cause him considerable expense and inconvenience to comply with Peacock's request, and he asked Wolfe for help. Wolfe, in turn, talked with Colonel Stump, who overrode Peacock's order. In the meantime, Stump mentioned Poss's possible involvement in the Grow incident to Wolfe, who found it hard to believe. He had always considered Poss to be a man of high caliber.

The HICOG official viewed Poss as no different from other Germans working for the occupation forces. His manner was always subservient and anxious to please. Wolfe found this attitude to be customary in individuals working as hotel managers and waiters, but he thought the position Poss occupied was evidence of a character weakness. Wolfe described Poss's wife, Helena, as a frugal, hardworking woman with good moral qualities and Poss as possessing a good character, honest, trustworthy, and completely pro-Western in political orientation. Wolfe told the CIC agent that the years Poss spent in America as a prisoner of war apparently helped form his character and political thinking. It was there that he had mastered the English language. Wolfe could not imagine Poss having the nerve to pick up Grow's diary. "He would have been such a nervous wreck that he would 'break' under questioning in five minutes." Wolfe was very emphatic: Poss did not have the "guts" to photocopy the diary. Politically, Poss was viewed as leaning toward the German Social Democratic party rather than Konrad Adenauer's Christian Democratic Union, which had the strongest party alignment within the newly formed Federal Republic. Wolfe concluded by asserting that Poss would be considered for a position of trust with the American authorities because he believed him to be thoroughly reliable and qualified.[16]

But Wolfe was the only one who gave Poss a good character reference; the employees who worked for and with Poss for years described him differently. To date, the CIC had considerable evidence pointing to Poss as the culprit in the diary incident. Nevertheless, the agents were in a delicate situation. They naturally suspected Poss but could not detain him on orders from McClure. Finally, the CIC persuaded Poss to agree to a polygraph examination on the morning of 17 April. Four CIC agents including Schroeder and Woods, were involved in the test. A polygraph technician and interrogation leader were brought in to administer and monitor the test.

Throughout the interview Poss maintained an "air of hurt indifference" and occasionally acted as if he saw the whole affair as "quite a joke." Nevertheless, in just a few hours the agents were satisfied that Poss had photographed Grow's diary. The following reasons were outlined in a verbatim report:

1. Poss had been described as untrustworthy and an opportunist . . . he is intelligent and would hardly fail to recognize the importance of General Grow's diary.

2. Poss definitely possessed a camera suitable for copy work.

3. Poss had sufficient experience in photography to have accomplished reproduction of the diary.

4. Poss visited the East Zone of Germany in early September 1951 and the first part of October 1951.

5. Polygraph examination of Poss indicated that he had lied about his knowledge of the diary and he had been in the Grow suite with a camera in September 1951.

6. Suessbrich made a signed statement that she had observed Poss leaving the Grow suite with a camera during September 1951. Her statement was borne out by a polygraph examination. Interview of Christ, his wife, and the employees of the hotel affirmed that Suessbrich had informed them of the incident in September 1951.[17]

On 22 April 1952, the 66th CIC Detachment submitted its final report to G-2, EUCOM. The agents were satisfied that Poss had compromised Grow's diary. They presented two alternatives in their recommendations: arrest Poss and intern him so a confession could be obtained, or close the case. Should the latter course be taken, they suggested that a bulletin be disseminated to all American agencies in EUCOM placing Poss on a restricted list, effectively banning him from employment. The agents admitted that "this seems too trivial a punishment for a Soviet agent," but a ban would ensure that he would not be employed in a position granting him the opportunity to perform acts detrimental to the United States. On 15 May the final report on Poss was submitted to Bolling's office, which had been monitoring all developments in EUCOM since January because of

Gerhard Poss (1952).
Courtesy of the U.S. Army

the existing communist controversy and especially the spy paranoia besetting the Truman administration.

The agents believed they had solved the diary compromise. Since January the investigation had been closely followed by Bolling and Taylor in the Pentagon. On the same day that it was determined Poss lied during the polygraph test, Bolling reversed his decision made on 5 February "that court-martial charges not be preferred against General Grow." In a memorandum to General Taylor dated 17 April 1952, Bolling recommended that "court-martial charges be preferred against Grow at once."[18] Since January, top army officials, notably Bolling and Taylor, had remained silent. Now an air of urgency accompanied their action.

In the meantime, employees at the Victory Guest House began to leave their jobs with the derequisitioned hotel. By early 1953, only two of the original employees were still working at the hotel, Poss and Suessbrich. The CIC was unable to obtain any information concerning Poss's sister's connection with the communists. A screening of several hundred refugees from Erfurt failed to establish whether Poss had contacted Soviet or East German authorities. Consequently, the case passed into an inactive file and Poss remained at the Victory Guest House, no longer under surveillance.

It is possible that, as a result of the diary incident, Poss was or became a counteragent, but no documents were unearthed suggesting such a double role. If it were the case, it would behoove McClure, Bolling, and Taylor to take proper measures to cover Poss's counter-espionage activities.

Command Influence

B Y NOW IT was evident that the Grow episode would remain an all-army affair, although two other institutions
had attempted to interject themselves into the investigation. On
14 January 1952, the American embassy in Moscow first notified the
secretary of state that excerpts from Grow's diary had appeared in an
East Berlin newspaper.[1] That same day, the State Department informed Bolling of the incident. Bolling in turn discussed it with Taylor. Subsequently, Taylor directed Grow not to return to Moscow and
ordered a complete investigation of the case. Accordingly, a message
was sent to Grow in Berlin saying the State Department did not wish
him to return to Moscow.[2] At the time, American intelligence agencies in Europe appeared to be unconcerned about the incident and accepted the article as part of standard Soviet propaganda attacks. The
State Department was also not overly concerned. Hence the monitoring and management of the affair were consigned to the army staff.
After the Western and then the communist media began their coverage of the diary's compromise in March, the State Department renewed its interest. By 14 March the State Department had a copy of
Auf dem Kriegspfad and photostats of the two East Berlin newspaper
articles—almost two months after the army had acquired Squires's
book and copies of the two communist newspaper articles. Shortly
thereafter, the *Literaturnaya gazeta* and *Bolshevik* carried Squires's exposé. Subsequently, the State Department, acknowledging a possible
propaganda coup for the Soviet government, reacted.[3]

The Central Intelligence Agency also attempted to involve itself in
the Grow affair. As early as January, the CIA had been interested in

General J. Lawton Collins (1951).
Courtesy of the U.S. Army, National Archives

Lieutenant General Maxwell D. Taylor (1958).
Courtesy of the U.S. Army, National Archives

Lieutenant General Alexander R. Bolling (1952).
Courtesy of the U.S. Army, National Archives

Major General Ernest M. Brannon (1950).
Courtesy of the U.S. Army, National Archives

Colonel Robert Bard (1954).
Courtesy of the U.S. Army, National Archives

minimizing Soviet propaganda opportunities provided by the episode and eventually advised against a court-martial. Since 15 January, the intelligence agency had repeatedly and unsuccessfully attempted to obtain a copy of Grow's diary from the army. On 5 March—the day before the *Washington Post* broke its exclusive—the CIA was informed by Brigadier General Robert McClure, chief of psychological warfare, that Grow's diary would not be made available. Even though Bolling was irritated over the agency's entrance into the case, a CIA agent drew up a program to capitalize on the disclosures from the diary. The result was the "Plan for Propaganda Counter-Offensive re: The Diary of General Grow" released on 18 March. The plan had supposedly received interim approval and been classified as "Eyes Only" before being forwarded through higher channels to the director, Walter Bedell Smith, for clearance, where it stalled. Smith had been appointed director in 1950 as a result of charges of inept intelligence against government and military agencies for their failure to preempt North Korea's suprise attack in June 1950. Years before that he was a Leavenworth classmate and close friend of Taylor's. But a month had passed during which the counteroffensive plan was not acted on, much against the wishes of the agent who initiated the program.[4]

Meanwhile, the State Department admitted that the propaganda effort aimed at the Soviet Union "has been very poor." An ad hoc working group was formed by the assistant secretary of state for public affairs to outline a competitive propaganda offensive against the Soviet regime.[5] An analysis of Soviet vulnerabilities and the principal assets available to the United States for their exploitation was outlined. The program was designed to discredit the Soviet government to its people by pointing out the differences between a democracy and a totalitarian regime. One medium to be used was the Voice of America, although it had failed in exploiting the counterpropaganda potential of the diary incident. Unfortunately, the proposed program did very little to outline ways to neutralize Soviet propaganda. Its psychological approaches were tame and lackluster in comparison to Soviet propaganda overtures. In general, the objective of an American psychological offensive was designed to enhance relations between the two superpowers. This approach was too broad, lacked a definite direction, and was poorly conceived.

The Truman administration had launched a policy of containment in 1947 to blunt Soviet power and expansion. According to this policy, concessions would have to come from Joseph Stalin even though negotiations would continue between the two contesting powers. The U.S. State Department Bureau of European Affairs and its representatives had had difficulty in establishing a program controlling Soviet-bloc propaganda, even in the United States. All they could develop was a plan to acquire all printed information circulated by Soviet-bloc missions located in the United States. This action was essentially defensive and aligned with the containment policy. Soviet propaganda was more innovative simply because the Kremlin was on the offensive. Regardless of how ludicrous it often sounded, it had a greater impact than American efforts did.

The State Department did attempt to react to the Grow case. On 9 April it requested a comparison from the Department of Defense of the quotations in Squires's book with the actual diary so as to confer with the Defense Department concerning tactics to be followed in countering anticipated communist exploitation of the diary. One possibility the deputy assistant secretary for public affairs, Joseph B. Phillips, had in mind was to challenge the Soviet Union over the validity of Squires's exposé. He believed that the Soviets feared making public the full text of the diary entries. Phillips asked that the ten diary excerpts from *Auf dem Kriegspfad* be authenticated. The State Department, like the CIA, was opposed to court-martialing Grow because of the possible international implications of such an action.[6]

Clayton Fritchey, director of the Office of Public Information in the Department of Defense, sent a request to General Dorn, deputy chief of information, suggesting that Bolling's office execute the analysis.[7] The action officer in Bolling's office was Colonel Gordon E. Dawson, chief of the Security Division. Dawson, who earlier had examined the diary for classified security information, went through the diary again in search of the excerpts that had appeared in Squires's book. Of the ten excerpts, six did not appear in the diary and four were taken out of context. Dawson discussed this with Bolling, who had also read portions of Grow's diary, comparing the extracts to see if they matched.[8] On 15 April both officers approached Grow, asking for his suggestions in finding an effective method for counteracting the propaganda advantage drawn from the diary. Stunned, Grow told

Bolling and Dawson "that they were three months late"—he had wanted such an analysis as far back as January. By now Grow suspected Bolling's duplicity. This was the first time Grow had been officially approached since the diary's existence had become public knowledge.[9]

During the rest of the day, Grow went over the diary twice, very carefully, because he had not seen it since it was confiscated on 28 January. At the end of the day, he returned the diary to Dawson along with an undated penciled memorandum. He reported that there was no doubt that the extracts were either forgeries or taken out of context.[10] It was evident to Dawson that the diary reflected Grow's estimate of Soviet intentions against the United States and did not reflect the American government's intent to take aggressive action against the Soviet Union as reported by Squires.[11] Grow's painstaking comparison and Dawson's comments were forwarded to Bolling and then to Taylor. But the analysis apparently never reached the State Department.[12] Later, Bolling would admit he regretted that Grow's penciled memorandum was ignored.

The State Department then raised the question of whether the Soviets might try to exploit the diary in the United Nations. To raise the incident in the United Nations would invite the truth of lax security in addition to Grow's carelessness, which Bolling, along with Taylor, had every reason to fear, especially in light of recent events in EUCOM. A friend of Grow's in the CIA, George L. King, told him: "State is sore that the Army let the case go by default."[13]

Bolling advised Taylor that the request by the State Department necessitated a review of the army's position regarding media releases. The Soviet press had not mentioned *Auf dem Kriegspfad* until after the incident had been publicized by the *Washington Post*. Moreover, the Department of the Army had informed Norris, the *Post* reporter, that "the diary was authentic." He added that the incident had caused adverse reaction to the army because of extensive editorial comments in the domestic press. The army, meanwhile, remained silent regarding the true nature of the diary extracts even though Dawson and Bolling were aware of Squires's propaganda efforts. Bolling explained to Taylor that the Soviet press had reported that official American representatives had recognized Grow's diary as being authentic. Moreover, Bolling asserted that certain congressmen had attacked Grow because "he kept secret notes and betrayed completely the instigators of a new war."[14]

Bolling told Taylor that in his own opinion an early public announcement should appear in the American press regarding the truth about the case. He then considered what should happen to Grow: should he "voluntarily" retire or be court-martialed? Bolling suggested that the possible ramifications of these two alternatives be explored and the conclusion disseminated to the press by McClure's Psychological Warfare Division. Bolling did acknowledge that the Soviets had enjoyed a propaganda victory because of domestic press announcements. "We have played right into Russian hands and they never suspected it would work out so well," he readily admitted.[15]

Bolling claimed that he consulted with the inspector general and the judge advocate general and both agreed that valid grounds existed for preferring court-martial charges against Grow. The G-2 noted that "the American public and the Congress will be satisfied with nothing less than a trial by court-martial for General Grow, and that course is the only fair one to him as an individual to afford him an opportunity to offer a defense of his actions." Also, no doubt, playing heavily on Bolling's mind were the results of the CIC investigation in EUCOM, which had uncovered a possible Soviet "mole" and deplorable security measures at a hotel used by ranking American officials. Perhaps the G-2 had much to lose—which was ample motivation for caution and silence.

Thus on 17 April Bolling reversed his position of early February and recommended that court-martial charges be preferred against Grow "at once." He suggested to Taylor that an announcement be made to the American press that no public reply or rebuttal had been made regarding Squires's book because an investigation was still pending to determine whether Grow would be tried. Upon the conclusion of the trial, Bolling promised to deliver a full explanation to the press outlining the true contents of Grow's diary in relation to Squires's distortion. Regarding the State Department request for assistance in a counterpropaganda effort, the G-2 recommended that an analysis of the diary be furnished upon the conclusion of the trial. Finally, Bolling suggested to Taylor that Parks, the chief of information, immediately prepare an exposition of the diary contents in rebuttal to Squires's version and that it be exploited by McClure's Psychological Warfare Division.[16]

On 18 April an updated inspector general's summary report of the investigation was received in the Office of the Chief of Staff. For the first time, it officially recommended that court-martial charges be preferred against Grow. Further investigation to determine the complicity of other individuals involved in the compromise of Grow's diary would require a long period of time "and can be expected to have no influence upon the conclusions and recommendations," noted the IG report. There was no mention of the European inquiry, which was suggested in the IG report in early February. Moreover, the original report was purportedly held in the inspector general's office "pending completion of coordination amongst Department of the Army agencies."[17] Indeed, the original report had been forwarded to Bolling on 4 February. He had read it, then recommended to the army chief of staff that no court-martial charges be preferred against Grow. Bolling believed the army's interests would be better served by waiting for the propaganda uproar over the diary to die down and not aggravating the situation with a court-martial proceeding. He added, however, that the IG "may recommend that Grow be tried by court-martial." It must be recalled that in early February the IG had made two recommendations: that appropriate disciplinary action be taken against Grow and that the investigation continue to determine who photostated the diary.[18] From 4 February to 18 April the IG made no other documented recommendations regarding the Grow case. Suddenly, after the eruption of the disquieting developments in EUCOM and the interjection of the State Department and the CIA into the affair, along with embarrassing media reports and congressional inquiries, Bolling and Taylor abruptly reversed course and took the initiative for an immediate court-martial.

Meanwhile, on 18 April, the CIA agent who had initiated the "Plan for Propaganda Counter-Offensive re: The Diary of General Grow" received some startling news. The plan "was not to be used at this time, owing to 'the absence of any policy group having the authority to pass upon it.' " The plan was to be "held in abeyance." He was perplexed. Upon further investigation the agent discovered that key personnel in the CIA who normally would have approved or disapproved of the plan were not even aware of its existence. This caused him to speculate that interference had come from certain top army officials in the Pentagon who had political connections within the CIA. Earlier, when the agent attempted to acquire the diary for analysis, he was told to forget he had ever asked. McClure advised the agent, in no uncertain terms and without providing a reason, that he would not acquire the diary for the CIA. It was also generally known that Bolling opposed CIA intrusion into the case.[19]

Moreover, CIA Director Smith, known for his role as Eisenhower's efficient chief of staff during the war and later as an ambassador to the Soviet Union, was of the same elite group as Taylor and Collins. Smith, Collins, and Taylor were part of General George C. Marshall's professional "family tree." Collins and Taylor were among the great battle captains of World War II, which assured their upward mobility. Grow was unable to penetrate this elite group because he did not achieve as much and made no imprint on Marshall's "family tree." Consequently, Grow's upward mobility was limited, and he lacked the influence and organizational strength possessed by the elite group. Grow was also a member of an army branch that had very little influence in the army hierarchy. Of the army combat officers who became members of the Joint Chiefs of Staff up to the Vietnam era, only one came from the armor branch, and that was Creighton Abrams in 1972.[20]

On 19 April an urgent top army staff meeting was held in Taylor's office regarding the disposition of the Grow incident. The conferences held in his office that week were usually attended by General Bolling and Colonel Dawson from G-2; Generals Brannon and Harbaugh and Colonel Bard from the Judge Advocate General Corps (JAGC); Generals Craig and Prickett from IG; General Parks, chief of information; General Reber, army liaison representative to Congress; General McAuliffe, G-1; and a representative from General McClure's Psychological Warfare Division. Taylor directed Bolling to prepare by Monday morning, 21 April, a memo draft from the chief of staff, Collins, to the secretary of the army, Pace. This draft would outline possible courses of action. Taylor had in mind a recommendation that the case be investigated with a view to a trial by general court-martial. Upon completion of the investigation, the incident would be reviewed again, and then it would be decided whether to proceed to a trial or request the secretary of the army to administer a simple punitive reprimand. Next, items were identified that would be needed to sustain the charge, such as Squires's book and a statement that it had been circulated in East Germany, handwriting testimony to show the extracts in the book were Grow's, and an examination of the diary and Squires's book in terms of AR 380-5 (Army Regulation: safeguarding security information).[21]

As directed by Taylor, Bolling on the twenty-first forwarded a summary sheet to General Collins giving a brief history of the diary incident. The diary, "in which classified security information was contained, was made public in a book written by Richard Squires, a British defector, and published in East Germany." On 6 March the American press began publicizing Squires's version of the diary excerpts. "This publicity has been extremely adverse to the Department of the Army," Bolling noted. The only public mention by the army concerning the incident was on or about 5 February, "when it was announced that the diary appeared to be authentic and the matter was being investigated." Bolling's meaning was confusing because the incident was not picked up by the news media until a month later. There was talk that the columnist Drew Pearson would break the story. Later that month, there was a rumor that the *Daily Worker* would come out with a report. Neither did. Not until Bolling released chapter 6 to Norris did the news media run the story. Bolling then advised Collins that the IG recommended a court-martial, and the judge advocate general advised that sufficient legal grounds existed to sustain the charge against Grow.[22]

Upon receiving Bolling's summary sheet, Collins prepared a memorandum for the secretary of the army. The first draft to Pace advised that the IG recommended a court-martial, and sufficient legal grounds existed for such action. If the incident proceeded to a trial, the results could not be fully predicted because so many varying factors existed, such as Grow's "many years of honorable service and technical rules of evidence." It was speculated that "the results might very well be a determination of guilty with the only punishment the imposition of a reprimand." Pace was to be presented with a recommendation for an investigation of the charge against Grow with a view to trial, based on Article 92 in the Uniform Code of Military Justice.[23]

In court-martial practice, the formal written accusation consists of two parts: the technical charge and the specifications. The technical charge against Grow was that he had violated the new *Uniform Code of Military Justice, 1951,* Punitive Article 92, which dealt with the failure to obey an order or army regulation (AR 380-5):

Any person subject to this code who—

1) violates or fails to obey any lawful general order or regulation; or

2) having knowledge of any other lawful order issued by a member of the armed forces, which it is his duty to obey, fails to obey the same; or

3) is derelict in the performance of his duties; shall be punished as a court-martial may direct.

The sample charge based on Article 92 read:

In that _____ at _____ on or about, _____, being in possession of classified military information in the form of entries in a diary, the publication of which tend to embarrass the United States in its relations with other nations, was derelict in the performance of his duties as United States Military Attaché in Moscow, by negligently leaving the said diary unattended, thus permitting its compromise by publication in a book, *Auf dem Kriegspfad.*[24]

Because portions of Squires's version had been demonstrated to be false, it would have been impossible to try Grow on the basis of the Soviet propagandist's accusation. Consequently, other grounds had to be found. A security violation was convenient because it could technically be proven based on an interpretation of Article 92 by selected experts. But it could not be made public. No doubt it was easier to prove a security violation than any other offense, provided the appropriate witnesses were presented.

The memo for Pace was reworded and altered by Collins. The words "so many varying factors existing, such as the officer's many years of honorable service and technical rules of evidence" were stricken, as was the sentence which made reference to the enclosed charge. The reworked memo was signed by Collins and hand carried to Secretary Pace, who noted it but indicated no approval. Pace did not receive the prepared charge under Punitive Article 92, nor was he advised that the diary quotes as they appeared in Squires's book were forgeries or taken out of context.[25]

Honorable Frank Pace, Jr. (1951).
Courtesy of the U.S. Army, National Archives

On the twenty-first another urgent development occurred. On the first day of a conference of judge advocates in Charlottesville, Virginia, Major General Ernest M. Brannon, the judge advocate general, received a telephone request to return to Washington immediately. Brannon informed his chief of the Military Justice Division, Colonel C. Robert Bard, that they must return to Washington promptly. They were ordered to "get working on the Grow case and try to finish it up that week so it could be turned over to Second Army, if possible, by Saturday." Bard had attended the meeting in Taylor's office on the nineteenth when the decision was made to proceed toward a court-martial. They had no sooner returned to Washington when Taylor orally directed Brannon to draft a set of specifications. On instructions from Brannon, Bard drafted five specifications acceptable under Article 92 and passed them on to Brannon. The first charge sheet was dated 22 April 1952 and listed five specifications. The first three dealt with Grow's "wrongfully, improperly and without properly classifying, recording in his personal diary classified military information" relating to the annual military attaché conference in Frankfurt, movement of a military unit to an overseas command, and a domestic tank production program. The fourth specification accused Grow of being derelict in the performance of his duties as an attaché in Moscow by failing to safeguard his diary, thereby permitting its compromise and publication in *Auf dem Kriegspfad*. The last specification accused Grow of failure to safeguard and protect information from diplomatic representatives from countries friendly to the United States. No doubt Bard constructed the charges from Dawson's and the IG's analysis of the diary made earlier in February. On the twenty-fourth, Bard's name was typed on the charge sheet as the nominal accuser.[26]

After viewing the specifications, Brannon suggested a closed proceeding because of the nature of the evidence. He declared that the secretary of the army would probably prefer a closed session, and the press release should contain only a paraphrase of the specifications, especially the first three charges, which appeared to him to have been based on entries in the diary.[27]

On the twenty-fourth, "pursuant to instructions of General Taylor," a copy of the court-martial charge and specifications against Grow were hand carried to Brigadier General M. F. Hass, secretary of the general staff, who was to forward the charge sheet to Collins so that he could review them that night in his quarters.[28] The charge sheet contained the charge, Article 92, and the five specifications prepared by Bard. The same day, Taylor, who had seen the prepared charge and specifications, advised Collins that "from a security point of view, these specifications may be safely published in the press if you so desire." Again, this raised the question of why Grow should be tried for a security violation if the specifications were to be made public. Taylor suggested that the reference "to an overseas command" be deleted from one of the specifications "to avoid stimulating discussion in Congress and elsewhere." Brannon, Taylor contended, had no objection, but Brannon suspected that Grow's defense counsel would move to make the specifications more pointed at the outset of the trial. If the notion was accepted, Taylor added, "the specifications could be amended without prejudice to the outcome."[29]

In standard court-martial procedure, as it existed at the time, before a charge sheet could be executed the actual accuser must initiate, prefer, and sign the sheet. According to the *Manual for Courts-Martial, United States, 1951 (MCM)*, any person subjected to the Uniform Code of Military Justice could prefer charges. This was one of the provisions of the new code. Usually the charges were preferred and signed by the commander who exercised immediate jurisdiction over the accused. In the Grow case, however, the army staff meeting in Taylor's office was hard-pressed to determine who should sign the charge sheet as the actual accuser or accusers. This action displayed the political rather than the judicial nature of the proceedings.

Eight witnesses were listed for the prosecution: four from G-2, Bolling, Dawson, Brigadier General John Weckerling, and Colonel Charles H. Ott; two from IG, Prickett and Ray; the assistant chief of G-3, Major General Reuben E. Jenkins; and an unidentified witness from Headquarters, EUCOM. Listed as documents and objects to be submitted as evidence were Squires's book, Grow's diary for 1951, his statement to the IG, and depositions from EUCOM. Also prepared on the twenty-fourth was a list of prospective court-martial members of Grow's rank and higher.[30] This action seemed premature because the charge sheet was not yet final, and an investigating officer pursuant to Article 32 of the Uniform Code had not been chosen to conduct an impartial pretrial investigation.

On Friday, the twenty-fifth, a second charge sheet was presented to Taylor during the staff conference. He read the specifications very carefully. Brannon recommended that the third specification, which dealt with tank production in the United States, be dropped because it was minor compared to the other charges. The number of witnesses remained the same, but penciled out from the evidence was "Depositions, Hq EUCOM," replaced with "Conference report OAC of S, G-2." Throughout the staff discussion on the charge and specifications, the question was raised as to who would be the proper authority to sign the charge sheet as the accuser. Neither Bolling nor Dawson wished to sign. They offered the excuse that neither one knew enough about the Grow case to qualify as an accuser. Their position was curious because both were actively involved. To be sure, neither Taylor nor Brannon would volunteer. The second charge sheet was not signed but again contained Bard's typed name.[31]

A group including Taylor, Bolling, Brannon, and Bard again went to see the chief of staff. Collins read the charge and specifications, which were discussed and some changes considered. The specifications were retyped and returned to Collins. The third charge sheet, dated 25 April, also contained changes. Added to the prosecution's witnesses were Major Edward S. Robbins from G-3, Colonel Harold R. Booth from the IG, and Warrant Officers George Henri and Gustav Bard from the 66th CIC Detachment. Missing were the CIC reports dealing with the EUCOM investigation. When the IG submitted its report early in February, one of the recommendations made was to "determine the person or persons and the methods or means by which Richard Squires obtained photostatic copies of the diary." There was no reference to the Poss affair. Brannon's recommendation that the specification dealing with U.S. tank production be stricken and Taylor's recommendation that the phrase "to an overseas command" be removed because it might cause a "discussion in Congress and elsewhere" were accepted.[32]

Shortly thereafter, Collins, along with Bolling and Brannon's assistant, Harbaugh, took the draft charge and specifications to Pace, who was joined by his assistant secretary, General Counsel Francis Shackelford. Collins read the specifications to Pace, who approved the recommendations of the chief of staff and the inspector general.[33] After the session with Pace, Collins telephoned Taylor at his quarters and instructed him to proceed in referring the charge and specifications to the commanding general of the Second Army after a final check with Brannon. Within thirty minutes, at Taylor's direction, a telephone call was made to the Second Army, where Grow was assigned.[34]

Early Saturday, 26 April 1952, Bard signed the third charge sheet again after much discussion among the army staff in Taylor's office. In the end, Bard was to act alone as the nominal accuser. He did as he was told or in accordance with implied orders from Taylor and Bolling. "I am an Indian, not a Chief," Bard would later admit. Moreover, by Bard's own admission, he was "not a security expert."[35] This requirement was necessary so the contents of the diary could be evaluated under AR 380-5. Only Bolling and Dawson and perhaps the IG were in a position to pass judgment on classification. They had controlled and analyzed Grow's diary. Thus how could Bard judge whether the diary should be classified? Because Bolling and Taylor were the prime movers in calling for a trial and instrumental in initiating and managing the preferring of the charge and specifications, they were really the accusers. But they preferred to be anonymous in the official proceedings; Bard was a figurehead, an instrument of command control. Thus Grow would find it difficult later to face and question the real accusers as is guaranteed under the new Uniform Code of Military Justice, Article 46, "Opportunity to obtain witnesses and other evidence."

Saturday morning another conference was held in Taylor's office, with two new members present, Brigadier General Leslie D. Carter, chief of staff, and Colonel Edward H. Young, staff judge advocate, from the Second Army. They were given a package containing the signed charge and specifications, the handwritten text of Grow's 1951 diary, *Auf dem Kriegspfad,* and statements from witnesses. Taylor told Carter and Young that the package was to be given to Lieutenant General Edward H. Brooks, commander of the Second Army, to institute an investigation in accordance with the Uniform Code. "These are charges being referred to you against a member of your command and the Manual covers you from then on," Carter and Young were advised. Taylor's and Bolling's actions of the past seven days indicated that Brooks would be the nominal convening authority.[36]

Historically, charges are usually associated with a military trial by the endorsement of the charge sheet by the commanding officer of the accused. This occurs after the signing and swearing to charges by an accuser who has personal knowledge of or has investigated the episode. Before the Grow case could proceed to a general court-martial, the charge sheet needed to contain the charge or charges and specifications, available information about the service of the accused, evidence, and proposed witnesses. The charge sheet had been firmly constructed with a view to a general court-martial under the control and direction of Taylor, Bolling, and their staff before the convening authority, the commanding general of the Second Army, had made any contribution to the proceedings.

When Grow returned to the United States in January, he was assigned to Headquarters of the Second Army at Fort Meade, Maryland, with temporary duty in the Pentagon, first in the office of the G-2 and then with the army's Personnel Board. So it was through command influence that Brooks of the Second Army became the administrative convening authority for a general court-martial, even though he was not involved in the judicial management until Saturday morning, 26 April 1952. Thus for practical expediency, he would get Taylor and Bolling off the legal hook and move the judicial proceedings to a nominal, inferior authority. In the end, Brooks was to enter the episode as the convening authority only after the mechanisms to try Grow were under way and firmly structured to be a trial controlled by Taylor's management group.

That same Saturday, Carter and Young, following Taylor's instructions, hand carried the package to Headquarters of the Second Army, where its contents were viewed by Brooks. There were no written instructions, but Brooks was advised by Taylor that the case should be considered classified "secret" to exclude the general public. This action had the effect of restraining the proceedings and severely limiting what could be explored as evidence, which could easily work against the accused by reducing the latitude of his defense. The "secret" classification allowed greater control by Taylor's management group and the designated convening authority by restricting possible admissible evidence and the cross-examination of potential witnesses. By placing a blanket of secrecy on the Grow case, it was possible to cloak the trial proceedings so as to prevent inquiry into either facts or reports by inquisitive reporters.

Though there is no documentation of duress, coercion, or limiting instructions given to Brooks, Carter, or Young, Taylor's and

Bolling's command influence prevailed and established a marked sense of direction. The charge and specifications were prepared at the direction of Taylor and Bolling against the advice of the CIA and the State Department, which had been concerned with the ramifications of international interest in a court-martial. Rather than referring the charge under Article 92 to a superior, as was usual, it was passed to an inferior command for trial. What else could be expected of the officers from the Second Army after Taylor and Bolling orchestrated the proceedings with Collins's endorsement and recommendation and Pace's approval? Command influence was overwhelming and positioned for a quick conviction even before the pretrial investigation of facts. Moreover, the army staff preordained guilt so no one was surprised when Brooks concluded that the charge and specifications warranted a pretrial investigation with a view to a general court-martial. Subsequently, Brooks appointed Colonel Frederick S. Matthews, a senior staff officer who began his military career as an infantry officer with the National Guard in 1914, as the investigating officer (IO). Matthews, whose career was at a plateau, was charged to investigate the Grow case pursuant to Article 32.

Article 32—embodying the same general concept and protection as Article of War 70, *MCM*, 1928, and Article of War 46, *MCM*, 1949—was designed to offer protection for military personnel. To Matthews fell the responsibility of conducting a "thorough and impartial investigation of all matters set forth." The new code required him to "extend the investigation as far as may be necessary to make it thorough," that is, to inquire into the facts of the Grow case and make a determination of the feasibility of a trial by general court-martial. His recommendations to Brooks were to be advisory only. Under the new code, the investigating officer was directed not to perfect a case against Grow "but to ascertain and impartially weigh all available facts in arriving at his conclusions." Failure to comply with the requirements outlined in Article 32 could cause Brooks to disapprove the proceedings.[37]

Early on Monday, McAuliffe, the G-1, called and advised Grow that he was ordered to stand trial for violation of AR 380-5. Relying on what he believed was "Army honesty and loyalty," Grow selected as his military attorney Lieutenant Colonel Robert E. Joseph from the Judge Advocate General Corps. One of the significant reforms of

the Uniform Code was that the accused had the right to be represented by a civilian attorney of his own selection, but Grow decided
to put his destiny in the hands of the JAGC even though some of his
close friends advised him to do otherwise. The next day, Tuesday,
Grow and Joseph discussed the situation at length. Joseph was aware
that politics from the top were influencing the proceedings. Both men
were optimistic, however, because they believed that the army did
not have a case. "We should be able to break it unless too much pressure comes in," Grow stated. He also decided to withdraw his application for retirement and take his chances with the military justice
system, which he was sure would exonerate him of the charge.
On Wednesday he talked to Brooks, who seemed friendly but as
expected would not listen to the details because of his position as
the administrative authority. Grow got the impression the pressures "came from top side," even though Brooks assured him he
would receive fair treatment and that no bias would influence the
proceedings.[38]

On Monday the Department of the Army released to the press information that charges had been preferred against Grow. The allegations listed were generalized, stating that Grow improperly recorded
classified military information in private records and failed to safeguard such information. The next day the media reported this news,
identifying Secretary Pace as initiator of the news release.

The *Washington Post,* under Norris's unrestrained pen, again repeated Squires's version, which called Grow a warmonger. The *New
York Times,* like the *Post,* left the impression that the diary excerpts
were authentic. Brannon, the *Times* wrote, had indicated that the
hearings and trial (if there was one) would be closed to the press because of the security aspects of the case. The influential paper also
quoted Parks, chief of information, who claimed he had attempted to
have the specifications drawn up in such a way that they could be
made public, but he had been overruled. The *Times* and *Post* quoted
top army officials who said that they could not recall charges for security violations having been brought against an officer of Grow's
rank in years.[39]

The communist media did not carry the news of the court-martial
charges to the extent that the American press did. After the March
and April propaganda bonanza, they lessened their attack on Grow.

The multilanguage weekly *New Times,* however, published by the Soviet Central Council of Trade Unions, which dealt with USSR foreign affairs and policy, did report that charges had been brought against Grow. "Pace admitted that Grow's bloodthirsty calls for war and his espionage and similar doings were official secrets of the United States Army Department." The *New Times* singled out Grow's diary excerpts, as depicted by Squires, as having been authenticated by the Pentagon.[40]

The original draft of the press release prepared by Taylor's staff stated that Squires's book contained greatly distorted quotes, especially those that portrayed Grow as a warmonger, and that upon completion of the court-martial, a further exposition would be made of those statements from the actual diary. Not one comment regarding the distortion of the diary, however, was released to the press because McClure believed no advantage could be gained by revealing the nature of Squires's propaganda effort.[41]

Another situation remained to be dealt with. The director of the Office of Public Information in the Department of Defense had requested an analysis for the State Department of ten diary entries listed in *Auf dem Kriegspfad.* The request was acted upon, and the Office of Public Information received Grow's and Dawson's comments that the excerpts were deliberately distorted and replete with misinterpreted segments and manufactured portions. But for some unexplained reason, no record existed of the State Department receiving the analysis. The army was concerned that the State Department would release a counterpropaganda effort while legal action against Grow was in progress. Furthermore, Bolling strongly emphasized that any action taken by the State Department must first be cleared by the Department of the Army.[42]

The actions taken by Taylor and Bolling strongly suggest that they were more interested in managing the embarrassing episode than in justice.[43] Perhaps Bolling was sensitive about charges leveled against agencies of the United States government regarding ill-advised intelligence arising out of North Korea's surprise invasion in June 1950. He was associated with that failure while serving as the deputy director of intelligence of the army.[44] Nevertheless, Bolling had reached the pinnacle of his career, and he had to protect his G-2 function at a time when heavy emphasis was placed on loyalty and security violations and recriminations. Bolling's next career move—providing his record was clean—might be the command of an army. Taylor was marked for greatness. He had more potential than Bolling, and his upward mobility, perhaps to army chief of staff, was a strong possibility.

To Taylor and Bolling, military justice reflected the status quo of command influence, which had had a long and very controversial history. After the Vietnam War, the watchdog agency of Congress, the General Accounting Office, concluded after a two-year probe that too much power was still vested in the convening authority. The study also noted that even though command influence was prohibited, "it can be exercised in many subtle ways that are not readily susceptible to detection."[45] Taylor and Bolling, with Collins's and Pace's cooperation, would be able to mask command influence in the Grow case, thus removing potential impediments to their careers.

★ ★ 6

Pretrial Investigation

GENERAL GROW WELCOMED the proceedings as a path to vindication.[1] Confident the pretrial investigation would put the matter to rest, he withdrew his request for retirement. Until 28 April, when the charge sheet was served, Grow was never advised by Collins and Taylor that disciplinary action was being considered. On 30 January, when he was interrogated by Colonel Booth from the IG Investigation Branch regarding security violations, Grow denied that he had violated such procedures. He first suspected that security was the issue while talking to the acting IG, General Prickett. This realization strengthened his confidence in his ability to defeat the charges. Though admitting he had not exhibited the appropriate discretion in safeguarding the diary, he believed the diary for 1951 did not contain security information. The material it contained was common knowledge. Moreover, Grow (or any American official) never was able to take a step or speak to anyone in the USSR without the knowledge of the Soviet security police. He was thoroughly familiar with security practices as indicated by his record in Moscow and elsewhere. He had been responsible for classifying material and did not breach security by recording information that was the basis for the classification of reports from "confidential" to "top secret."

In addition to the charge sheet, Matthews received written documents, statements, and affidavits pertaining to the charges.[2] Missing, however, were numerous documents dealing with the origin and management of the charges and the CIC reports from EUCOM (except a TWX from Bolling, the G-2, to McClure, EUCOM G-2, dated 22 April 1952, and a reply thereto from McClure to Bolling).[3]

116

At least four charge sheets were prepared between 22 and 26 April. Bard had finally signed at 0900 hours on the twenty-sixth as the accuser, and Colonel Young signed for the commanding general of the Second Army on the same day. A review of the four charge sheets indicated that Taylor and his management group were unable to agree on the number of prosecution witnesses and documents. The final charge sheet, which was received by the Second Army and Matthews, contained additional witnesses. Deleted from the prosecution documents were the depositions from Headquarters, EUCOM, perhaps to prevent the interjection of the Poss incident or any evidence reflecting unfavorably on the army staff, especially the G–2 function in EUCOM and the Pentagon.

All CIC reports from EUCOM were eliminated to avoid embarrassment, especially to Bolling. Army staff records, not available to Grow and his counsel, reveal that Taylor, along with Bolling, were the actual accusers, not Bard. The "Chronology of Events," Records of the Army Staff, noted: "The DC of S [Taylor] directed G–2 [Bolling] to prepare a recommendation that this case be referred to CG, Second Army, for investigation with view to trial." This decision was made on 19 April. Until the Second Army received the case at 0900 hours on Saturday, 26 April, Taylor and Bolling were actively maneuvering the proceeding toward a general court-martial.[4] In this respect, their thinking tended to exhibit the traditional style of military management, but it was modulated because of the demands caused by the army's expanded role. Taylor's management process was a cross-fertilization of the military industrial combination, which had become so pronounced because all resources were pooled to fight a global war and deal with the expanded role of the military in the postwar period. In February 1951, when Taylor became the assistant chief of staff, G–3, he admitted to the army chief of staff, General Collins, that he lacked experience in such management matters as personnel, procurement, logistics, and budget. Knowing this, the secretary of the army, Pace, made a point of giving Taylor administrative experience. That August he was promoted to deputy chief of staff for operations and administration (DC of S, OA) and continued a close working relationship with Collins, who had been his corps commander in Normandy.[5]

Before his appointment as DC of S, OA, Taylor had become the senior American representative in Berlin (1949–51) through the efforts of John J. McCloy, the United States high commissioner for Germany. The two had been friends since before World War II. Taylor, who possessed a powerful ego, claimed that he had gained considerable insight into Cold War tactics, including experiencing anti-American propaganda disseminated by Soviet-controlled media in East Berlin. While in Germany, Taylor established a reputation by his management of the volatile situation following the West Berlin blockade. Preserving his reputation was necessary for a professional aspiring to career advancement, and it was of the utmost importance that no unfavorable residue be deposited along the way. Taylor had an important stake in developments in Germany because of his military career and his relationship with McCloy and HICOG.[6]

On 29 April, Colonel Joseph requested that the charge sheet be declassified without deletion or alteration so he could prepare the defense. General Brooks released the charge sheet but disapproved of the "Top Secret" declassification because the document had been transmitted to Headquarters of the Second Army with that classification and with instructions that it continue to bear that classification.[7] This action again demonstrated command influence emitting from Taylor and Bolling. It also offered the army staff an opportunity to localize and control the evidence against the accused. Joseph then requested temporary duty (TDY) to EUCOM so he could interview potential witnesses. He wanted to contact officers and civilians known to Grow who had knowledge and information about the question of security as related to certain entries in Grow's diary. For the accused and his defense counsel, this information was pertinent to the pretrial investigation. Matthews did not agree with Joseph's request, and Second Army Headquarters subsequently disapproved on the basis that it did not include adequate justification for temporary duty.[8] This was the first hint that the pretrial investigation would not follow Article 32 of the Uniform Code. If Joseph had been allowed to go to Europe, it would have created a difficult situation for Grow's accusers. The investigation of Poss was almost completed, and if Grow's counsel had access to that material, it might affect the outcome of the trial, or at the very least, injure the careers of Taylor and especially Bolling. If the defense was denied the results of the

EUCOM investigation, Taylor and Bolling could more easily monitor the proceedings.

At 0900 hours on 13 May 1952, Colonel Matthews began the investigation of charges at Fort Meade, Maryland. He instructed Grow and his counsel: "You have the right to present anything you may desire in your own behalf either in defense, extenuation or mitigation" and the "right to have the investigating officer examine available witnesses requested by you."[9] Matthews, however, already had acted to counter this assurance by denying the defense the right to interview potential witnesses in EUCOM. This was just the beginning, for Matthews's actions during the month of May would make a mockery of Article 32.

It now was Joseph's turn to respond to Matthews's opening remarks. He first noted that Grow was withdrawing his request for retirement submitted in late February. Next, defense counsel reiterated the request for declassification of the charge sheet. He argued: "This action is deemed necessary to protect adequately the rights of General Grow in the preparation of his defense of the charges." In addition, he requested the return of Grow's 1951 diary because it had been turned over to the inspector general in January under duress. Joseph was applying Article 31 of the Uniform Code, which dealt with the prohibition of compulsory self-incrimination. He moved to have the first two specifications on the charge sheet dismissed on the grounds that each failed to allege an offense. These specifications dealt with Grow's diary entries. Joseph argued that the third and fourth specifications be consolidated because "only one offense, if any, is alleged in said specifications." These specifications were concerned with the security nature of maintaining a personal diary. Finally, Grow's counsel renewed his request to be placed on temporary duty in EUCOM so he could interview potential defense witnesses. Matthews demurred, and the first witnesses were called.[10]

The initial prosecution witnesses were from the Inspector General's Office. The first to give testimony was Brigadier General Fay B. Prickett, the deputy inspector general. He testified about a meeting on 28 January in Taylor's office, at which Taylor directed him to secure the diary after Bolling stated it was imperative to gain its possession. Prickett, who viewed the request as an order, was taken by surprise because he felt that the IG office was being used to obtain the diary before receiving a request to conduct an investigation. When Joseph attempted to pursue the content of the discussion in Taylor's office, Matthews objected. The more Joseph attempted to pursue his right as counsel to question the witness, the more Matthews moved to deny the defense access to all matters dealing with the diary incident.[11] Matthews's objections, which were frequent throughout the pretrial, were always accompanied by the statement that Joseph's questions were not applicable.

The next witness was Colonel Edward J. Maloney, chief of the Investigation Division, who was called after Prickett remembered that he had asked Maloney to send an officer to contact Grow and secure his diary. Like Prickett, Maloney noted that there was no investigation pending against Grow at the time. When Joseph attempted to establish the time when consideration was given to a trial by court-martial on the grounds of security violations, Maloney became evasive. He could not specifically state what security violations were at issue, and he did not remember who had signed a statement from the G-2 office directing an investigation. At this juncture, Joseph requested that the statement signed by G-2 be made available. Believing the answer lay in the document listed on page 1 of the charge sheet entitled "Conference report—OC of S, G-2," Joseph requested access under Article 32. Matthews replied, "The documents listed on the front page . . . don't have bearing." Stunned, Joseph then followed suit: "It is requested that in the interest of justice and to protect the accused's rights that this G-2 document be brought before the IO and made available to defense counsel at this time." Again, Matthews was unyielding. Joseph's purpose in requesting the G-2 document listed on the charge sheet was to ascertain who had influenced the IG's action and the relationship between the action officers, Taylor, Bolling, and Prickett.[12]

Following Maloney was Colonel John E. Ray, who had been detailed to secure Grow's diary. Ray was a bit agitated over his assigned mission because he considered the directive by Taylor "a rather unusual request." Again Joseph raised the question of the G-2 document. Counsel wanted to know if the document was available for perusal during the pretrial. "I see no reason why it would not," replied Ray, at which point Matthews intervened once again, thwarting the defense's efforts.[13] Joseph's purpose in pursuing the admission of the G–2 document was to ascertain the actual accuser's identity, which Grow and his counsel had been unable to determine.

Joseph's reasons in questioning Prickett, Maloney, and Ray were twofold: first, to determine if the diary was involuntarily delivered, and second, to determine who was the actual accuser (or accusers). To these questions, the defense counsel found no clear answers; however, his questions began to raise serious doubt about the roles of certain top army officials.

The next witness called was Colonel C. Robert Bard, who had signed the charge sheet. No sooner was Bard sworn in as a witness when Joseph asked: "Who directed you to prefer the charges?" Matthews quickly responded that the question was immaterial. Joseph disagreed and argued that the defense was entitled to know who was the actual accuser. Citing the *Manual for Courts-Martial,* he pointed out that the accused was entitled to have the accuser made known, and Bard, as nominal accuser, received his orders from above. Finally, Joseph was able to solicit an answer from Bard, who contended that in February he had been assigned by General Brannon to determine whether offenses had been committed. But there was no record in any of the army documents indicating that Bard had prepared specifications in February. The first recorded documentation of specification was dated 22 April 1952. Following up on Bard's answer, Joseph asked him who had instructed Brannon. Bard refused to answer, basing his response on the attorney-to-client relationship, which made the conversations with Brannon privileged. According to Joseph, this privileged relationship would not apply in this case. He maintained that it was an official army matter and therefore had a bearing on the question of identifying the appropriate and proper convening authority. Moreover, it would have an important bearing on Grow's position because he would have the opportunity to confront the real accuser. [14]

Again Matthews intervened. Joseph was advised not to worry about the convening authority. Joseph responded that the defense did not realize a convening authority had been established before the completion of the pretrial investigation. Matthews then replied that the commanding general of the Second Army would be the convening authority if a court-martial followed. [15] Joseph's comment about the established convening authority seemed to be a ploy because one of the defense's arguments dealt with the validity of the appropriate convening authority, the Second Army. To muster a pretrial investigation there must be a convening authority. If the pretrial investigating officer recommends a court-martial, it is usually the same convening authority who calls for a military tribunal to decide if a person subjected to the code had violated it.

Joseph decided to question Bard about the specifications he had prepared dealing with the classification of certain military information. He startled the defense counsel by admitting he was not a security expert; however, he had received information from two G-2 officers who were security experts, Colonel Gordon E. Dawson and Major Edward S. Robbins. Bard then remarked that he was more or less a conduit for the actions of others, and his routine duty was accomplished when he finally signed the charge sheet on 26 April. Joseph could not understand why it took from early February to 26 April to make a determination and draft charges. In February, Bolling had recommended that no court-martial charges be preferred against Grow, then in April changed his mind.[16] Regarding the urgency in April, Bard stated he was an "Indian," not a "Chief," but that he had acted quickly on 21 April on Brannon's orders. There was a sudden urgency to settle the Grow case in five days. Joseph maintained that his client was not advised that charges were being contemplated until 28 April, which indicated to the defense counsel that Bard was inserted as the nominal accuser to cover up the real accuser. When pressed by Joseph, Bard finally remarked that he had worked on the case per instruction from his immediate supervisor, General Brannon.[17]

The last witness called on the thirteenth by the defense was Colonel Joy R. Bogue, the assistant commandant of the Strategic Intelligence School, G-2. He recalled that Grow had been an excellent student and highly regarded by the school staff and his peers. Bogue rated Grow in the top third of his class in consciousness of security measures. When asked if there was an army regulation or policy against keeping a personal diary, he replied, "None that I am aware of." He added that no instructions were given at the Strategic Intelligence School to the effect that personal diaries should not be kept. Surprisingly, during this testimony, Matthews offered little interference.[18]

On Wednesday, Colonel Booth was the first witness for the prosecution. It was Booth who had taken testimony from Grow "pursuant to a directive from the Chief of Staff."[9] When Major Edward L. Stevens, Jr., the assistant individual defense counsel, requested the directive, Booth stated that he had no authority to present the document. That responsibility was held by the secretary of the army. Nevertheless, Booth did attempt to recall the contents of the directive. Stevens's questioning was designed to establish the origin and identity of the real accuser. Stevens moved to establish the application of Article 31 of the Uniform Code of Military Justice which prohibited compulsory self-incrimination. Before Booth took Grow's testimony on the thirtieth, he had the opportunity to read the translated copies of Squires's book, the East German newspaper reviews, and Grow's diary. At no time during the testimony did Booth read Article 31b to Grow as required under the Uniform Code: "No person subject to this code shall interrogate, or request a statement from, an accused or a person suspected of an offense without first informing him of the nature of the accusation and advising him that he does not have to make any statement regarding the offense of which he is accused or suspected and that any statement made by him may be used as evidence against him in a trial by court-martial." Because Booth had read Grow's diary and the enclosures from the chief of staff's memorandum, he was in a position to make some judgment as to the possibility of guilt, Stevens argued. Therefore, a reading of subparagraph b was mandatory. Booth disagreed because of Grow's rank and thirty years of military service. Stevens asked Booth if he at any time advised Grow of Article 31, subparagraph d, which read: "No statement obtained from any person in violation of this article, or through the use of coercion, unlawful influence, or unlawful inducement shall be received in evidence against him in a trial by court-martial." Booth had no idea at the time that there would be a court-martial and saw no reason to so inform Grow.[20]

Booth did mention, however, that he had recorded in his report that there had been a compromise of classified information through the disclosure of the contents of Grow's diary in Squires's book and in the two East German newspapers. If he had read chapter 6 of *Auf dem Kriegspfad* and compared the excerpts to Grow's diary, which he had also read, he would have seen that Squires's notes were false or taken out of context. This Booth did not mention, nor did Stevens pursue it.[21] Thus the discrepancy was not admitted. Grow was understandably disturbed by Booth's testimony. He noted: "Booth is a slick customer and obviously out to get me."[22]

Robert I. Henderson, shorthand reporter in the Investigations Branch, testified that he did not see a *Manual for Courts-Martial, 1951,* in Booth's possession when testimony was taken on 30 January.[23] Though Booth gave some explanation on the "compulsory self-incrimination prohibited" article, he did not provide Grow with the complete contents. Consequently, Grow was not clearly informed of his rights under Article 31, the individual defense counsel argued.

Colonel Gordon E. Dawson, chief of the Security Division, G-2, and one of Bolling's right-hand men, testified that he had closely examined Grow's diary on two different occasions and had determined that it contained classified information.[24] He was assisted by another officer in G-2 who early in February had identified dates and entries that were considered classified such as movement of the 1st Armored Division and status of tank production in relation to the division; information from friendly attachés and diplomatic personnel; information about the attaché conferences in Frankfurt; the views of the American ambassador on the USSR; and Grow's comments and opinions. In April Dawson, along with Bolling, had approached Grow and requested a review of Squires's excerpts for the State Department. Dawson admitted that the diary reflected Grow's estimation of Soviet intentions against the United States and did not reflect an aggressive attitude toward the Soviet Union by the United States as reported in *Auf dem Kriegspfad.* The witness noted that he wholeheartedly supported Grow in turning the incident into an antipropaganda effort. His actions, however, indicated otherwise. The information forwarded to the State Department did not contain a request from Dawson or even the G-2 to initiate any action to counter Squires's excerpts. The effort, therefore, was never carried to its conclusion even though Dawson and Bolling were aware that Squires's excerpts were false or taken out of context.[25] When Dawson completed his testimony, Grow and his defense counsels felt some good points had been made for the defense. Even Dawson commented that he had heard that Grow's performance in Moscow was "excellent" and even "superior."[26]

Another officer from G-2, Colonel Charles H. Ott, turned out to be a splendid defense witness. Ott noted that while serving as attaché, Grow had exercised considerable responsibility in security matters.[27] Major Edward S. Robbins from G-3 (Operations) was the next witness. Very early in May, after the charge sheet was delivered to the Second Army, Robbins had made a statement regarding the parts of Grow's diary (entries from 13 July and 27 September) dealing with the status and deployment of the 1st Armored Division to Europe. This appeared in the second specification on the charge sheet. Robbins's analysis was not documented until 2 May, a week after Bard signed the charge sheet. Under questioning by Matthews, Robbins said that he was called into Major General Reuben E. Jenkins's office on 1 May and instructed to work with Bard on a statement about the classification of certain passages in the diary. Jenkins was the assistant chief of staff, G-3 (Operations), under Lieutenant General Maxwell Taylor. Robbins and Bard had determined that the passages in the diary dealing with the 1st Armored Division were classified information, but Robbins admitted he had never been involved in security or intelligence work and, like Bard, had acted as "an Indian and not a chief." The fact that Robbins's action occurred after the drafting of charges and was then interjected into the proceeding out of G-3 rather than the Second Army again demonstrated that command influence was emitting from Taylor's management group.[28]

During the "thorough and impartial investigation of all matters," Joseph was not permitted to view all the documents pertinent to the defense. For example, on 14 May he requested a document dated 29 January 1952 from the chief of staff ordering the Office of the IG to conduct an investigation into the possible security violation or misconduct by Grow. Joseph also requested Bolling's written opinion dealing with alleged security violations. General Brooks's acting chief of staff denied the request and advised Joseph that the documents would be addressed to Matthews. His only action was to make Joseph's request a matter of record entered in the report on the proceedings. Grow was again denied his rights under Article 32 of the Uniform Code of Military Justice. He was not given full opportunity to examine all the facts or documents pertaining to the investigation of charges.[29]

Joseph then moved to dismiss and consolidate the charges and to suppress and return Grow's diary. Joseph argued that a careful examination and analysis of AR 380-5 dated 15 November 1949 (question of properly classifying) clearly indicated that the army regulations do not prohibit recording classified military information in a personal diary. On 18 March 1952, an army directive was issued prohibiting the keeping of a personal diary. Because the diary referred to in the specifications was by its very nature a confidential record in Grow's possession, AR 380-5 did not apply to the classification of entries, Joseph contended. Matthews replied that the first two specifications contained no reference to "failure to properly safeguard" classified military information, but on the contrary, merely referred to recording such information in a personal diary without classifying it. Grow's professional duty as an army attaché, Joseph responded, required him to record in some private and personal document important information of military significance so he could refresh his memory and draw on the data from time to time. It would be impossible to recall all noted material, with relevant dates, without some documentation. Finally, in regard to the first and second specifications, Joseph observed that the history of the armed services was filled with diaries similar to Grow's. He listed three prominent examples: those kept by Generals Dwight Eisenhower, Omar Bradley, and Mark Clark, all later rewritten and published as books.[30] Bradley and Clark were still on active duty at the time their books were published. Rather than being condemned for writing these books or keeping the diaries on which they were largely based, both had received public commendation and increased prestige. To try Grow for keeping a diary, Joseph argued, was hardly consistent with the accepted custom of leaders of the army. Since AR 380-5 did not prohibit the alleged act and personal diaries of ranking officers were commonly published, it followed, the defense argued, that neither of the first two specifications of the charge alleged an offense.[31]

Taylor also maintained a diary during this period, but it was a handwritten appointment book that was used to verify daily contacts and meetings when he wrote his autobiography years later. Grow's counsels, no doubt, were not aware of Taylor's diary–appointment book, and if they were, they would not have raised the issue because of Taylor's prerogative of rank and the potential damage to their careers if they did so.

Now Joseph acted to consolidate the third and fourth specifications into one issue. These specifications addressed dereliction in the performance of duties relating to Grow's alleged failure to safeguard his diary. Joseph felt that this constituted one transaction. There was only one diary, and the defense contended that to make it the basis for a multiplication of charges by splitting it into two specifications was unreasonable. Joseph rested his argument on *MCM, 1951,* paragraph 5a, which says the convening authority can correct an error in the event the charges are referred to trial.[32] Joseph's motion for dismissal of the first two specifications was denied, and he was informed that relief sought in basic communication of the third and fourth specifications would be properly considered upon the Second Army's receipt of Matthews's report of the investigation.[33]

Grow's counsel now moved to suppress and return the diary. In support of the motion, reference was made to the statements of Brigadier General Fay Prickett and Colonel John E. Ray from the Office of the Inspector General on 1 May 1952 and the testimony of Prickett, Ray, and Maloney before Colonel Matthews on 13 May 1952. Joseph argued that in *Boyd* v. *United States* (1886) "the unreasonable searches and seizures condemned in the Fourth Amendment are almost always made for the purpose of compelling a man to give evidence against himself." In other words, Joseph argued that the diary was not voluntarily surrendered but had been turned over to the IG on an order from the chief of staff and therefore should not be admissible as evidence against Grow.

Joseph based his argument on the events that occurred 28 January 1952 during a conference in the office of the deputy chief of staff. Bolling had told Taylor it was imperative to obtain the diary. Taylor requested Prickett to secure it. Prickett, questioning Taylor's request, consulted with Judge Advocate General Brannon as to the best method for obtaining the diary. As a result of Prickett's consultation with Brannon, Ray prepared a letter for Prickett's signature, addressed to Grow, stating that the IG had been directed by the chief of staff via Taylor to turn over his diary, and Ray had been instructed to receive it. Subsequently, Ray contacted Grow and presented

Prickett's letter. Though Grow protested and at first refused to surrender it, he decided to give the diary to Ray because the request came from the chief of staff and was considered to be a directive. Joseph noted that for an officer to obtain the diary in this manner from the IG's office was unusual when no formal investigation was pending. Moreover, Grow at no time was advised by Ray of his rights or that the diary could be used as evidence against him. The next day, a directive from the chief of staff ordered a formal investigation, and on 30 January Booth took testimony from Grow with reference to his diary.

Grow's counsel's argument was impressive. Military law prohibits unreasonable searches and seizures and renders such evidence inadmissible.[34] It also prohibits compulsory self-incrimination.[35] Based on the Uniform Code and *MCM, 1951,* Grow's counsels argued that the diary had been obtained illegally. Further to support their position, they cited opinions of the United States Supreme Court and other federal courts.[36]

On the basis of the cited legal military authorities and federal decisions, the individual defense counsels summarized their motion. They established that Taylor had unequivocally directed Prickett to secure the diary, that Ray had sought out Grow and presented him with a letter signed by his chief stating that he had been directed by the chief of staff to acquire the diary, and that Grow had properly interpreted the letter as an order from his superior. In addition, the defense asserted that military custom dictates that a request or an expression of a desire by a superior "has all the force of a direct order," requiring obedience by the subordinate.[37] Grow had demonstrated by his apprehension that he did not wish to relinquish the diary, which could later be considered an admission of guilt and used against him in court. Although Grow had requested a written stipulation from Ray that the diary would not be used against him in any proceedings, Ray had refused, claiming that he lacked the proper authority. Nor did Ray advise Grow of his rights under Article 31 of the Uniform Code. As soon as the diary was acquired and examined and Grow was questioned by Booth, the Office of the Inspector General recommended, in vague terms, disciplinary action against the former attaché, which culminated months later in the preferring of charges. Concluding, the defense counsel reiterated that the method used to acquire Grow's diary amounted to unlawful search and seizure as well as compulsory self-incrimination. Grow had been compelled to produce evidence (the diary) against himself. The use of command influence to procure the diary and then use it as evidence was clearly illegal according to both military and civil law, the individual defense counsel argued.

The defense counsel's brief to suppress and return the diary was forwarded to the secretary of the army through General Brooks. On 16 May Joseph was notified that his motion would be considered by Matthews in his report and by Brooks upon receipt of the final report of the investigation.[38] It seemed certain that Grow had lost a critical legal motion. Meanwhile, the next group of officers were ready to be questioned.

The day of 16 May turned out to be critical in the pretrial investigation. Testimony would be heard from personnel from the office of the deputy assistant chief of staff, G-2. Grow's attorneys did not consider the testimony of Brigadier General John Weckerling important or damaging to the defense.[39] But Brigadier General James Phillips's testimony was damaging. After reading the diary, he believed that Grow had violated security classification. Yet on cross-examination by defense counsel Phillips said that he had known Grow for almost thirty years, held him in high esteem, and considered his judgment to be sound.[40]

The next witness proved to be most interesting primarily because he exposed the true nature of the proceeding. Throughout the testimony of this witness a degeneration of military ethics prevailed. Major General Alexander R. Bolling was sworn in and began his testimony. Bolling related how he had learned about the diary incident and that it was Taylor who "directed a complete investigation of the case and that all possible information be furnished at the earliest date." Joseph began to question the G-2 about the conference held on 28 January with Taylor and Prickett regarding the acquiring of Grow's diary. Bolling replied that he did discuss the diary, but "I will not ——." Before he could complete the sentence, Matthews interrupted, characterizing the question as "objectionable." Thereafter, Bolling declined to answer any question relating to conversations held on the Grow matter in either Pace's, Collins's, or Taylor's offices. When Joseph pressed for specific dates, Bolling responded with a "no recall." Again Matthews's cryptic interruption: "Any question with references to a conversation has no part in this case." When Joseph asked Bolling about his knowledge as to how Grow's diary was obtained, Bolling lied: "I do not [know], merely hearsay."[41]

Joseph observed that on 7 February Bolling had told Grow that he did not think the inspector general would make a recommendation on the investigation. Bolling agreed. But the IG, Booth, had indeed made a recommendation on 4 February that appropriate disciplinary action be taken against Grow and that the investigation continue to determine how Squires obtained access to the diary.[42] Bolling knew this. In fact, the day after the IG report, Bolling sent a memorandum to the chief of staff recommending "that court-martial charges not be preferred against General Grow." He then added that "to sustain any charges, the diary itself would have to be offered and received in evidence," which constituted a clear violation of Article 31 dealing with the prohibition of compulsory self-incrimination. Bolling concluded his recommendation to Collins by observing it would be best "not further reviewing the entire matter in a court-martial proceeding." Unfortunately, Bolling's memorandum of 5 February was among many documents Grow and his counsels would never see. When further questioned about the IG investigation concluded on the fourth, Bolling commented that on 7 February he "had attempted to find out what the final outcome of the investigation would be and . . . was told that no recommendations had been made as yet."[43] It seemed that Bolling was unable or reluctant to tell the truth.

Joseph quickly moved to question Bolling about Grow's character and performance. The G-2 said that the former military attaché possessed an outstanding memory for detail, rated his performance of duty as "superior," and claimed that Grow's character was "unquestionable." Joseph then changed his line of questioning. He reminded Bolling about a cable addressed to General McClure, G-2, EUCOM, dated 22 April 1952, and the reply to Bolling, dated 25 April 1952. The cable had dealt with the distribution of Squires's book and the CIC agent who had purchased a copy in East Berlin in January. Both cables made reference to the Grow matter. Bolling was evasive: "I can assure you if it was detrimental to General Grow, I would answer, but there was nothing in that, that affects General Grow."[44] When Joseph appealed to Matthews for a ruling, he was advised "that the information is not necessary in the investigation." Again the door was closed to the defense regarding the events in EUCOM. No doubt Bolling's evasiveness made it possible to cover the embarrassment of having discovered a communist operative working in the Victory Guest House in Frankfurt where ranking American military and diplomatic figures were housed. To bring the results of the CIC investigation into the Grow pretrial investigation would surely affect the proceedings, if not Bolling's stature and career.

When Joseph asked Bolling if he had made any recommendations with respect to the preferring of charges against Grow, he again refused to answer, and once more Matthews called the question "improper." It seemed that the defense had little chance with Bolling's evasive answers and Matthews's pronounced partiality. Every attempt by Grow's counsel to determine the identity of the convening authority was blunted by Matthews. At this point, Joseph became heated, turned to Matthews, and remarked: "General Grow's reputation, his profession, his life is affected by the investigation and the possible trial of these charges. I think that latitude should be permitted me, as Individual Counsel, who has never had an opportunity to talk to General Bolling or any of the other witnesses, to develop the facts."[45] Matthews replied that his request would be noted.

Joseph decided to analyze the memorandum from Grow to Bolling dated 17 March 1952, regarding action to be taken against use made of Squires's exposé in the *Washington Post*.[46] Bolling agreed with certain portions of the memorandum. He added: "I am not here to defend *The Washington Post* because they take exception to many things we have done here." Bolling admitted that his G-2 function had been ineffective in controlling adverse publicity with the result that "the entire case was poorly handled and played into the hands of the Soviets." Joseph asked Bolling if he ever made any releases to General Parks (chief of army information) or to the press. "Yes, but I made no releases to the press," Bolling responded. When pushed by counsel, Bolling reconsidered and admitted that a translated copy of chapter 6 of *Auf dem Kriegspfad* was furnished, through Parks, to the *Washington Post*. Bolling's statement does not coincide with the CIA report, which quoted the G-2 as stating that Norris from the *Post* "had in effect forced him (Bolling) to release the incident to the press."[47] Bolling then protested that he did not hold press conferences.

According to Lloyd Norman from *Newsweek,* however, Bolling held monthly news briefings for selected newsmen who covered the Pentagon beat.[48]

Concluding, Joseph asked whether Grow cooperated regarding the diary incident. "Fully," responded Bolling, "but I am sure you understand the investigation was not part of G-2 nor did we conduct an investigation other than attempt to secure the individual who is alleged to have supposedly photostated that diary, and that we continue to do." "Has that been done?" questioned Joseph, to which the G-2 responded: "I refuse to answer that."[49] Again Bolling was less than truthful. He had been fully aware of the results of the investigation in EUCOM and of the implication of Poss.

That evening Grow recorded: "Bolling certainly did not tell the whole truth and that is a generous statement." He also believed Phillips's testimony was damaging and noted, "although expressing deep friendship . . . he gave expert opinion so bad . . . convinced me that he was pressured and was afraid." To Grow, the sixteenth had been a depressing day, and his optimism began to wane.[50] The pretrial hearings were recessed until 21 May. On that day, a third member, Major Roger M. Currier, joined the defense team.

When the hearings resumed, General Brannon, the judge advocate general of the army, made his appearance. The defense counsel wanted to continue the questioning so as to determine the identity of the real accuser and to prove that the diary had been delivered involuntarily. Earlier Bard had testified that Brannon directed him to prepare the charges. Once more, Matthews prevented Grow's counsels from developing their premise regarding the nature of the real accuser. On every question Matthews threw up a roadblock. Finally, Joseph, perturbed and frustrated, turned to Matthews and said, "If I am going to have to be restricted to tell you in advance what I expect to prove by each witness, I might as well stop right now." Again Joseph attempted to question Brannon about the nature and circumstances surrounding the procurement of the diary and the identity of the real accuser, but again he was overruled. Matthews became markedly protective of Brannon's testimony. Brannon stated that he could not answer certain questions because of his capacity as legal adviser to the secretary of the army and army agencies. To answer would affect the confidentiality of attorney–client relations.[51]

Major General Reuben E. Jenkins, assistant chief of staff, G-3, was considered a suitable witness for the defense. Jenkins thought Grow's judgment was "first class." Jenkins, however, believed that the recording of the movement of the 1st Armored Division in the diary was worthy of a security classification.[52]

The next witness gave the most absurd testimony to date, full of distortions and supported by vague, evasive terminology. When Joseph asked Lieutenant General Maxwell D. Taylor to comment on the conference held in his office on 28 January, he arrogantly stated: "Frankly, I can't. I have had so many things happen in my life that to recall what happened on 28 January, I couldn't do that any more than I could fly." Yet later during the sworn testimony, he said: "I watched this case closely, the G-2 and IG aspects of it. I can't say I participated in more than a monitory position." In fact, numerous discussions and conferences were held in Taylor's office, including the initiating, monitoring, and execution of the charges against Grow. When asked by Joseph who directed the charges, Taylor replied: "I don't know how to answer the question, frankly, because I don't know which of the senior individuals involved individually cleared this case to say he made the final decision. It went through me but it was decided far beyond me. It was cleared higher than my office." Taylor threw up a smoke screen by moving the responsibility away from himself and Bolling. The situation as documented on 19 April in Taylor's office indicated that Taylor had in fact directed Bolling to prepare a recommendation to Brooks of the Second Army for the pretrial investigation with a view to a court-martial. When questioned why there was such an urgency in April to execute the charges, Taylor responded: "I could answer in very general terms. I don't know when they preferred charges. I don't know who initiated charges to be drawn at any time. This whole thing was watched very carefully for the reaction overseas and the propaganda effect. I don't recall any particular decision being made at any given date."[53] Numerous documents dealing with the Grow case indicated otherwise and that both Taylor and Bolling had lied. Unfortunately, the defense did not see these documents, which were purposely excluded from the proceedings.

Following the last witness on the twenty-second, including several requests and motions made by Joseph, Matthews decided to execute a disposal of the pretrial investigation. The motion to suppress and return the diary and declassify the charge sheet was denied. The request by Grow's counsel for the summary sheet on the inspector general's report of investigation was considered by Matthews not to be pertinent to the investigation. The request to obtain the directive to the inspector general to initiate the investigation, likewise, was considered not necessary. Frustrated, Joseph requested that all documents and adverse rulings in question be attached to Matthews's final report. Again Grow's counsel requested action on the request for TDY orders to EUCOM. Once more Joseph argued that he needed to go to Europe so he could interview potential witnesses and prepare the defense. Matthews, as had by now become his custom, noted that the TDY request would be made part of the report of investigation, effectively putting off another request by Grow's counsel. Joseph believed that the trip to Europe would uncover documentary evidence applicable to the hearings. He was right, but he and Grow would not have the opportunity to explore the CIC investigation, which had drawn to a close. Grow's counsel also requested time to prepare and submit several briefs on substantial points raised by the defense. To this Matthews responded that he had heard all the testimony, examined all evidence and documents, and a brief was unnecessary. Reluctantly, he gave Joseph until the twenty-eighth to submit a brief, noting, "the investigation will be closed on that date." Not all the witnesses listed on the charge sheet had been called, Joseph reminded Matthews. He called attention to Warrant Officer George Henri from the 66th CIC Detachment, whose unit was responsible for investigating the compromise of the diary in Europe. Matthews responded that the situation would be taken care of later, possibly knowing that Henri's testimony would have opened a "bag of worms."[54]

The following day, for the fourth time, Joseph submitted a request for TDY orders to EUCOM because it was "essential to the proper and adequate preparation of General Grow's defense." This time the request was simply ignored.[55] Naturally these repeated requests raised the question of the defense's right to investigate events in Europe at government expense. Two prosecution witnesses from the 66th CIC Detachment in Berlin were listed on the charge sheet, and perhaps Grow's defense counsel could have handled the requests by telephone. Because the CIC was listed on the charge sheet and Poss was associated with the government's main source of evidence—the diary—"a thorough and impartial investigation" was needed and it "should extend . . . as far as may be necessary to make it thorough." The investigation should also be "limited to the issues raised by the charges," which were initiated as a result of the events in Europe that surrounded Grow's indiscretion in 1951. It could be argued that the entries in Grow's diary provided a prima facie case for the government. But the defense was entitled to pursue the issue until the government's evidence was challenged by other evidence. In other words, each party was entitled to produce evidence that was relevant and necessary for a thorough and impartial investigation.[56]

Grow's counsels hurriedly prepared a brief to meet the deadline set by Matthews. Their main argument dealt with the propriety of Brooks, as commanding general of the Second Army, acting as the convening authority. It was their contention that the authority who directed the charges against Grow was superior to Brooks and thus he lacked the power to convene a court-martial to try Grow. Joseph and Stevens argued that Bard, performing a "routine duty," prepared and signed the charges per instructions from his superior, General Brannon, on or about 21 April. Brannon had testified that Taylor directed him to prepare charges based on the findings of the inspector general. Also Bolling and Prickett, in their testimony, had made recommendations concerning the preferring of charges. Taylor in turn testified that individuals senior to him were involved in the decision to prefer charges. Thus, the defense counsel argued, an authority superior to Bard had directed the decision. Therefore, under the Uniform Code, said authority was also an accuser. Grow's counsel supported this argument by citing two recent decisions handed down by the United States Court of Military Appeals (USCMA) in which it was determined that a competent superior to the accused must convene the court-martial. This procedure was necessary so as to identify the actual accuser and limit command influence by persuasion or subtle influence.[57] Congress, Joseph argued, intended to eliminate the vices innate in the convening authority's ability to influence the court-martial by enacting the new code. It would be easy to act through a subordinate like Brooks because he would find it difficult to ignore "even the unannounced desires of his superior." The defense counsel summarized by observing that Brooks was junior to one or more accusers. Hence he was without power to convene a court-martial, and any court he appointed would be illegally constituted.[58]

It appeared that, despite Matthews's obstacles, Grow's counsel was presenting a persuasive defense. Perhaps it was too persuasive because on the morning of 27 May Joseph received a long distance phone call from Lieutenant Colonel Charles M. Munnecke, the acting staff judge advocate of the Second Army, requesting that Grow and his counsel report to Fort Meade promptly. Munnecke was told to expect them to arrive at Fort Meade at noon the following day because Joseph was in Fort Monmouth, New Jersey, and Grow at home in Falls Church, Virginia. Later that morning, Munnecke called Joseph again, informing him that the following day would be too late and requesting that he get Grow to Fort Meade immediately. Because this was logistically impossible, it was agreed that an army car would pick Grow up at Falls Church at 0800 hours on the twenty-eighth. Again Munnecke called back and changed the time to 0700 hours. At 0700 hours, Joseph and Stevens picked up Grow at Falls Church, proceeded to Fort Meade, and reported to Headquarters, Second Army. When they arrived, Grow and his counsels were astonished to learn that an additional charge had been presented and would be investigated that afternoon. The defense had not suspected an additional charge to be filed. Joseph immediately requested a copy of the newly filed charge sheet and was refused on the ground that the charge was classified "Top Secret." When Joseph formally requested from Matthews a week's continuance so he could evaluate and prepare a suitable defense, he was told that "it is not practical to delay the beginning of the investigation." Grow and his counsels were stunned. What had happened to the legal rights that the Uniform Code offered? Pentagon intrigues had once more made a mockery of the Uniform Code by continuing to direct and influence the proceedings.[59]

The new charge accused Grow of recording in his diary on 24 March 1951 reported plans of the Soviet Far Eastern Revolutionary Committee for a large-scale offensive in Korea in April 1951 by the Chinese Red Army, an alleged violation of punitive general article "Article of War 96."[60] But this was an incorrect listing of the general article; the Uniform Code identified it as Article 134. This minor confusion arose from inability to use the Uniform Code correctly. General Article 134 was indicative of the morass in which the real convening authority was lost. General Article 134 and Article of War 96 were not specifically dissected in either the code or the previous Army Articles of War. It is a vague and indefinite catchall that could be used indiscriminately by the convening authority or accuser for the benefit of discipline or personal interpretation of military conduct. Thus the excuse of urgency so often used in the Grow case once again justified questionable methods.

The new charge sheet listed two witnesses for the prosecution: Major Nicholas A. Povendo and Colonel Gordon E. Dawson, both from Bolling's G-2. Documents included Grow's diary, a message from the United States Army military attaché in Ankara, Turkey, and a message from Department of the Army to the army military attaché in Moscow. Dawson had appeared as a witness for the prosecution on 14 May and had testified that he had examined Grow's diary on two occasions and determined that it contained classified information.[61] Dawson now claimed that in February 1952 he had identified the entry Grow made on 24 March 1951 as a subject for a military security classification that could have been included in the first charge sheet. Accordingly, after testifying, he hastily prepared a statement covering the entry on the twenty-fourth, which he then handed to Major Povendo, chief of the Message Center Branch, G-2, for evaluation. Dawson had earlier discussed this move with his friend Colonel Bard, the nominal accuser on the first charge sheet. Both officers joked about how different people classified communications. Dawson suggested to Bard at "one time or another" after 20 May 1952 that he considered the entry in question to be grounds for an additional charge. There just happened to be another nominal accuser in the Judge Advocate General's Office, Major Arthur M. Scheid. He signed the additional charge sheet and dated it 26 May 1952.[62] As before, the charge did not originate from the Second Army—the so-called convening authority—but from the Pentagon. On the same day the charge sheet was turned over to the Second Army for disposition. Two days later, Matthews was ordered to investigate the additional charge. He did not waste time; it was one of the shortest pretrial investigations of charges against a general officer in the history of modern military justice.

Grow's counsels vainly protested. They quickly prepared a brief, arguing that the specification in the charge sheet did not allege an offense because the mere personal recording of classified information without classifying it was not a violation of AR 380-5. Moreover, the additional charge was improperly designated. Joseph and Stevens called for a dismissal.[63]

Matthews was adamant. This was it; the pretrial investigation had ended. The motion for a dismissal was denied, as was the continuance to analyze and prepare a defense to the additional charge. All motions and briefs of the defense counsel, Matthews asserted, would be attached to the final investigation officer's report. At 1510 hours on 29 May 1952, the pretrial investigation adjourned, and on 31 May Matthews recommended a general court-martial.[64] Matthews violated the most important and legally vital responsibilities of a pretrial investigation officer. He did not conduct a complete and impartial investigation. He controlled the proceedings in a way that effectively prevented a thorough investigation of the specifications as listed on the two charge sheets, acting more like a prosecutor for the real and nominal convening authority. At times, it seemed, Matthews resembled a prosecutor by assuming an adversary position, especially when handling efforts by the defense to determine all facts. Surprisingly, Squires's false accusations were never brought into the proceedings. Also, Matthews did not properly perform his duty because Grow was not fully informed or allowed to pursue all documents pertaining to his case. Grow and his defense counsels were only given the opportunity to review the actual charges and prescribed evidence. Many documents were withheld, including the CIC report in EUCOM. Thus Grow was not afforded all the applicable rights or the latitude connected with the investigation as outlined under Article 32 of the Uniform Code. Matthews's actions provide an excellent example of how not to conduct a pretrial investigation under Article 32 and the role political interests played in usurping the judicial process.

Finally, Brooks of the Second Army did not ensure a thorough and impartial pretrial investigation by selecting Matthews. Matthews was not attuned to the true meaning of Article 32, and his role as investigating officer indicated that the military judicial system was only as effective and fair as the individuals responsible for its execution. There was a constant denial of military due process because Brooks and Matthews were affected by command influence and acted according to the desires of Taylor's management group.

The General Court-Martial

O<small>N 3 JUNE</small> 1952, the Second Army chief of staff, Brigadier General Leslie D. Carter, notified Taylor that
Brooks had decided that a trial by a general court-martial was warranted after receiving Matthews's report. Carter also gave Taylor a
list of twelve general officers, none of whom were below Grow in
grade, relative rank, or on the same promotion list. These officers
were to be detailed to the general court-martial serving as the military jury.[1]

Shortly thereafter Taylor met with Brannon and Parks and outlined three steps to be taken in regard to the general court-martial.
First, he along with Brannon and Parks picked eight general officers
from Carter's list to sit on the court. The Second Army, as the designated convening authority, would have no say in picking the court
members.[2] The selection of court-martial participants is the duty of
the convening authority. Usually selection cannot be delegated, yet
Taylor, along with Brannon and Parks, decided who should constitute the court and presented the list to Brooks. This action reflected
command influence. Thus the army staff under Taylor's guidance
failed to sever political, command interests from the judicial process.

Second, Taylor directed Parks to issue a press release announcing
the court-martial. Finally, the assistant chief of staff, G-1 Personnel,
Lieutenant General Anthony C. McAuliffe, was to inform members
of the court-martial by phone before Parks's press release appeared.
McAuliffe was a close associate of Taylor's and followed Brooks as
G-1 Personnel. Brannon remarked that he would detail members of
the JAGC to the court, and they would probably come from the

Lieutenant General Anthony C. McAuliffe (1951).
Courtesy of the U.S. Army, National Archives

Pentagon.[3] Taylor's action again revealed the direct route he had taken since January in not only monitoring but actually constructing and directing the trial procedures.

An article in the *Saturday Evening Post* on 14 June entitled "Tomorrow They'll Be Famous" depicted Taylor as "better known inside the Army than outside it." The author, Demaree Bess, praised Taylor while chiding Grow for letting his diary fall into communist hands. Bess virtually paraphrased Norris's article in the *Washington Post* early in March. He accused Grow of using his diary to record whatever influence he possessed to hasten a war with the USSR. Bess commented on the army staff's long months of delay in bringing charges, for which he blamed the army as much as Grow: "They surely must have sensed that the policy which made the mistake possible was as much to be condemned as the man." A month later, shortly before the trial, the *Washington Post* reported that, according to an army spokesman, the delay was allowed "to permit General Grow and his counsel to thoroughly prepare his case."[4]

Shortly after the court members were picked, Bard informed McAuliffe that General Harold R. Bull was scheduled for retirement on 31 July. Bard suggested that Bull be recalled to active duty on 1 August. Meanwhile, General Collins, army chief of staff, was notified that General Carter, chief of staff of the Second Army, believed the trial would last at least a month. It was then recommended that retired officers be substituted for certain members of the court. With a month-long trial in mind, McAuliffe proposed that General John R. Hodge be excused because of the pressure of other duties. It was Brannon's idea that the court consist of nine members so as to permit both sides an opportunity to challenge members without imperiling a quorum. Major Generals William R. Schmidt and John B. Anderson were brought out of retirement, establishing a quorum of nine. McAuliffe remarked that when the challenging was completed, consideration needed to be given to excusing General Bull. Bull, a very good friend of Grow, did not want to serve on the court-martial.[5]

On 13 June the Board of Governors of the 6th Armored Division Association wrote a letter to Brannon supporting their former commander: "We believe . . . that General Grow should not be punished merely because a thief stole his private possessions and used them for propaganda; we believe that in the event this officer faces trial, that justice will be served if the board or Department of the Army announces that General Grow's views were his own views, and while perhaps indiscreet ones, do in no way represent the views of the Department of the Army or any other governmental agency."[6] About the same time, Grow's G-1 during World War II and an association member, Colonel James S. Moncrief, Jr., recalled the general visiting him at Walter Reed Hospital and intimating that he could beat the army's case.

Meanwhile, the trial counsel, Colonel John S. Dwinell, JAGC, notified Grow's counsel that the date for trial had been set for 23 July 1952. Shortly thereafter Brooks declared, "in the best interest of national security," that all evidence would be classified; therefore, the general public and spectators were to be excluded from all trial sessions. This decision provided an environment favorable to the prosecution because it controlled all information arising from the trial, thus negating any advantage Grow might gain from media exposure. Moreover, any adverse publicity arising out of the court-martial would hardly enhance the careers of the army staff engaged in managing the Grow case.

As late as 1988 an article in the *Military Law Review* noted that closing courts-martial to the public to protect classified information and limiting the defense counsel to classified documents "can prevent the accused from receiving a fair trial." Thirty-six years after Grow's court-martial the dilemma of balancing national security interests with the rights of the accused was still an issue. The author admitted that "there is little indication that current classified information procedures guarantee fair trials."[7]

The second problem to occur was in the picking of defense witnesses. On 2 July Joseph and Stevens submitted their list of witnesses for the defense; it included General Bolling. On the tenth and again on the twenty-second, Bolling was requested to appear as a witness. Grow's counsels were advised without an explanation that Bolling was away on official business and not in the immediate vicinity of Washington. The *MCM* clearly states that the trial counsel (the person who prosecutes a case for the military) "will take timely and appropriate action to provide for the attendance of those witnesses who have personal knowledge of the facts at issue in the case for both the prosecution and the defense."[8] Who else but Bolling fit this description in the Grow trial? Yet in spite of all efforts by Grow's counsel to acquire Bolling as a witness, he was conveniently unavailable. Even an attempt by the trial counsel and individual defense counsel to get Bolling to stipulate failed. During the trial, Dwinell astonished Grow and his counsel by stating, "General Bolling is not a necessary witness."[9] He never did appear. Instead, limited portions of his testimony taken on 16 May during the pretrial investigation would be admitted, a very meager concession which was useless to the defense.

On 18 July the defense counsels requested as a witness General Parks, along with all press releases and other documents within his authority or control. Dwinell hedged, and Joseph repeated the request on 25 July. It became so difficult to obtain witnesses for the defense that on 22 July Joseph and Stevens requested a postponement until 28 July or a later date. They gave three reasons.[10]

First was the important information regarding the issue of jurisdiction of the general court-martial based on the deposition obtained from the secretary of the army at 1545 hours on 21 July. Earlier in the day, Secretary Pace had received a briefing on the Grow case from his department counselor, Francis Shackelford. Pace was advised that the statutory definition of accuser as stated in the Uniform Code was vague. The question of vagueness was based on a standard which determined the degree to which a person has an interest, other than official, in the matter. In addition, Pace was made aware of the pretrial testimony of three witnesses: Bard, Taylor, and Brannon. Bard, under sworn testimony, had stated: "I am an Indian, not a Chief." Pace was also advised by Shackelford that Bard did not know why the charges were drafted so quickly. Taylor was quoted as stating that the decision to prefer charges was made at a level beyond his authority. And Brannon was cited as refusing to answer a question by Grow's counsel regarding the knowledge of whether Taylor received orders from higher up.[11]

The interrogators at Pace's deposition were Joseph and Lieutenant Colonel Paul J. Leahy, JAGC, assistant trial counsel. When questioned, Pace denied signing charges or directing any other person to sign charges in the Grow case. When pressed by Joseph, Pace admitted that he concurred with the recommendations made by the inspector general and army staff, Collins and Taylor. Pace did not know nor was it brought to his attention that the quotes from Grow's diary in

Squires's book were forgeries. When asked if had he known, whether it would have affected his decision, Pace replied, "I should say not." Pace's judgment again was not based on his personal assessment of facts but on recommendations by the army staff (Taylor through Collins) and the inspector general. Pace thus assumed a passive role.[12] The decision had been made below his level. All that was required was his confirmation.

Another aspect of the question of jurisdiction was General Taylor's stipulation dated 21 July. Before submitting to the stipulation Taylor consulted with Brannon on Friday, 18 July, and again early on Monday, 21 July. Taylor admitted that he had taken the initiative against Grow in Collins's name and on Bolling's recommendation in January, including issuing the request to Prickett to obtain the diary from Grow so it could be turned over to Bolling for analysis. At the same time, according to Taylor, Bolling recommended that the diary incident be investigated by the inspector general. Taylor approved this action. As soon as the IG investigation was completed, it was referred to Brannon's staff for legal study, where it remained for over two months. Then on 21 April, Taylor directed Brannon, who was in Charlottesville, to return to Washington to put the charge and specifications together as soon as possible. This decision was taken after Taylor consulted with Collins. When Brannon and Bard returned to the Pentagon, Taylor informed them that Collins had directed them to draft typed specifications. They did so within a week, and Taylor then hand-carried the specifications to Collins for approval. Taylor admitted that a serious dispute arose over who would sign the charges, and "I did not clear the charges with Secretary Pace" but decided to refer them to Brooks of the Second Army. His reason for this decision was because Grow was assigned to duty in the Second Army. Action on the Grow situation lay dormant for several months, Taylor explained, because senior authorities of the general staff were watching foreign and domestic reactions arising from disclosures in the diary. He also recalled that no action was taken at first because it might augment the propaganda effort of the Soviet government. Concluding, Taylor believed his role in the affair was that of a monitor at the general staff level, which was "the ordinary function of a Deputy Chief of Staff. My actions and orders in this matter, as in all matters, were taken by me in the name of the Chief of Staff."[13] Thus

Grow's defense was based on establishing the identity of the real convening authority above the Second Army, not Taylor or Collins but the secretary of the army. This was done so as to challenge the jurisdiction of the Second Army to try Grow.

The second reason the defense requested a postponement was to allow time for pretrial interviews of essential witnesses. Grow's defense counsels requested testimony from General J. Lawton Collins, army chief of staff; Brigadier Robert A. McClure, chief of the Psychological Warfare Division; and two colonels from his division, Wendell W. Fertig and John B. Stanley. Once more, unfortunately for Grow's defense, these witnesses were not afforded the opportunity nor did they want to give testimony. In fact, Grow's counsel would never have the opportunity to place on the witness stand any officer of equal rank or above the rank of major general who was involved in the management of the trial with the exception of the G-3, Major General Reuben Jenkins, and Major General Floyd L. Parks.

The third reason Joseph and Stevens gave for their request for a postponement was the persistent unavailability of Bolling. The defense maintained that he was an essential witness, if not the most important, and urged that the court-martial be postponed until he was available. Bolling's presence would throw light on the issue of jurisdiction, they reasoned, and they also anticipated that he would give testimony indicating that the real accuser in the Grow case was somebody other than Bard.

Colonel Dwinell rejected the request for postponement because of the time element. This denial would also blunt defense efforts to acquire numerous stipulations, including those from Europe. It was evident that, as in the pretrial investigation, the convening authority was using time against the accused. Very little latitude was offered to Grow's defense counsels to allow them to develop a proper and effective case. As a result, the Second Army told Joseph and Stevens that their request had been received after the "close of business." Dwinell then advised that the matter would be referred to the court for a decision.[14]

In the end, the real accusers never appeared as witnesses. Taylor's only "appearance" was in a stipulation introduced during the motions at the court-martial. According to the noted military jurist Edward M. Byrne, a witness has a greater impact on court members if he appears in person than he does through the presenting of a stipulation.[15] Bolling remained unavailable throughout, with no reasonable explanation given. Also, there was a possibility that if Bolling was available the embarrassing events in EUCOM would be brought up during the trial and the whole issue of Poss's involvement laid bare. This would change the whole direction of the trial. Collins and McClure and the two colonels from his Psychological Warfare Division did not testify, stipulate, offer a deposition, or appear as witnesses as requested by the defense counsel. Pace would submit to a deposition, which was admitted as evidence for the prosecution. Throughout the hearing, the action of controlling witnesses exemplified the vices of command influence which permeated the whole proceeding. The Sixth Amendment to the Constitution sustains the right of the accused "to be confronted with the witnesses against him, to have compulsory process for obtaining witnesses in his favor." Article 46 of the Uniform Code states: "The trial counsel and defense counsel shall have equal opportunity to obtain witnesses and other evidence." Grow never had the opportunity "to obtain witnesses and other evidence" or to confront his real accusers.

On the morning of 23 July the general court-martial proceedings began with the introduction of counsels.[16] The members of the court were sworn in: the law officer, Major General Hubert D. Hoover, JAGC; the trial counsels, Colonel John S. Dwinell, JAGC, Lieutenant Colonel Paul J. Leahy, JAGC, and First Lieutenant Donald M. Stearns, JAGC; the defense counsels, Lieutenant Colonel Robert E. Joseph, JAGC, Major Roger M. Currier, JAGC, Major Edward L. Stevens, Jr., JAGC, First Lieutenant Seymour Weil, JAGC, and Brigadier General Adam Richmond. Richmond, the new member of the defense team, was a retired general officer in the judge advocate general's corps and former staff judge advocate for General Eisenhower in Africa.

As soon as the court was convened, Dwinell gave a brief summation of the charges and specifications. The initial charge was preferred by Bard and the additional charge by Scheid. Dwinell then moved to exercise the trial counsel's right to one preemptory challenge in the case of one court member, General Bull, who withdrew and took no further part in the proceedings. The defense counsel then challenged the remaining court members on whether they held any biases or should be precluded from sitting in the trial. After the remaining eight members were challenged, Dwinell read the charges and specifications in full.

Next came the arraignment. Before entering a plea, the defense moved to dismiss all charges and specifications for lack of jurisdiction. The convening authority, General Brooks of the Second Army, was inferior in rank and command to the actual accuser. To argue its point, the defense called Colonel Bard.

Under questioning by Currier, Bard recalled how he drafted the charges and specifications and that conferences regarding the charges were held in Taylor's office. These conferences were attended by Bolling and Dawson; Reber of the Legislative Liaison Division; Parks, chief of information; Craig, the inspector general, or Prickett, the deputy inspector general; and Fertig from Psychological Warfare. Bard also recalled that McAuliffe, along with Brannon and his assistant, General Harbaugh, was usually in attendance. Bard referred to the conferences as "progress reports." Recollecting the events on Friday afternoon, 25 April, Bard stated that Taylor went to Collins's office with the charges and specifications. Accompanying him were Brannon, Bard, and Bolling. After a short conference in Collins's office, with Taylor doing the talking, the group went to meet with the secretary of the army. Collins then did the talking. Pace listened but did not suggest any action. Collins informed the secretary that a package of evidence and the charge sheet would be turned over to the Second Army the following morning, and Pace concurred. When questioned by Currier regarding the conflict over who would sign the charge sheet in Taylor's office on Friday, Bard explained that it had been suggested that Bolling become the accuser. He resisted and said something like "I don't want to get mixed up in it." Then Dawson was suggested. Dawson was under Bolling's command. He also resisted. Bard admitted: "The two people who normally would sign the charges didn't want to do it." Someone had to sign, "so I volunteered," recalled Bard, "after other people showed reluctance." The package containing the charges that was served to the Second Army on Saturday, 26 April, was executed in Taylor's office. In attendance were Carter and Young from the Second Army, Bolling, Dawson, Parks, Reber, and Bard.

Under cross-examination by trial counsel, Bard admitted that no one had ordered him to sign the charges but that he had volunteered. Because so many general officers were involved in the conferences, it would, given the military respect for hierarchy, offer the lowest-ranking officer a chance for group identity and influence. Even Bard recognized this; he mentioned to the court that he would not normally have signed the charge sheet if he had not been at the various conferences in Taylor's office.

After Bard withdrew from the courtroom, the prosecution and defense offered Taylor's stipulation, which clarified his involvement in the proceeding since January. It also clarified Collins's role in the case. Along with Bard's testimony, Taylor's stipulation confirmed Bolling's actions. Again it was evident, if not critical, that Bolling's presence as a witness was mandatory for Grow's defense. After Taylor's stipulation was read, the court recessed. The next witness called by the defense in its motion for a dismissal was Colonel Dawson, who until 26 May had been with Bolling's G-2 but who was then assigned to the army language school. He was questioned about his role in the additional charge and the specification signed by Scheid on 26 May. Dawson admitted that after his testimony during the pretrial investigation, "as a matter of academic interest," he had checked the Cable Section to correlate top secret cables with entries in Grow's diary. Shortly thereafter, he paid a personal call to the IG and on his way back walked into Bard's office and mentioned his assignment. Bard suggested that Dawson acquire a statement from the officer in charge of the G-2 Cable Branch, Major Povendo. Bard recalled that the pretrial investigation officer, Colonel Matthews, who happened to be in the Pentagon that day, had visited Dawson's office to pick up the additional charges.

After questioning Dawson, the defense for the fourth time requested the appearance of the elusive General Bolling. Currier argued that the defense could not proceed on the motion for dismissal until Bolling presented himself. Dwinell felt that Bolling's presence was not warranted. Nevertheless, Currier argued: "It seems peculiar that the prosecution has an opinion as to the necessity of the defense witnesses that the defense needs." Dwinell responded by citing *MCM,* paragraph 115 (Attendance of witnesses), which states that the trial counsel will provide attendance for all witnesses "except that where there is disagreement between the trial counsel and the defense . . . the matter will be referred for decision to the convening authority or to the court." This action was one of the limitations of the Uniform Code because it could place control of witnesses in the hands of the people who exercised command influence. Grow's counsel was at a marked disadvantage because the trial counsel monitored and controlled the witnesses requested by the defense.

Joseph pointed out to the court that Bolling had refused to answer questions on jurisdictional matters during the pretrial investigation. But General Anderson, a court member, responded: "I don't see what Alex Bolling has to do with the jurisdiction of the court or why we need to wait to have any further testimony." Anderson, one of the general officers called back to active duty to serve as a court member, apparently supported the prosecution. Members of courts-martial assume the responsibilities of an impartial jury. Anderson's comment indicated otherwise; he offered an opinion in favor of the prosecution covering Bolling's absence. This was a biased remark.

General Hoover, selected from Brannon's JAGC as the law officer (title given to the military judge in a court-martial), ruled that a decision on whether to call Bolling be delayed.

Major Scheid was called as a witness for the prosecution. He told the court that he had been detailed as a liaison officer between the office of the army staff judge advocate and Colonel Matthews, the IO of the original charges. No one ordered or directed him to sign the additional charge, contended Scheid, even though the charge was called to his attention. Scheid had acted more as a designated action officer representing Bard and Dawson than as a liaison officer.

After Scheid gave his testimony, Pace's deposition was presented by the prosecution and received as evidence. Immediately, Leahy objected to Joseph's questioning Pace as to why the charges were directed to a lower level, the Second Army, rather than being referred to the president of the United States. Joseph based his question on the recent *LaGrange* case, which held that if an officer was shown to be an accuser, it was incumbent on him to refer the case to a higher rather than a lower command.[17] Joseph argued that if Bolling would present himself to the court, he could show how the innumerable sections of the army staff and a multitude of high-ranking officers had debated the matter since January. The urgency during the eventful week in April, disagreement over who would sign, and the unusual means of delivering the charges from one echelon, the Pentagon, to another, the Second Army, indicated that the charges had been purposely directed to a lower command. Since Pace and Collins were among the superiors involved, it would stand to reason, based on the *LaGrange* case, that the charges should have been referred up—to the president.

Colonel Joseph explained to the court that Squires's book contained certain alleged statements that were attributed to Grow's diary "and which to this day the people of the world . . . think Grow said" but were in fact forgeries. When this fact was brought to Pace's attention, he said he was not aware of the forgery. Joseph moved to his next premise, arguing that Pace did not have all the facts before him and thus was not in a position to make a decision or recommendation.

Colonel Leahy objected: "We are concerned only with whether or not he [Pace] is the accuser." General Hoover, the law officer, sustained Leahy's objection. Joseph added one further comment. Referring to the misleading article in the *Washington Post* on 6 March, he reminded the court that the Soviets had picked it up and released it for public consumption and that the American press had acknowledged the authenticity of all statements. The defense counsel then noted that Pace's deposition indicated he was not aware that the *Post* article had "influenced not only our government but certain other ones." Again Leahy's objection was sustained by the law officer.

After a short recess, Currier made one serious questionable concession: the defense withdrew its request for Bolling to testify on the motion for dismissal. Grow's counsels failed to exploit this situation in that the wrongful denial of a defense witness would require dismissal of the related charges under the confrontation clause of Article 46, Uniform Code, and the Sixth Amendment of the Constitution. From a judicial perspective, witnesses established by Grow's counsels were required by law to be readily accessible. With Currier's action, for all practical purposes, that the direction of the trial would go against Grow was a foregone conclusion. The proceedings now clearly reflected political, command interests that were separated from the judicial process, thus making the judicial process unreliable by unlawful command influence.

When the court reconvened at 0830 hours, 24 July, Dwinell announced that Lieutenant General William M. Hoge had been relieved from the court by order of the convening authority, the Second Army. The reason given was "good cause." The defense was again in an awkward position; not only were key witnesses denied but a court member had been lost. This could work against Grow because military juries do not have to be unanimous. With eight members sitting on the panel, the prosecution would need an affirmative vote from six to get a conviction. Likewise, for an acquittal, Grow would have to get a vote from three. But with the panel now reduced to seven members, the prosecution would require only five affirmative votes and the defense would still be required to get three votes for an acquittal. Based on mathematical determination alone, the defense's chances were negatively affected by the excusing of Hoge.

In the meantime, Brooks's deputy commander at the Second Army, General Clift Andrus, was appointed court president, and the order for Hoge's relief was approved by General John E. Hull, vice chief of staff to Collins and Taylor's predecessor. Joseph asked the military judge, General Hoover, if Hoge had in fact been relieved for a good reason. At 1800 hours, two hours after the court recessed on the twenty-third, the defense was advised by the convening authority that a good cause existed. This fact was substantiated when the court opened the next day and Joseph requested General Brooks and General Hoge to appear before the court and state if there, indeed, had been a good cause. The Uniform Code provided that a member may be excused for such a reason, Dwinell retorted. The court took a short recess, and when it reconvened, Dwinell stated that he had been officially informed by the Department of the Army that the convening authority relieved Hoge from the court because of pressing military duties at the Fourth Army. Collins was advised that Hoge was relieved because the trial was expected to last a month. In addition, there was no deputy commander at the Fourth Army.[18] Joseph accepted this decision and withdrew the defense's request for General Brooks's and Hoge's presence.

The law officer, General Hoover, was now ready to offer a decision on the defense's motion for dismissal. He denied the motion that the commanding general of the Second Army lacked authority to convene a court. First, Pace, as the secretary of the army, was not an accuser within the meaning of the code, in view of the requirement of Article 22 (Who may convene general courts-martial). Second, Pace did not direct the signing or swearing of charges. According to Hoover, there was no evidence that Pace had any interest in the case other than that which was incidental to his administrative duties as secretary of the army. In addition, the code provided the convening of a general court-martial by an accuser who was the "commanding officer." Thus a "commanding officer" must be in the military service, whereas the secretary of the army was a civilian and not subject to limitations under Article 22. The motion to dismiss the first two specifications of the charge and the additional charge and its specification was also denied. In Hoover's view, the omissions of acts as alleged in the three specifications did, as a matter of law, "constitute violations of AR 380-5 and AW 96." Joseph responded that the defense had no further motions.

In retrospect, the defense counsels' effort to challenge jurisdiction was misdirected. Rather than challenge Pace, they should have looked at Taylor and Bolling and even Collins. Personal interest rested with them. Bolling's interest in the case was readily distinguishable from the official interest displayed by Pace. Taylor's actions pointed to him as the action officer who, in fact, managed the proceedings. After all, as the Records of Army Staff indicated, the collective power of the army staff was the real mover in support of a court-martial. Unfortunately, Grow's counsels did not have access to the staff's records. The army staff was where the seed of jurisdiction was planted, nurtured, and grown. But could the defense counsel overcome the preponderance of command influence within the military hierarchy? It was highly unlikely. The graph, "Progenitors of Command Influence," provides an example of the overwhelming effect the army staff had on the court-martial proceedings. With the introduction of counsels, challenges, arraignment, and motions completed, it was time for the plea, to which Grow responded: "Not guilty." It was time for the lengthy litany of witnesses, stipulations, and evidence to begin, as it did on 24 July.

Throughout the trial, evidence and testimony presented either personally or by stipulation highly commended Grow's intelligence, character, integrity, and ability. In some respects, these witnesses

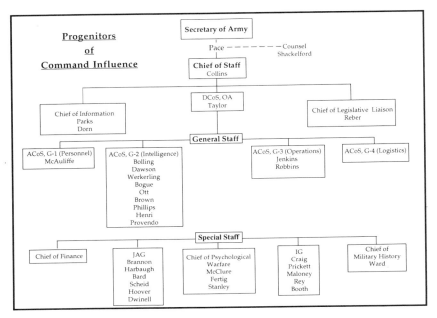

Progenitors of Command Influence

constituted a "Who's Who" from World War II. They included General Thomas T. Handy, Lieutenant General Willis D. Crittenberger, Lieutenant General Manton S. Eddy, Lieutenant General L. K. Truscott, Jr., Major General David G. Barr, Major General Hobart R. Gay (Patton's chief of staff in World War II), Major General George W. Read, Jr. (Grow's assistant division commander during the war), Brigadier General Thomas J. Camp, Colonel William J. Given (Grow's divisional signal officer during the war), and Congressman J. Caleb Boggs from Delaware. Truscott—at the time a coordinator and special adviser to HICOG—considered Grow "a man of outstanding ability especially marked by superior quality of character, intelligence, courage, energy and devotion to duty." Truscott also deemed Grow "to be one of the outstanding officers of the Army." General Gay informed the court that he kept a diary during the war on instructions from General Patton. Gay considered Grow's character "irreproachable." Grow's subordinates in Moscow, Lieutenant

Colonels Reuben B. Thornal and Eugene P. Sites and Majors Frank D. Bush and James W. Dean, were unanimous in praising his ability, character, and security consciousness. Captain Nicholas A. Drain, the navy attaché, and Colonel Frank B. James, air force attaché, who served with Grow in Moscow, emphasized that security there had improved during his tenure.

Shortly after the parade of witnesses began, Grow's counsels objected to the admission in evidence of the diary. Using the same argument presented during the pretrial investigation of charges, defense counsel argued that the diary had been acquired under circumstances amounting to an unlawful search and seizure leading to compulsory self-incrimination evidence. Conditioned by decades of obeying orders, Grow had been influenced by official pressure from his superiors to produce his diary. Summing up his objections, Stevens noted: "The utter illegality of such a method of procuring the evidence and its consequent inadmissibility in evidence is clear under both military and civil law." Thus the procurement of the diary ran afoul of the Fifth Amendment privilege against self-incrimination. The prosecution had known well in advance of the defense's argument, and Dwinell was ready. Grow had waived his rights under the Fourth Amendment because he freely surrendered the diary: "It was very fundamental and has been so stated a number of times by our courts that when an individual consents to a seizure, no question of unlawful seizure under the Fourth Amendment arises." Dwinell cited a federal case in which reference was made to a military Board of Review decision which determined that when an individual consents to a search, no question of unreasonable search under the Fourth Amendment exists. Touching upon paragraph 152, *MCM,* the trial counsel stated that the manual clearly sets forth a list of lawful searches, including the right of the commanding officer to have jurisdiction over the place where the property was situated. Dwinell noted that in another military Board of Review decision, the evidence obtained by seizure would not affect its competency in a court-martial proceeding because immunity from searches and seizures guaranteed by the Fourth Amendment does not extend to military reservations. Finally, Dwinell cited a Supreme Court decision wherein the Court stated, "when papers in the possession of an accused contain public information, there is no longer any privilege to be asserted by the accused and he cannot, by any act of his, forever seal off the Government from taking the necessary steps to protect its interests." Thus the prosecution's contention was that the evidence (Prickett's, Maloney's, and Ray's testimony) had indicated the diary had been legally obtained.[19]

The law officer then determined that the diary was admissible evidence because Grow understood his rights at the time he handed over the diary to Ray. He was not coerced, and his consent had been freely given. In addition, statements made by Grow suggested that he was fully aware of the situation. Hoover concluded, "The circumstances here bring this case within the principle that the authority of a Commanding Officer to conduct a search is the equivalent of a search warrant." However, the events surrounding the rendering of the diary to the IG and subsequently to Bolling were conditional by the nature of military orders that by its very nature established the mind-set of mental compulsion. The events late in January indicated that Grow, under the duress of the IG and the vagueness of the order to render, was impelled to surrender the diary, thus questioning the nature of inadmissibility of involuntary evidence.

The quartet from IG, Prickett, Maloney, Ray, and Booth proved again to be valuable witnesses for the prosecution. When Prickett was cross-examined by Joseph, he suddenly experienced a lapse of memory. During the pretrial investigation, Prickett had, under sworn statement, viewed Taylor's request to obtain Grow's diary "in the nature of an order." But now Prickett stated: "I am not sure I considered it an order or not." Joseph asked Prickett: "Did you make this statement, 'General Taylor then directed me to secure the diary from General Grow'? " Prickett replied: "I now can't remember whether I got the word 'direct' or whether I was ordered; I do not remember." Joseph facetiously asked Prickett if he recalled testifying at the pretrial investigation. Finally, he stated that he did. Years later, Prickett would admit that some irregularities took place at the trial and that he had not told the truth. He believed he should have changed his testimony.[20] Maloney and Ray outlined their roles to demonstrate that Grow's diary was acquired with his consent. Booth, when giving his testimony, requested that he be allowed to refer to notes taken on or about 30 January. Under cross-examination, Booth did admit that even though he had a directive from the chief of staff, he did not read

Brigadier Fay B. Prickett (1948).
Courtesy of the U.S. Army, National Archives

or advise Grow of Article 31 in its entirety. When asked if he compared chapter 6 of *Auf dem Kriegspfad* with Grow's diary, Booth replied: "No, I don't recall that I did that." But indeed he had. Booth read the diary and chapter 6 before he took Grow's testimony. And yet when asked if he evaluated the so-called alleged facsimiles in Squires's book, he responded: "No, I couldn't answer that." Finally, when questioned if it occurred to him that the investigation on 30 January might result in a court-martial, Booth stated: "I had no intimation it would or would not."

On 11 June 1951, Grow had recorded the following entry in his diary: "At 1420 final session of conf. I gave Comm. A (Items) report. Followed by 'Trends' and 'Areas' Committees who practically echoed our report. Gist then was better work needed in Wash. & a big step from up in CIA covert espionage. Heubner replied he was delighted & CIA welcomed our support."

This entry was the basis for the first specification of the charge. The most damaging witness for Grow's case was one of Bolling's deputies, Brigadier General John Weckerling. Weckerling claimed that the entry of 11 June was "Top Secret" and would endanger any covert operation mounted against the Soviet Union. Dawson from Bolling's G-2 testified that in 1949 he had assisted in revising AR 380-5. Dawson claimed he would have assigned some form of "Secret" classification to Grow's entry. To controvert the testimony of Weckerling and Dawson, the defense introduced the testimony of Colonel Paul G. Cramer, who had served as chief of the Security Division, G-2, until mid-July 1950. Cramer, who was familiar with AR 380-5 and had attended the attaché conference in Frankfurt in June 1951 along with Weckerling, testified that there was nothing in the diary entry of 11 June which would be of value to the Soviets. In his opinion, the entry was common knowledge because the press had reported the need for an increase in espionage activities. Grow's statements would not endanger national security or cause serious injury to the interest or prestige of the United States.

Lieutenant Colonel Eugene P. Sites, formerly assistant military attaché in Moscow under Grow, believed the entry of 11 June did not violate the provisions of AR 380-5 because it was common knowledge regarding the function of the CIA. Lieutenant Colonel Reuben B. Thornal, Grow's executive officer in Moscow, testified that the entry in question, like the others, did not violate security. The subject matter contained in Grow's diary was freely discussed in the diplomatic colony in Moscow, Thornal told the court. Major Frank D. Bush, who had been an assistant army attaché in Moscow until June 1951, testified that the entry of 11 June did not violate AR 380-5 nor did it need classification. The court was then advised by defense counsel that the diary entry in question did not indicate the contents of the committee report emitting from the attaché conference.

The second specification dealt with an entry in Grow's diary for 13 July 1951: "I learned for the first time that the 1st Armd Div. is to be the sixth division for EUCOM & will fill the place of the dissolving Constabulary which has been referred to in the press as the '6th division'. " On 27 September 1951, he wrote: "There are not enough tanks to equip the 1st Armd Div so it probably will be late coming over here."

Major General Reuben E. Jenkins, the G-3, was called as a key witness for the prosecution. Jenkins, who had been an understudy to Taylor when he was G-3, recalled that the entries for 13 July and 27 September should have received a "Top Secret" classification. Under cross-examination he admitted that before returning to America early in 1951, he had heard of the movement of various divisions overseas and some reference to movement had been made in Congress. The prosecution called Brigadier General James H. Phillips, deputy assistant chief of staff to Bolling. Phillips looked at the diary entries and announced to the court he would have classified them from "Confidential" to "Top Secret." To controvert Jenkins's and Phillips's testimony, the defense attempted to establish that the movement of the 1st Armored Division and status of tank production were common knowledge. The defense's key witness was again Colonel Cramer. He testified that before Grow made the diary entry, American diplomats in Europe were discussing the plan to send several army divisions to reinforce NATO. "It was in the press and released by the State Department," Cramer stated, and "no doubt the Russians knew as much about it."

The basis for the third specification of the charge dealt with diary entries pertaining to the identification of antiaircraft positions, military targets, and railroads in the Soviet Union. The most influential witnesses for the prosecution were again General Weckerling and

Colonel Dawson. Some of the diary entries, taken by themselves, according to Dawson, required no classification, but if grouped together, some form of classification would have been appropriate. Dawson agreed that the information contained in the diary was of little importance; however, it became an issue when the contents were listed in Squires's book. Concluding, he stated, "The collection of individual items which in themselves might be unclassified about a potential enemy's troops and so forth, but the denying to that potential enemy that we have that information is classified 'Secret'. " To counter Dawson's testimony, the defense argued that the entries needed no classification, either individually or collectively. It was obvious that the entries contained nothing Soviet state security did not already know. Grow's counsel once again called on Cramer. He told the court that the Soviets knew Grow, they gave him permission to be in the country, and they would have stopped him if he had attempted to enter a sensitive area. Cramer added that it was common knowledge that everywhere Grow went at least two cars of Soviet state security followed him. Both Sites and Bush recalled that the antiaircraft positions identified in the diary were in nonrestricted areas, and their location was common knowledge. The diary entries did not violate security, nor were they detrimental to the interests of the United States, they testified. Regarding Soviet activity, Sites stated: "They are not stupid. They know where their weaknesses lie. As to the fact we traveled—they gave us permission. We military attachés knew our single job was to find things of military significance. It was obviously no revelation to them."

General Weckerling commented for the prosecution: "I have been in every intelligence assignment I think you could possibly name" and "security has always been highly stressed wherever I have been on duty." However, when questioned by court member Major General Orlando Ward regarding note-taking during the gathering of military information in a foreign country, Weckerling admitted he did not write such words as "Confidential," "Secret," or "Top Secret" on his raw notes. Weckerling, however, did recover his role as a prosecution witness under timely examination by General Hoover, the law officer. "I kept my raw notes in a safe," Bolling's deputy replied.

The fourth specification involved the following entries in Grow's diary:

> 19 January 1951—Pope dropped in to compare notes and insists that we have not seen all the positions. Quite true but we unearthed 4 that he had not seen and I believe that several have been moved in the past year.
>
> 2 March 1951—Had debriefing of Maj. Bush & Col Guimond (Can) on their Tbilisi trip for 2 hrs in AM. They found no unusual military activity altho there is a big garrison there.
>
> 26 January 1951—Sqourdeous the Greek is equally anxious for a bold showdown. He is one of the few fighters among the Europeans;
>
> 9 March 1951—Got off . . . another report by sites on observations by the Turk Att. reported to us.
>
> 14 Mar 1951—Pope called & we had a long talk on the probable strength & probable intentions.

Once again Dawson took the stand as the prosecution's key witness. If the entries mentioned in the specification revealed the sources of information as representatives of friendly foreign governments, then classification was indicated, he surmised. During the pretrial investigation, Dawson admitted that he would have assigned a classification of "Confidential," but now after further consideration, he decided that the proper classification was "Secret." The defense responded with the testimony of Cramer, Sites, and Bush. They agreed there was no violation of security because the missions and activities of Colonel C. D. T. Wynn-Pope, the British military attaché, and Lieutenant Colonel Bernard J. Guimond, the Canadian military attaché, and American attachés were well known to the Soviets. Moreover, it was pointed out to the court that Grow's diary did not mention methods of operations regarding attachés.

The specification of the additional charge was based on a diary entry dealing with intelligence information relating to a Chinese offensive that had been obtained through Turkey. The diary entry of 24 March 1951 reads: "Just as I got home, the code room called me to reply to a message from G-2 that Turkey reports Chinese offensive in Korea will start late April with Soviet volunteers 'of Mongolian origin.' We suspect as much but have no evidence."

The prosecution structured its argument on a message (MATUR 17180) received on 24 March 1951 by army G-2, Washington, from the military attaché in Turkey with a request that it be forwarded to the military attaché in Moscow. The message was classified "Top Secret." The information on the Chinese offensive and the use of Soviet volunteers of Mongolian origin originated from the former Polish ambassador to Turkey, who was at the time a political refugee in Ankara. The message also explained that V. M. Molotov, the Soviet foreign minister, had planned a large-scale offensive by the Chinese Red Army in Korea during April 1951. The plan considered the extensive use of Soviet aircraft and regular Soviet troops of Mongolian extraction who were to be introduced into combat units as so-called volunteers. An evaluation of MATUR 17180 indicated that the source was considered a man of high integrity, but G-2 needed further information and requested Grow to comment. On 25 March Grow replied: "Top Secret" that "Local confirmation Ankara report impossible, however, Soviet action in line with our suspicions. Unlikely that volunteers will come from Russia but from FE forces." When Dawson was asked to comment on the diary entry of 24 March and MATUR 17180, he responded: "That would be classified at least 'Secret' and perhaps 'Top Secret.' " He then added: "As far as the security classification, it would have several international implications," especially because the information came from a friendly nation. The forecast of a Chinese offensive was at the time common knowledge and thus did not constitute a violation of security, the defense rebutted. Again Cramer was used as the main witness for the defense. He claimed that the cable had been overclassified and answered: "There is nothing in there except that Turkey reported they were going to have an offensive. It was quite evident at the time." Sites stated, however, that the MATUR message should have been classified; nevertheless, he and Thornal believed the remaining information was common gossip and generally known among the diplomatic colony in Moscow. Bush added that he considered the MATUR message classified because it revealed a source, whereas the diary entry needed no classification because it did not reveal a source. To controvert the prosecution witnesses, Grow's counsel presented as evidence articles that appeared in two widely distributed weekly magazines, *Newsweek* and *Time.* One article in *Time,* dated 19 March 1951, stated: "The decision still rested with Red China. Washington knew that Mao was planning one more offensive." And on 9 April *Newsweek* wrote: "The

English Army is forecasting the Chinese counter-offensive." On 10 March 1951, a weekly service journal published in Washington with a general circulation, the *Army-Navy-Air Force Journal,* printed: "During the past week the Communist forces south of the 38th parallel have been heavily reinforced. . . . This suggests the strong possibility of a new Red offensive."

In June, when Demaree Bess of the *Saturday Evening Post* wrote a critical paragraph on Grow's conduct, Grow had written to Bess, suggesting that the reporter talk with some of the general's friends who had served with him in Moscow. Perhaps Grow thought Bess would change his opinion. It was not until ten days before the court-martial began that Bess followed through on Grow's recommendation. The startling discovery the reporter made "was that the most damaging quotations attributed to General Grow by communist propagandists were forgeries, and had never appeared in the diary." Bess was bewildered that nobody in the Pentagon had challenged the falsified quotes. The defense counsel thus called Bess as a witness, but Richmond failed to exploit the reporter's recent discovery that nobody had challenged the authenticity of the quotes. When asked if he had the authority to incorporate the correction in a new article, Bess responded: "I do." Surprisingly, Richmond replied: "That is all." The prosecution then had no need to cross-examine, and Bess was excused. The result was that Grow's defense counsels failed to use an important witness who could have explained the diary fiasco as a result of "fantastic security regulations" and the army's seven-month verification of a communist lie.[21] Also perplexing is why no attempt was made to have the *Post* reporter, John Norris, appear as a witness. Only the *Post* article on 6 March marked "Top Secret" was introduced as an exhibit by the prosecution.

The defense was able to call one of the major players in Taylor's management group, Major General Floyd L. Parks, chief of information, to determine how the *Post* and its reporter acquired Squires's book. It was Parks's understanding—he was out of the office at the time—that on about 4 or 5 March Norris visited the office of chief of information to obtain additional data on Squires's revelation. According to Parks, Norris claimed he had learned of the diary compromise through another reporter and subsequently ordered *Auf dem Kriegspfad* from Germany. Parks declared that his office did not furnish

Norris material "or pass on information on which to write this story." Parks's testimony, however, differed from Bolling's sworn statement in May during the pretrial investigation. Bolling had alleged that Norris was furnished a translated copy of chapter 6 through General Parks's office. This was a contradiction between Parks's testimony and Bolling's sworn statement. The CIA agents who interviewed Bolling on 6 March recorded in the CIA Daily Log that he commented that he was forced by Norris to release information on the incident. Parks's testimony is also questionable regarding the perusal of *Auf dem Kriegspfad* by Norris. Agents from the 66th CIC Detachment in Berlin visited at least eight bookstores in West Berlin but were unable to locate copies of Squires's book. It was not until a German national on instructions from the CIC agents entered East Berlin in January 1952 that at least three copies were obtained. By April, the CIC concluded that there had been "no report of sale of book elsewhere than East Berlin."[22] Perhaps the most surprising aspect of Parks's role as a defense witness was that Grow's counsels failed to pursue the obvious contradiction between Parks's and Bolling's statements. Parks was excused, and again no thought was given to calling Norris as a defense witness.

On the morning of 29 July 1952, General Grow took the stand. In regard to the first specification, he told the court that his entries did not in any way compromise security. Commenting on the second specification, Grow noted that he obtained information on the armored division and tank production "through different conversations with different officers on different occasions, all occurring in Germany during a period of about a month or six weeks, in the summer of 1951." He added: "I have no means of knowing what the Department of the Army had in a planning stage or, as a matter of fact, under any other stage until the thing was consummated because in Moscow we did not receive such information except through the press and through conversation." In respect to the third specification, relating to antiaircraft targets and bridges, Grow recalled that he was always directed by one pertinent question: "Is it all right to put this down? If it is all right to put it down, all right, I'll put it down." He added that whenever he wrote in his diary he was guided by security based on judgment, opinion, and considerable experience. Reflecting on the fourth specification, dealing with the listing of information obtained from representatives of other countries, he responded that even though the diary was full of names, it never compromised security sources. Moreover, he added, those sources mentioned "are in the same business and are recognized as being colleagues in a joint matter." On the additional specification dealing with the G-2 message, Grow replied: "I did not identify this message in the diary or indicate in any way that I had received a classified message." To Grow it had been a wide-open subject and common gossip. He then drew a comparison between the source, the former Polish ambassador residing in Ankara identified in MATUR 17180, and his fellow attachés in Moscow. "The source in the message was extremely covert and needed to be closely protected, but sources, such as Pope and Guimond, who were openly known as colleagues, obviously required no classified contact protection," he explained.

The most damaging statement Grow made under cross-examination was when he noted: "I treated the diary in about the same manner as you would treat a personal letter . . . I did not treat it in the sense of a military classified document but rather in the sense of a personal classified document." The court also took note of a comment Grow made on 18 January 1952 in his diary in response to the East German newspaper articles: "Done in Germany when my security was lax." The court considered Grow's statements a significant indication that the former attaché was aware the information recorded in his diary needed protection. After Grow's testimony, it was evident that the court members viewed his actions as careless.[23] This observation would be voiced again years later by Collins and Taylor, yet they emphasized that they had no part in influencing the court-martial proceedings.

At approximately 1040 hours, Grow completed his testimony. The court took a short recess during which time a hearing was held out of the presence of the court members between the law officer, trial counsel, defense counsel, and the accused. Dwinell contended that AR 380-5 sets out certain rules "specifically to paragraph 3c which says, 'It is of paramount importance that all who engage in administering these regulations preserve a common sense outlook toward the subject.' " Currier then stressed that the record in the Grow case was replete with evidence that the routine duty of a military attaché in Moscow was unique and not controlled by security action applicable in the United States. Currier was attempting to identify the difference between the "Washington atmosphere" and field duty.

In less than half an hour, the court came to order and both the trial counsel and defense counsel presented brief summations. The prosecution contended that security violations were obvious. Cited as examples were entries in the diary that revealed sources of information from friendly attachés; followed the movement of the 1st Armored Division; noted intelligence missions in the Soviet Union; and recorded a top-secret coded message without a classification. The court recessed. At 1300 hours it came to order and Hoover advised and instructed the seven court members on the substance of the specifications and their responsibility in rendering judgment. The court adjourned at 1340 hours; in less than an hour Hoover and the court reporter were called back into the courtroom. General Andrus, the court president, read the findings. They had reached a decision in fifty-five minutes.

Certain rules guide court members. First and foremost, they are expected to be fair and impartial. When determining guilt or innocence, a free and full discussion of the facts of the case is paramount. Usually all questions—and there were many in the Grow case—should be thoroughly discussed. Then, and only then, the members vote by secret ballot. In the Grow trial, however, the court members acted with such rapidity that serious question arises as to how freely discussion and deliberation were exercised. Early in the proceedings, the designated convening authority had indicated that the trial would last a month—information that was passed to the media and also passed up through the army staff to Collins. In reality, the trial lasted five days and the court had reached a decision in less than an hour.

The maximum sentence for the offense called for dismissal from the army (discharge), three years at hard labor (confinement), and total forfeiture of pay. General Andrus, the court president, announced the verdict:

Of Specification 1 of the Charge: Violation of AR 380-5 at Frankfurt, Germany, on 11 June 1951 by recording, without classifying, in his personal diary classified information relating to a conference of U.S. Military Attachés and representatives of U.S. Intelligence agencies: GUILTY.

Of Specification 2 of the Charge: Violation of AR 380-5 at Frankfurt, Germany, on 13 July 1951 and 27 September 1951, by recording, without classifying, in his personal diary classified information relating to the movement of a unit of the Armed Forces of the United States: NOT GUILTY.

Of Specification 3 of the Charge: Dereliction of duty at Moscow, USSR, and Frankfurt, Germany, from 4 June 1951 to 14 July 1951, by failing to properly safeguard classified information pertaining to execution of his intelligence mission: GUILTY.

Of Specification 4 of the Charge: Dereliction of duty at Moscow, USSR, and Frankfurt, Germany, from 4 June 1951 to 14 July 1951, by failing to safeguard properly information, the unauthorized publication of which would be detrimental to the United States: GUILTY.

Of the Specification of the Additional Charge: Violated AR 380-5 at Moscow, USSR, by recording, without classifying in his personal diary classified information relating to plans of the Soviet Far Eastern Revolutionary Committee: GUILTY.

Andrus turned to Grow and announced: "It is my duty as president of this court to inform you that the court in closed session and upon secret written ballot, two thirds of the members present at the time the vote was taken concurring, sentences you to be reprimanded and to be suspended from command for a period of six (6) months."

On Wednesday, 30 July, the *Washington Post* reported on the front page: "Gen. Grow Held Guilty, Suspended Six Months. 'War Diary' Diarist Convicted of Two Offenses by Army Court-Martial."

During the trial, the news media constantly mentioned the diary episode. Following the line taken by the *Post* in March, Grow was again and again accused of calling for war with the USSR "now as soon as possible" and the need for "hitting below the belt." After the verdict, the *Post* again repeated the all-too-familiar theme established in March that Grow had called for a war against the Soviet Union. It was the familiar warmongering theme. In its editorials, the *Post* bragged that its reporter, John G. Norris, had been the first to disclose the diary exposé. The *New York Times* added: "According to the Army, the diary was photographed without Grow's knowledge during a visit to Frankfurt." The *Times* gave credit to General Parks and his assistant General Dorn from the Office of Information for releasing some of the facts in March, which, according to the newspaper, led to intense controversy within the army staff and among officials in the Department of the Army. Neither the *Times* nor the *Post* questioned the accuracy of the diary excerpts.[24] In a major turn of events, the next day the headline over an article by John G. Norris in the *Post* declared: "Army Says Reds Fabricated 'Quotes' from Grow's Diary." This was the first time the *Post* was told the true story by army officials. Parks, a key player in Taylor's management group, who like Taylor had been a Berlin commandant during the war as well as an airborne chief of staff, was responsible for public information. Finally, after months of delay, Parks's Office of Information reported that communist propagandists had deliberately distorted Grow's writings. Naturally, Norris raised the question, Why the disclosure now? The answer, offered by an official army spokesman, was that releasing the information earlier would have interfered with the court-martial proceedings. Another official, according to Norris, suggested that the information was released "to offset any feeling that Grow was let off too lightly." The *Post* reporter recovered from his embarrassment by writing: "The fact that portions of the diary are false does not alter the fact that he was responsible for compromising classified data but it does indicate that he was not as vociferous for a 'preventive war' as had appeared it was indicated." Finally, he wrote that the army gave examples of Grow's statements which were twisted; "he was made to appear to be urging war, he was merely giving his estimate of Soviet aggression and not urging an American attack."

Like the *Post,* the *Times* reported on the surprising change in events. Portions of Grow's diary, which were supposedly a violation of AR 380-5 worthy of classification, were now released to the media. Only those entries that "had been most-widely disseminated by the Communists in East Germany" were released, the army explained to the media. Parks was generous to a fault in giving the media a full disclosure of how the entries had been distorted.[25] He, like other army staff members, had been anything but truthful to cover up the institutional embarrassment caused by the compromise of the diary. Not only was the truth elusive among the army staff, but it was also evaded in sworn statements and testimonies.

During July the trial counsel and the law officer, like the investigating officer earlier, frequently indulged in flagrant disregard for military justice. Indeed, though they displayed a degree of incompetence by compromising the code, there were obvious hints in their actions that they were following the implied wishes of the army staff in the Pentagon under Taylor's direction. For example, on 2 July Grow's counsel formally requested the following general officers to appear as witnesses: Lieutenant General Maxwell D. Taylor, Lieutenant General Anthony C. McAuliffe, Lieutenant General Edward H. Brooks, Major General Alexander R. Bolling, Major General Ernest M. Brannon, Brigadier General Leslie D. Carter, and Secretary of the Army Frank Pace, Jr. No subpoenas were issued by trial counsels, and not one of the generals appeared in person in spite of their obvious involvement and the three-week lead time before the trial. Attempts by the individual defense counsel to postpone the trial until the witnesses were available and the subsequent five-day trial, which had been expected to last a month, once again suggest that the army staff monitored and controlled the trial proceedings.[26] In addition, the other paramount question raised by the IG was never resolved by the defense counsels. This question would be raised later during the appeal process and again handled without a resolution. The IG had recommended as early as February that an investigation should be aggressively pursued to ascertain the methods and personnel involved in surreptitiously photostating Grow's diary in Frankfurt. The CIC not only identified Gerhard Poss as the possible perpetrator but also reported to Bolling's G-2 that the Victory Guest House was "entirely lacking in security features." Only select members of Taylor's management group were aware of the events in EUCOM, and it behooved them to avoid a discussion of the CIC security investigation at the Victory Guest House for fear that the information would affect their careers or even possibly the outcome of the pretrial investigation and the court-martial. There was also a strong possibility that the CIC report or parts of it, if made public or leaked to the media, would place the army staff in a more precarious position, especially in light of the emotional setting and paranoia provided by Senator McCarthy's red hunt. Taylor, in his *Swords and Plowshares,* would comment on McCarthy's "savage" attacks against the army. Thus a very important aspect of the Grow episode was circumvented.

General Grow leaving court-martial.
UPI

170

Collins, Taylor, Bolling, Brannon, Parks, and the rest of the management group could have been injured by a revelation in the media that inappropriate command influence was involved in the Grow proceedings. The new code had just been implemented with provisions to guard against command influence, which, since World War I, had been a major complaint leveled against the military justice system. The last thing Taylor and his group wanted was an incident that would place the military justice system on public trial through media and even congressional exposure.

CONCLUSION

COMMAND INFLUENCE, WHICH permeated Grow's pretrial investigation and general court-martial, has a long, controversial history. To understand the actions of Taylor's management group it is necessary to trace the institutional establishment, implementation, and dynamics of U.S. military justice, its detachment from civilian justice, and the heated attempts at reform. In spite of the far-reaching reform of the 1950 Uniform Code of Military Justice, Taylor's group adhered to the traditional formalism of military justice while at the same time attempting to apply the new managerial model arising out of the experience of World War II.

The most important court test of the military legal system occurred in 1858. The Supreme Court, dominated by Chief Justice Roger B. Taney and reflecting a Jacksonian attitude toward states' rights and private property, held valid in *Dynes* v. *Hoover* that courts-martial are established under executive article II of the Constitution, which made the president commander in chief, and legislative article I, which authorized Congress to make rules for government of the military forces. It declared that courts-martial are not established under judicial article III of the Constitution.[1] Thus the Supreme Court solidified the notion that military courts are not part of the federal judiciary and accepted the two systems of jurisprudence. This decision proved the legal precedent for the application of the agency theory of separatism and enhanced command influence.[2] Consequently, an enclave beyond the civilian courts was established, producing a dichotomy between civilian and military law and justice. Courts-

172

martial were sustained as executive agencies independent of the federal judiciary and not subject to review by direct appeal, writ of certiorari or error, and collateral review. The acting judge advocate general during World War I, Brigadier General Samuel T. Ansell, commenting on the military code, noted that it had "changed little or none in system, principle, or procedure" since the adoption of the British Articles of War in 1775. The system, he attested, was retained so long because Americans lacked interest in military matters, particularly military law.[3]

It was not until the rapid expansion of conscripts as well as the volunteer military force in World War I that the agency theory of separatism was for the first time seriously challenged. The movement for reform came from within the army.

The judge advocate general of the army, Brigadier General Enoch Crowder, was appointed to the post of provost marshal general in 1917 to administer the Selective Service Act. The wartime administration of the Judge Advocate General's Department, in turn, was conducted by Brigadier General Samuel T. Ansell, who became acting judge advocate general in Crowder's absence. Ansell would soon emerge as the progenitor of reform of the military justice system. He vehemently challenged the traditional role of the military commander in the court-martial process as the executor of the agency theory of separatism. General Crowder supported the agency theory of separatism, a reactionary position that caused an antagonistic relationship between him and Ansell.[4]

Appearing before the Pennsylvania Bar Association on 26 June 1919, Ansell continued his attack on the entire court-martial system. The power exercised by military courts, he argued, "should be in keeping with the progress of enlightened governments and should not be inconsistent with those fundamental principles of law which have ever characterized Anglo-American jurisprudence."[5] The following month, Ansell resigned from the army. The American Bar Association's committee acknowledged that the system probably needed some reforms but found it generally satisfactory. A Cornell University law professor and Crowder supporter, George Gleason Bogert, commenting on the report, declared that the agitation for reform was grossly exaggerated and had inflamed the minds of congressmen and the public.[6]

In haste, Ansell—now a civilian attorney—prepared an article for the November edition of the *Cornell Law Quarterly.* It was an explosive piece, attacking the court-martial process and especially the agency theory. "The court-martial is not a court at all; it is but an agency of military command governed and controlled by the will of the commander," Ansell wrote. He added: "There is no right of review; there is no legal supervision."[7] Ansell sincerely believed that the military mind was intolerant of methods and processes necessary to execute justice. In the same edition of the *Cornell Law Quarterly,* Professor Bogert attacked Ansell and his proposed reforms.[8] Opposition to Ansell continued. Professor John H. Wigmore, speaking before the Maryland Bar Association, declared: "The prime object of military organization is victory, not justice. . . . But justice is always secondary, and victory is always primary."[9] The New York National Guard judge advocate general, Howard Thayer Kingsbury, like Wigmore, strongly endorsed the agency theory. "In the military organization, each member owes obedience to an individual—his commanding officer," he wrote, "and any proposed reform of court-martial procedure which contemplates setting up a military judiciary, independent of executive command, proceeds upon an unsound basis."[10] The eminent Yale University jurist Edmund M. Morgan, an Ansell supporter, raised questions regarding the court-martial process and the arbitrary control of the commander. When analyzed, Morgan argued, these questions indicated a noticeable deficiency in military justice.[11] Reactionary fever, however, was too strong, and not until another world conflict would agitation for reform again be set in motion.

The pressure for reform did produce some changes in the military legal system, but they did not interfere with the agency theory of separatism. On 4 June 1920, the postwar National Defense Act was implemented. It included a new statute for the government of the army. For the first time, a system of review was established. One of the most important reforms was the abolition of the right of the appointing authority to return an acquittal to a court-martial for adjustment of the verdict. Military control of court-martial proceedings remained firmly entrenched. The agency theory of separatism still existed, but it had been disturbed by Ansell's attack.[12]

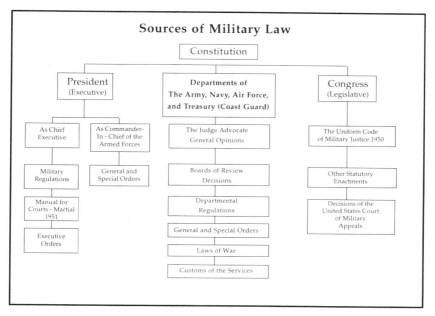

Sources of Military Law

Constitution

President (Executive)	Departments of The Army, Navy, Air Force, and Treasury (Coast Guard)	Congress (Legislative)
As Chief Executive / As Commander-In-Chief of the Armed Forces	The Judge Advocate General Opinions	The Uniform Code of Military Justice 1950
Military Regulations / General and Special Orders	Boards of Review Decisions	Other Statutory Enactments
Manual for Courts-Martial 1951	Departmental Regulations	Decisions of the United States Court of Military Appeals
Executive Orders	General and Special Orders	
	Laws of War	
	Customs of the Services	

Sources of Military Law

World War II brought an expansion of American armed forces that was more far-reaching than had occurred in World War I and continued the old conflict of constitutional legal rights.[13] Unlike events of World War I, the movement for legal reform came mainly as a result of complaints of returning servicemen rather than pressures from inside the military. The former dean of Catholic University Law School, Rear Admiral Robert J. White, explained that the complaints were a reaction to the demands on military authority made by large numbers of draftees and by worldwide global commitments.[14] In March 1946, Secretary of War Robert P. Patterson appointed a board to view relationships between officers and enlisted men. Though not specifically established to examine the military justice system, the Doolittle Board, as it was called, noted many inequities and injustices and recommended a general review of military justice procedures. At the same time, Patterson appointed the former president of the

American Bar Association, Arthur Vanderbilt, to head an advisory committee on military justice. The *New York Times* lauded the action of the War Department and reported that wartime court-martial procedures had drawn wide criticism in both the House and Senate.[15] After an intensive investigation of the wartime army judicial system, the committee submitted its report on 13 December 1946. The voluminous report found major problems in the court-martial process and recommended corrections. One such problem was command influence, which the committee considered wrong and subversive of morale. Military courts should be protected "from the influence of the officers who authorize and conduct the prosecution." The commander, as the appointing authority, selected all court members, including the trial judge advocate (prosecutor) and defense counsel, and the law member, who as a part of the court performed duties pertaining to questions of military law. In addition, the appointing authority had the power to review and pass on the court findings. It appeared that Ansell's arguments were being resurrected by the Vanderbilt Committee, which challenged command control and the complete domination of the court and counsel by the commanding officer.

While the Vanderbilt Committee was concluding its lengthy study, the civilian call for reform continued. An article in December 1946 in the *Atlantic Monthly* noted that there was "an irreconcilable conflict between law and militarism, between the mind of the lawyer and that of the military commander." The latter stressed discipline; the former stressed legality and justice. Regarding courts-martial, the article stated that it was "understood that [the commanding officer's] reference of a matter for trial is an indication of his belief in the guilt of the accused." In concluding, the author made a pertinent statement: "No system of law is better than the men charged with its enforcement. On the other hand, a legal system which offers to unscrupulous men obvious temptations for abuse can never be equitable or just."[16]

As a result of the outcry for reform of military justice, the Truman administration endorsed legislative programs for both the army and navy to update military law and justice. Secretary of Defense James Forrestal took the initiative for unifying diverse legal codes by appointing a committee to review military law with the purpose of creating a uniform code for all the services. The highly respected and renowned jurist Edmund M. Morgan was appointed to chair the committee.[17] Morgan had served under Ansell during World War I and supported his reforms. Like Ansell, Morgan was interested in altering the system that promoted command control and influence. Unfortunately, Morgan's drafting committee was so structured as to favor the agency philosophy, which endorsed command authority, and his sentiments on altering command control and influence were not shared by the majority.[18] Morgan apparently attempted a compromise, working primarily to establish a civilian review court like Ansell had called for many years before. By February 1949, the draft was completed and sent to Congress. In March and April hearings were held in both houses on the Uniform Code of Military Justice and eventually passed with minor changes. On 5 May 1950, President Truman signed the Uniform Code into law, and on 31 May 1951 it went into effect. This was a year before the Grow court-martial. In 1951 the *Manual for Courts-Martial* was published to explain and supplement the various provisions of the new code. The military, nevertheless, was not inclined to relinquish its prerogative of command control. Appearing before the New York Lawyer's Club in November 1948, the army chief of staff, General Dwight D. Eisenhower, declared: "The Army . . . was never set up to insure justice. It is set up as your servant, a servant of the civilian population of this country to do a particular job." He continued: "Division of command responsibility and the responsibility for the adjudication of offenses and of accused offenders cannot be as separate as it is in our own democratic government."[19] The most noted spokesman for the status quo was Frederick Bernays Wiener. He proclaimed that the "object of civilian society is to make people live together in peace and in reasonable happiness. The object of the armed forces is to win wars, not just fight them." Wiener had been adamant in expressing his opposition to any alteration of the agency theory of separatism. Moreover, Wiener added his own rationale regarding the agency theory. He held that sentencing was not designed to restore the offender to civilian status but was to act as "a slug" so that other military offenders "will profit by that example and not do likewise." Other influential military attorneys concurred with Wiener. The president of the Judge Advocate Association, William J. Hughes, Jr., and the judge advocate general of the army, Major General Thomas H. Green, were strong supporters of command control.[20]

There were, however, those who disagreed with Wiener, Hughes, and Green. The chairman on military law of the War Veterans' Bar Association, Arthur E. Farmer, was particularly critical of the commander's domination of the military court. He wrote that the military legal system was so structured that it made oppression and tyranny possible. In such an atmosphere, according to Farmer, a fair and impartial court-martial was difficult to achieve. Professor Arthur Keeffe of Cornell Law School, appearing before the House Committee on Armed Services in 1949, called the proposed uniform code a sorry substitute for the attempt at military justice reform after World War II. A few years later, commenting on the Uniform Code, Keeffe would argue in an apparent restatement of Ansell's views that there had been no substantial change in the level of command influence. It still existed under the cloak of the agency theory of separatism. He stated, "The commander still draws the charges, selects the judges, appoints the law officer, names the prosecutor and defense counsel and himself reviews the results of the hearing." In an editorial, the *New York Times* contended that the new code fell short in eliminating command control from the court-martial proceedings. The *Stanford Law Review* also persuasively argued against command influence. It held: "A soldier, like any other American citizen, is entitled to a fair trial. There can be no assurance that military trials will be fair, as long as it is possible for commanders to influence others."[21]

In answer to those critics, the supporters of the new Uniform Code could point to some of the most far-reaching changes in the history of United States military justice. Of note were alterations in the pretrial proceedings, the role of the commander or the appointing authority (now called the convening authority), and the post-trial proceedings.[22] The Uniform Code provided that any person subjected to the code could prefer charges and specifications against another individual also subjected to the code. Compulsory self-incrimination was prohibited. Before any charge or specification was referred to a general court-martial for trial, a pretrial investigation was required. Article 32, a revision of the old Article of War 70, provided for a thorough and impartial investigation and gave the accused the full opportunity to cross-examine witnesses against him.[23] In the

Grow case this article was not adhered to by Taylor's management team and the investigating officer. The one striking drawback of Article 32, even though it was binding on all persons administering the code, was that failure to follow the requirements set forth in the article did not constitute jurisdictional error.

The Uniform Code also attempted to place some limitations on command influence with the provisions of Article 37, the intention of which was to avoid improper command action designed to influence the action of the court. This article was also disregarded in the Grow case. The commander was still in control of the court-martial machinery. He would still determine whether to prosecute and in a general court-martial appoint the pretrial investigating officer, appoint the members of the court, the trial and defense counsel, and the law officer. The latter, who was analogous to a civilian court judge, was responsible for the fair and orderly conduct of the general court-martial proceedings, ruled on all interlocutory questions, and advised the court on questions of military law and procedure. He was not a member of the court, nor did he have voting privileges, but he could instruct the court on the elements of each charge, the burden of proof, reasonable doubt, and presumption of innocence. The senior officer of the general court-martial, called the president, would still preside and execute many judicial and administrative functions. The law officer along with the court members, nevertheless, remained subject to the pressures of command influence. Thus command pretrial and trial influence was to continue, and the convening authority still retained his function to review the record of the trial and approve the findings and the sentence.

Thus on the eve of the Grow court-martial two pronounced and conflicting notions existed regarding command influence in relation to the court-martial process: those who argued that commanding officers should be deprived of command influence, and those who viewed such prerogatives as essential for discipline and cohesion. In 1953, a year after the Grow court-martial, an article by Chester Ward appeared in the *Vanderbilt Law Review* declaring that command influence had been abolished under the Uniform Code. He further stated: "This has been made trebly clear . . . by actual day-to-day experience in administration of the Code for more than a year and a half." In 1970, Homer E. Moyer, Jr., wrote in the *Maine Law Review* that "military justice is clearly superior." He strongly defended the existence of command influence, rationalized its prevalence, and dissected the arguments of the critics.[24]

Hence the purpose of this book examining the Grow pretrial investigation and general court-martial is to identify subtle command influence under the Uniform Code and its use as a management tool and to show that the system—firmly institutionalized over many decades—was not capable of dispensing impartial military justice. The episode demonstrated that the failure to sever political, command interests from the judicial process produced unlawful command influence, thus degenerating the whole legal proceedings. The Grow trial also provides a classic example of the negative side of military management and the continued problem of command influence. As a result, the highest order of military ethos in the Grow legal case became self-serving rather than service. The institutionalization of the agency theory of separatism provided a means for managerial implementation in a negative way. By improperly using the military justice system, the procedure thus became destructive rather than constructive.

The Grow trial occurred during a period when military law and justice were moving away from an antiquated system borrowed from the British code and adopted by the Continental Congress in 1775. The original intentions as outlined in the American Articles of War no longer reflected the times. The Uniform Code was an attempt to provide a military legal system suitable to the time, but it fell short of resolving the problem of command influence. Extraordinary political, diplomatic, and technological demands and commitments resulting from America's acceptance of a greater role in world affairs restructured the military's mission so it could deal with global needs.[25] The Uniform Code was an attempt at military judicial activism so as to meet these new demands by reforming the legal system. But the perpetrators of command influence in the Grow trial in 1952 adhered to the original intent as set down in the Articles of War which Ansell and Morgan had found so distasteful and not applicable to the times.

To be sure, Grow's court-martial record was on the surface entirely proper. Nevertheless, the trial process was actively controlled to follow the implied wishes of the army staff. This attitude, though subtle, would produce an aura of command influence, thus negating military due process as outlined by the code. After all, officers in any command structure—more so when closely associated with the army staff in the Pentagon—depend on the military hierarchy for favorable reports and recommendations necessary for upward mobility. The trial counsel and the law officer, along with the other JAGC officers involved in the Grow case, owed their career advancement to the judge advocate general, General Brannon, who was a key player in Taylor's management group. Without doubt, they were subject to the pressures of command influence.[26]

The prosecution was well prepared for the court-martial and was able to get Grow to admit he was "lax." Not all the credit for a five-day trial should be given to the prosecution, however, who after all had behind them the overwhelming support, direction, and influence of the army staff. Grow was found "not guilty" of the second specification mainly because the G-3, General Jenkins, had finally testified and the testimony had been successfully challenged. Yet when the G-2, Bolling, was summoned as a witness for the defense, the Department of the Army said he was "not available." Grow maintained later that he had Bolling's affidavit indicating that he was, in fact, available and expecting a call to testify to the effect that there was no compromise of national security in respect to the specifications pertaining to G-2.[27] Why Grow's defense counsels did not pursue the request for Bolling's appearance is perplexing. One of their main arguments dealt with the question of jurisdiction, and in particular the validity of the specifications to which Bolling could certainly have testified. The defense's retraction of the request for Bolling made it possible for the prosecution to conclude the proceedings. In fact, the course of events to that point had already satisfied the managers of the court-martial. In addition, the defense had the opportunity to challenge the members of the court serving on the military jury, who had been selected based on criteria established in Taylor's management group and not by random selection. Grow's counsel did not exercise the right to one preemptory challenge against any court member. Even Brannon had expected more from the defense counsel.

It would be difficult to measure the degree of pressure affecting the performance of Grow's counsels. It was exercised in numerous subtle ways. Nevertheless, it should be kept in mind that Grow's counsels were members of the JAGC commanded by one of the active participants in Taylor's management group, General Brannon. The careers of JAGC officers may well have been threatened had they raised issues infringing on the army staff's claimed areas of responsibility. As members of a hierarchical system, Grow's counsels would naturally regard proper adherence to army policy as a prerequisite for entering the promotion lists. It would not take much of an imaginative leap to visualize undesirable duty assignments resulting from the challenging of superiors. Even the retired Brigadier General Adam Richmond, who had played an innocuous role during the trial, served as a token defense counsel so as to set a suitable protective environment for general officers required to give testimony. Richmond did admit that the case was "supercharged . . . you can't put your finger here and say, 'This is right and this is wrong.' " He added: "It involves Army Regulations about which we can gather no positive testimony. We have no experts." During the trial summation Richmond noted two letters of commendation, one submitted by General Eddy, the other by General Handy. Eddy's letter was marked "Top Secret" while Handy's letter was unclassified. Richmond pointed out that if two generals differ as to the interpretation of a security regulation, "how can you charge anyone else with having divergent views?"

The first step in the post-trial proceeding was the administrative review of the court-martial by the staff judge advocate of the Second Army. Three JAGC officers from the Second Army, Colonel Edward H. Young, Lieutenant Colonel Charles M. Munnecke, and Captain Abraham Nemrow, viewed the transcripts of the trial and provided the following opinion:

> There were no errors which materially prejudiced the substantial rights of the accused.
>
> The competent evidence establishes that the findings of guilty are correct in law and fact.
>
> The sentence is legally correct.[28]

On 19 August General Brooks, commanding general of the Second Army and designated convening authority, approved the findings. Thus Brooks became the reviewing authority and as such maintained the designated power to judge the court findings and sentence. He was now involved in the judicial decision and relied on the advice of his staff judge advocate. Another question arose at this administrative level on the impartiality of Young and his staff, who had acted in a sense as Brooks's lawyers, thus compromising the independence and disinterestedness of the Second Army's staff judge advocate's review of the trial.

The next administrative level affecting Grow's general court-martial was the Board of Military Review. A board of review for each military service was located in its Judge Advocate General's Office. It consisted of three lawyers, either military or civilian. The question of command influence again arises because of the board's subservient position under Brannon. Professor Edward F. Sherman argued that the board of review was not consistent with civilian standards found in independent appellate courts.[29] On 12 November the board of review affirmed the findings of the designated convening authority as "correct in law and fact and having determined, upon the basis of the entire record," that the findings of guilty and the sentence be approved. The board noted that it is "significant that the accused, himself, must have been aware that the information therein [the diary] needed protection when he made the comment on 18 January 1952: 'Done in Germany when my security was lax.' " The action by the board was noted by its members, Stanley W. Jones, Ralph K. Johnson, and Arthur P. Ireland.

The Board of Military Review based its decision almost entirely on the testimony from personnel in Bolling's G-2 who analyzed the diary. The most prominent was Dawson, with support from Weckerling. The defense witnesses' testimony was also noted, especially Cramer's and the former assistant military attachés in Moscow under Grow's command. Nevertheless, in spite of the persuasive testimony of the defense, Dawson's words had the greatest impact in the board's analysis of the merits of the trial. The board did remark: "In some manner, as yet unexplained, the contents of the accused's diary were photostated and a copy thereof made available to Richard Squires."[30] Bolling knew because of the investigation in EUCOM; he had the complete answer in April before the pretrial investigation. But like so many facts, it was kept out of the proceedings, making the Court of Military Review's role perfunctory.

While the trial record was proceeding through the various levels of administrative review, the first criticism of the proceedings and the Pentagon's handling of the diary incident appeared in the press. It was not the *Washington Post* or its paraphraser the *New York Times* that first noticed this possible unjust use of military judicial machinery, but the *Saturday Evening Post*. Demaree Bess, whose earlier criticism of Grow was based almost exclusively on the article in the *Post,* acted after receiving a letter from Grow in late June. In this letter Grow suggested that Bess talk with some of his friends familiar with the facts. After an investigation, Bess was astonished and bewildered that nobody in Washington had challenged the authenticity of the diary quotes in Squires's book. "When I began to track down this mystery," Bess wrote, "I unraveled a situation which sounds like something out of *Alice in Wonderland*." The villain was not Grow but "the sprawling network of commissions, committees, boards and liaison groups from various governmental departments and agencies." Bess believed that when army information distributed the reports of the court's verdict to the press immediately after the conclusion of the trial, the army would break "its inexplicable silence" about the forgeries of the diary. "To my amazement," he wrote, "nothing of the sort occurred." Bess did not blame the press but rather the army's silence and, by inference, the new managerial style of command. As a result of army management techniques, the court-martial's verdict made front-page headlines throughout the world: "The American Army, by its mysterious silence . . . virtually confirmed, for the American people and for the peoples of the world, a deliberately false picture created by communist forgers." Bess added: "Our Army had, in effect, verified a communist big lie for seven months, and kept on verifying it right through the official announcement of the court-martial's verdict." It was not until thirty-six additional hours had passed that an army spokesman suddenly released portions of the diary showing Squires's forgeries. The army's belated release, according to Bess, was picked up by the newspapers, but the story was given minor treatment as in the *Washington Post* or buried in inside pages. Grow's court-martial, Bess argued, had been caught up in the institutional machinery of the military, in part because the case was investigated by a dozen or more government departments and agencies, producing "an almost unmanageable confusion of authority." He added that "an unreasonable excess of so-called security" was applied to the Grow case leading to "incalculable damage by fooling the American people and friends of the United States throughout the world." Regarding the true contents of the diary, Bess quoted from an anonymous Washington official who had read it in its entirety and commented that it "revealed no really vital information to the Russians, nothing more than what could be considered nuisance value."[31]

Though Bess was the first knowledgeable outside commentator to head in the right direction, he did not have all the facts, and his noteworthy attempt fell short of revealing the complete truth. He was unable to isolate the activities of Bolling and Taylor and the roles they played, which were more than official in the usual sense. Furthermore, he was not privy to the CIC summary of the investigation in EUCOM. One result of the Taylor–Bolling management-control process was that the board of review, and later the U.S. Court of Military Appeals, would comment that "persons unknown photostated a diary kept by the accused." The question of the "persons unknown" was raised on several occasions by counsel during the proceedings, but Bolling was determined to suppress this information by isolating the answer so that it would not work in Grow's favor during the trial or appeals that would follow. Grow, for his part, had no knowledge of all this managing until the late 1970s, when he was finally shown the material from the CIC and Records of the Army Staff, indicating Taylor's and Bolling's active involvement in the court-martial process.

In spite of Bess's surprising revelation, the profile of Grow established by the *Washington Post* and the army staff in the Pentagon prevailed. Ten years after the court-martial a Pulitzer Prize winner from the *New York Herald Tribune,* Paris correspondent Sanche de Gramont, wrote in a book on international espionage since World War II that the diary quotes were never refuted by the military. Like the *Washington Post* earlier, Gramont gave Squires credibility and chastised Grow for his carelessness, thus providing one of the most embarrassing espionage coups against the West during the Cold War period. Gramont's book overall received good reviews; however, his own employer, the *Herald Tribune,* noted: "How he performed his research is a mystery." His book was void of sources. Even in the Soviet Union the Grow issue had surfaced again after years of silence. A propaganda piece designed for domestic consumption entitled *Front Tayoy Voyna* (The secret war front, 1965) repeated the falsified diary quotes. The article claimed that Grow's diary "was successfully photographed during a conference" in Frankfurt. Furthermore, the authors noted, the diary "became the property of world society."[32]

After his trial Grow had no future in the army, and he retired in January. Bolling received his third star on 1 August 1952 and became commanding general of the Third Army. He retired on 31 July 1955. Taylor remained deputy chief of staff until February 1953, when be became commander of the Eighth Army in Korea. On 30 June 1955, he became army chief of staff. His star and prominence continued to rise, and eventually he became involved in the controversial management of the Vietnam conflict.[33]

Years later, Taylor was noticeably evasive regarding his involvement in the Grow trial proceedings. On three occasions he noted: "I was not involved in the court-martial of General Grow . . . never got into it because of command influence . . . I have no side and had no personal involvement." The Records of the Army Staff, however, unavailable to the defense during the review process and appeals, indicate otherwise. He programmed the entire proceedings. No doubt Taylor was able to master political intrigues necessary to enhance his ambitions even if it meant compromising the truth; he relished the opportunity to manage the case for Collins. Frank W. Moorman, an airborne corps G-4 during World War II who had interacted with the airborne triumvirate of Matthew Ridgway, Maxwell Taylor, and James Gavin, facetiously recalled that "Taylor would cut your throat and think nothing about it."[34]

Even Collins displayed considerable lack of recall years later. He strongly defended Taylor's management group and commented that "only constructive criticism is permissible; however, at times criticism is to be let alone in order to uphold the army's integrity."[35] The court-martial of a general officer is not a regular occurrence in American military history, and to recall nothing about such an event is ludicrous, especially since the Records of the Army Staff and Records of the Trial for the first half of 1952 are replete with documentation involving Taylor, Bolling, the army chief of staff, and the army staff. Moreover, the autobiographies of Taylor (1972) and Collins (1979) demonstrate the ease with which both officers recollected events of their careers.

Grow continued a legal battle that was to last for many years. On 7 April 1953, he asked the Court of Military Appeals to reverse the general court-martial conviction. The United States Court of Military Appeals (USCMA) is the highest military court, consisting of three civilian judges appointed by the president for a term of fifteen years. The USCMA is the last resort for military cases.[36] The new Uniform Code had established for the first time in American military law an appellate court consisting of professional civilian judges. This provision was designed to eliminate the potential for command influence in the military justice system.

At the time of the conception of the USCMA, the selection of appointees resulted in political and media opposition. Two appointees, Robert E. Quinn and George W. Latimer, were political office seekers. While serving as governor of Rhode Island, Quinn had been accused of exercising nearly dictatorial powers by altering the legal process so as to crush a political foe. Latimer was seen as an old Truman crony. And Paul W. Brosman, perhaps the most able, was nevertheless a questionable candidate because he had not been appointed from civilian life as the law required, having been in the air force during the Korean conflict. He was also a close friend of Major General Reginald C. Harmon, the judge advocate general of the air force.[37] Even Quinn admitted that the court had been established in "the crucible of controversy." In Luther West's extensive study of command influence, he noted that the USCMA's efforts to "insure that military justice is administered in accord with the demands of due process" were neither effective nor consistent. Among the guarantees of military due process are the right of an accused to confront witnesses testifying against him, an impartial tribunal of competent members, and meaningful appellate review.[38]

In spite of the political accusations leveled against the composition of the USCMA, it did attempt during its early history to address the issue of command control. For example, in *United States* v. *Marsh,* decided a week before the Grow decision, the appeals court held that the convening authority was the accuser because of his personal interest in the case.[39] In other cases the civilian military appeals court found incidents of prejudice and jurisdictional error. In view of these decisions, it is difficult to understand the court's action in the Grow case. Frank Fedele, an authority on the early history of the USCMA, considered the impact of public opinion and political considerations on the case and the fact that Grow was a general officer. Fedele, however, left the answers to be resolved at a later date by "the searching mind of the student." Years later, the USCMA admitted its dilemma: "In the nature of things, command control is scarcely ever apparent in the face of the record."

In representing Grow at the USCMA, Roger M. Currier based his argument on three assignments of errors: that the convening authority (Second Army) was inferior in rank and command to the accusers, and, therefore, lacked the power to appoint a general court-martial; that the specification of the charge and the specification of the additional charge failed to allege offenses; and that the evidence was insufficient to support the findings. Currier presented virtually the same argument expressed during the trial. However, he failed to deal with the denied requests for defense witnesses which would have made a persuasive argument under Uniform Code, Article 46, and the confrontation clause of the Sixth Amendment. At this point in the proceeding, Currier could have considered the importance of Article 98 (Noncompliance with procedural rules), which provided the teeth to Article 37 (Unlawfully influencing the action of the court). Congress, when considering the Uniform Code, attempted to place some deterrent on unlawful command influence by making any violator subject to punishment. Article 46 (Opportunity to obtain witnesses and other evidence) was violated due to command influence, and thus Article 98 could have been utilized to redress wrongs and obtain relief. Grow's defense counsels, however, would never consider such action because of the nature of the command structure that placed their superior, General Brannon, as head of JAG and a major player in the Pentagon management team that orchestrated the trial proceedings.

On the first assignment of error or agreement, the court commented that a "person unknown photostated" Grow's diary and portions appeared in a communist publication, setting off a series of events. Because of the extremely serious nature of the charges and the rank of the accused, various army staff members became involved. In an ironic twist, the court stated that "the absence of even a suggestion of personal interest impels the conclusion that neither [Taylor or Bolling] was an accuser." The court also noted that the convening authority was not under compulsion or moral suasion when Taylor handed over the specifications and charges. On the question of compulsion or moral suasion, defense counsel Currier relied on the relief of General Hoge early in the trial, which placed the accused at a possible numerical disadvantage. But the court determined that the relief had been in line with Article 29 of the Uniform Code, which held that military exigencies were a reasonable cause for the transfer of officers from court-martial duties; moreover, the defense counsel had not introduced any evidence during the trial indicating that Hoge's relief was tainted by abuse of discretion. In conclusion, the appeals court paraphrased the Court of Military Review, noting that "if any numerical disadvantage resulted to the accused, appropriate relief could have been afforded upon a request for the appointment of an additional member."[40]

In the second assignment of error, defense counsel contended that the first specification and the specification of the additional charge failed to allege offenses. This argument had been advanced earlier by Grow's counsel. The appellate court, relying on AR 380-5, stated that "failure to classify military information recorded in any manner (personal diary or otherwise), according to the degree of protection needed" constitutes an offense.[41] Currier argued that regulations do not prohibit the keeping of a diary. He also asserted that if the alleged acts are prohibited by army regulations, "the violations are purely technical, administrative infractions of such an insubstantial nature as not to amount to offenses at all." But the appellate court responded that any technical and administrative malfeasance constituted some violation, and this violation normally had to be determined by the convening authority.

In the third assignment of error, Currier argued that the evidence was insufficient to support the findings. Once again, the court disagreed. It concluded that the two witnesses from Bolling's G-2, Dawson and Weckerling, had unquestionable qualifications. Their combined testimony, along with relevant exhibits, was enough to influence the appellate court. The court rejected defense counsel's argument that information regarding an offensive in Korea by Soviet surrogates was common knowledge and had been recorded in the press. The chief judge of the court, Robert E. Quinn, wrote: "It requires little knowledge of military affairs to conclude from this alone that the disclosures of the source of information advises the Communists where their counter-espionage efforts should be concentrated."

He chastised the diplomatic colony in Moscow for discussing the offensive and added, "This type of irresponsible talk eloquently bespeaks the necessity for further and more stringent enforcement of security measures."

The court found a statement made by Grow about the diary during the court-martial seriously damaging to his case. Grow had treated his diary containing reported classified information "as a letter from a Congressman or a copy of the *Saturday Evening Post.*" In conclusion, the court unanimously upheld Grow's conviction and found no merit in any assignment of errors.

The action taken by the USCMA is paradoxical in light of its decision a year earlier in *United States* v. *Clay* (1 USCMA 74, 1 CMR 74). The court held that the accused be given the rights granted by Congress which paralleled those accorded to defendants in civilian courts, such as to be confronted by witnesses against him, and to cross-examine witnesses for the government. The USCMA had the powers as an appellate court to reverse errors of law which materially prejudiced the substantial rights of Grow. This action it had taken earlier in the Clay case. In its inception the court adopted the judicial philosophy "to free those accused by the military from certain vices which infested the old system." Even though the court claimed that a conviction supported by a proceeding lacking in correct procedure "should fall on its own weight," it failed to consider the recognizable, the command management of the pretrial investigations and the court-martial.

On 18 July, the day after the military appeals court rendered its unanimous opinion, Grow requested a new trial. He argued: "Only a new trial at which all witnesses requested by the defense (but strangely unavailable at the court-martial) are made available, can rectify the injustice done . . . and prove that the charges were but a flimsy coverup."[42] In December he withdrew his request because one of his military counsels during the court-martial, General Richmond, advised him to keep the trial "clean." This argument may have influenced Grow, who had serious reservations about displaying the army's dirty linen in public. He did regret having relied on timid JAGC officers and wished he had "retained a good civilian counsel." Furthermore, Grow regretted not having vigorously demanded such witnesses as Bolling, which would have exposed the entire story while his superiors were under oath. Perhaps the most overriding influence on Grow's decision to back down was the serious consideration he had given regarding the future impact a vigorous continuance would have on his military-career-oriented family. There was a strong possibility, in view of the informal network of communication within the army, the politico-military relationship, and the importance of upward mobility dependent upon peers and mentors in the professional hierarchy, that continuing his defense would impede the necessary socialization and career development of his sons and perhaps his grandchildren.[43] Nevertheless, for years Grow periodically sent letters to the president of the United States and the secretary of the army pleading his case.

The final action on the Grow case was taken by President Eisenhower on 2 July 1957. Under Article 71 of the Uniform Code (Execution of sentence; suspension of sentence), no court-martial sentencing involving a general officer can be executed until approved by the president. The decision was made at the highest level "that the findings . . . be approved but that the sentence be remitted." To Grow, having the sentence remitted by the president had little significance. The real sentence was the termination of Grow's active military service and his prohibition from seeking further employment in any field in which his long military service could be of value. To Grow it was a life sentence handed down in relative secrecy and never fully justified; he gambled with the integrity of his peers and the military justice system and lost.

Grow then asked the president that he direct the declassification of his case so he could clear his name.[44] On 30 July the acting judge advocate general, Major General Stanley W. Jones, notified Grow that a copy of the trial record, including the unclassified exhibits and the decision of the Board of Military Review, was being assembled for transmission. He was advised that the diary, which had always been regarded as unclassified, was being transmitted with the declassified trial records. One year later, despite promises by Jones and Eisenhower's counsel, Grow had received neither the records nor the diary. Another letter to President Eisenhower finally prompted action. On 15 July 1959, Grow received virtually all the trial documents and his diary for 1951—all declassified.[45]

The ordeal was over, but the psychological scars remained. The Grow case demonstrated a profound example of unlawful command influence, a vice the new Uniform Code, Article 37, had attempted to eliminate. It had been exercised in such a devious and manipulative way that it was not easy to detect. The Grow case provided excellent proof that the Uniform Code had not solved the problem of improper command influence, a system that allowed extralegal interference in the execution of military justice. Thus Samuel T. Ansell's comment in 1919 identifying the court-martial as "an agency of miltary command governed and controlled by the will of the commander" was still valid in 1952 in spite of attempted reforms. Furthermore, Professor Edmund M. Morgan, a proponent of Ansell's position, wrote in 1919 that command abuses prevent "a fair and impartial presentation of the facts" and of the extent to which the court was subjected to the control of the appointing (convening) authority and "other superior military authority." In addition, Morgan, like Ansell, was critical of the limited review procedures and guarantees extended to the accused.[46] Very little had changed since 1919.

In spite of the reforms in the postwar periods, defects in military due process remained uncorrected.[47] The Grow general court-martial had indicated as much. Command influence, as a nineteenth-century notion of the agency theory of separatism, remained institutionally intact in spite of the attempts in 1920 and 1950 to bring the military justice system more in line with civilian legal procedures.

The Grow episode developed during a period when traditional army formalism and bureaucracy were being challenged by geographical, political, and diplomatic complexities of the Cold War period. Furthermore, since Marshall's reorganization of the army during World War II, there had been greater emphasis on applying corporate business practices to army management. Accepting this approach, according to Richard A. Gabriel and Paul L. Savage, planted the seeds for blatant careerism and self-interest. The bases for this, they argued, can be found in American history, whose past embraced the free economic enterprise of Adam Smith, the political laissez-faire of James Madison, and the Social Darwinism of Herbert Spencer. They blamed the business model Marshall adopted for weakening traditional military values such as honor and selflessness, leading to an ethos of self-interest and exaggerated careerism.[48]

James E. Hewes, Jr., in his study of army organization and administration, noted that General Marshall decentralized army administrative responsibilities to resemble the procedures the major pioneer industrialists had implemented earlier. Marshall, however, was able to retain the center of authority based on the established military principle of unity of command. But as America's commitment expanded and became more complex, Marshall's reorganization required modification. Consequently, the traditional formalism and bureaucratic outlook inherited from the bureau and branch chiefs came in stark conflict with the business rationalists, who called for stronger civilian control and involvement based on proven corporate management practices. The business rationalists were strict constitutionalists in that they believed the military should be actively governed and controlled by the "civil power" as designated by the Constitution's war power clause.

Less than a year after the Grow court-martial, President Eisenhower appointed the Rockefeller Committee to examine the organization of the Department of Defense. The committee was critical of interservice rivalry and the passiveness exhibited by the civilians who held the highest positions in defense. These civilians deferred to traditional military control as Secretary Pace had done in the army's management of the Grow case. Moreover, they were loose constitutionalists, tending to let the power center for management rest in the domain of the traditional military formalists. The counsel for the committee, H. Struve Hensel, criticized army formalism and bureaucracy, noting that an active civilian secretary was needed to manage the defense establishment. This active civilian—provided he was a strong executive with adequate powers—could implement successful business practices of decentralized operations and delegate downward clear lines of command. During the Grow episode, the spirit of the traditional army formalist came in conflict with the ongoing trend to modernize the military system following current business management practices.[49] The trend toward centralized business authority continued until the 1960s, when the McNamara "revolution" took place. The Ford industrialist and management activist Robert S. McNamara became secretary of defense in January 1961 and subsequently introduced a wide range of reforms. His aggressive management style prevailed, and eventually greater civilian control of the Pentagon was achieved.

Appearing before the Rockefeller Committee, General Collins stated that the chiefs of the services should be left "as free as possible to pursue their duties as members of the JCS by being able to delegate responsibility to their Vice Chiefs" and that loyalty from subordinates "is a prime requisite in any organization." Collins's notion of loyalty was a lofty quality as long as it did not obscure a higher loyalty to truth, which was a virtue absent during the Grow incident. The late Sir Basil H. Liddell Hart wrote that as noble as the quality of loyalty may be, it can become a substitute for "a conspiracy for mutual inefficiency;" ultimately leading to selfishness. Selfishness, in turn, becomes a companion to obtrusive careerism. Collins also believed that civilian leaders should establish policies for guidance and not concern themselves with the day-to-day operations of the military. Regarding military justice, Collins opposed the separation of judicial from command functions and supported absolute military control of the military judicial system. His comments and his relationship with Secretary Pace during the Grow episode were indicative of Collins's desire to retain traditional formalism rather than accept the application of modern business practices to military management.[50] Taylor, a loyal formalist who executed command influence in the army's traditional way as it had been inherited from the nineteenth-century notion of the agency theory of separatism, was strongly supported by his superiors. When he arrived in the Pentagon in February 1951, however, Taylor admitted that he lacked administrative skills. Later he would thank Secretary Pace for providing the opportunity to gain such skills.[51] In the Grow case, Taylor's mismanagement led to a bureaucratic blunder because he and the army staff relied on a managerial style based on traditional institutionalized formalism. Collins's and Taylor's decisions were rooted in bureaucratic routines that required them to use the traditional military justice system to continue the orderly progression of their military careers. Rather than viewing the Uniform Code as a living military code designed to meet the needs of a changing military role, Taylor's management group relied on a system that in general followed the original intentions of the Articles of War, which changed very little with respect to command influence until 1950. Nevertheless, the Pentagon group was able to isolate and control the incident so as to avoid repercussions and thus protect their self-interest.

General Grow had admitted that he did not exercise appropriate caution in securing the diary during a politically volatile period. The world war and the postwar period had placed new demands on the military professional. More than ever before, the American military was subjected to a greater and expanded role in diplomacy, administration, and management. Grow was a traditional heroic leader molded after the Patton image. He could cope with rapid technological changes, but he was not able to adjust to the expansion of military management and its political accompaniment created by the Cold War. Even though the argument that the former attaché used bad judgment in recording possibly sensitive information in his personal diary is persuasive, it does not excuse unlawful command influence and mismanagement. The key event was the decision by Taylor's management group to prosecute Grow rather than issue a reprimand outside the court-martial process or go along with his retirement request and refute the charges as suggested by the CIA, the State Department, and even Grow. Influencing this event was the acrimony of the times: McCarthyism and the communist controversy, the hysteria created by the Cold War, the spy paranoia besetting the Truman administration, and the CIC report, media pressures, and altered military careerism brought about by the incursion into traditional military formalism of modern business management techniques.

The Grow case was also unique because historically inappropriate command influence was usually exercised in ranks below general officers. It was rare for a general officer to be court-martialed. As in many professions, disciplinary action is usually handled outside the legal system. The military is no exception. The decision by an army staff management group to try the attaché was an uncommon procedure.

In 1977 the comptroller general of the United States reported to Congress after a two-year study that the aura of unfairness surrounding military courts still existed, and command influence, although prohibited, was still exercised. Quoting from a 1967 decision by the U.S. Court of Military Appeals, the report noted: "In the nature of things, command control is scarcely ever apparent on the face of the record." Twenty years later, a military law instructor for the Command and General Staff College's Center for Army Leadership,

Lieutenant Colonel Jonathan P. Tomes, wrote an article in *Army* outlining the difference between legal and illegal command influence. The commander acting as the convening authority who adheres to the true meaning of the Uniform Code and uses it to deal appropriately with the needs, purpose, and unique organization and mission of the military exercises legal command influence.[52] Illegal command influence must be distinguished from the lawful execution of the Uniform Code. When the army staff management group made the decision to prosecute Grow, illegal command influence occurred because the management group directed by Taylor interfered with the rights of the accused guaranteed under the code, thus undermining the credibility of the military justice system. It became a tool for inappropriate command influence.

Leadership instills discipline through actions and examples, not through the improper manipulation of the military justice system. Moreover, the system is only as fair as the individuals entrusted with its implementation. Even-handed justice was not applied during the Grow episode. As a result, the ingredients that should exemplify military leadership—selflessness, service, honor, duty, and moral integrity—gave way to command influence and career management. This ethos had replaced justice. An officer in the JAGC, Joseph B. Kelly, writing an article in 1953 for civilian attorneys interested in the new code, concluded by quoting from Scriptures, Paul to Timothy, "We know the law is good, if a man uses it rightly." Years later, in March 1987, lecturing at the U.S. Army Historical Institute in Carlisle Barracks, the eminent military jurist and a current member of the Court of Military Appeals, Walter T. Cox III, succinctly summed it up when he stated that "morale and discipline are enhanced when the troops understand that they are being treated with dignity, fairness, and equality under the law."[53]

By the mid 1980s the U.S. Supreme Court was not only reviewing court-martial proceedings when they were collaterally attacked but also reviewing direct petitions from decisions of the Court of Military Appeals. The agency theory of separatism was now questioned because certain legalities of the military court system were subjected to judicial article III of the Constitution.[54] No longer were the military courts an instrument of executive power provided by Congress.

As in all systems there are and will be malfunctions because of inertia caused by traditional self-serving bureaucracies that resist change. The call for legal reform, however, was generally resolved only after the United States experienced the trauma of four major military conflicts during the twentieth century. Unfortunately, like the Grow case, further limitations of command control were at times evasive and resistive, not so much because of the essence of the code, but because it was manipulated and used as a tool to satisfy the discretion of the commander, or as in the Grow court-martial, the army staff in the Pentagon.

NOTES

1. THE MAN, THE TIMES, AND THE COLD WAR

1. Thomas C. Reeves, *The Life and Times of Joe McCarthy* (New York: Stein and Day, 1982), 187–664.

2. Walter Lippmann, *Liberty and the News* (New York: Harcourt, Brace, 1920), 8, 71. Also see Ronald Steel, *Walter Lippmann and the American Century* (Boston: Little, Brown, 1980), 170–73.

3. Grow, "The Ten Lean Years," MS (1969), Hofmann files (hereafter cited as HF), p. 8. Also see edited versions in *Armor*, Jan.–Feb., Mar.–Apr., May–June, and July–Aug. 1987.

4. "Organization and Tactics" in "The Armored Force Command and Center," MS Study No. 27, Historical Section, Army Ground Forces, 1946, RG 407, National Archives, p. 42; Martin Blumenson, *The Patton Papers, 1940–1945* (Boston: Houghton Mifflin, 1974), 421, 425, 610; and Verbatim Record of Trial, Grow Files, HF, p. 240.

5. "USA-Diplomat auf dunklen Wegen. Wofür sich Generalmajor Grow interessierte/Aufzeichnungen des englischen Offiziers Squires," *Berliner Zeitung;* "Die Aufzeichnungen des britischen Majors Squires. Zu seinem Buch *Aug dem Kriegspfad/ Wie Westdeutschland kolonialisiert wurde,*" *Neues Deutschland.*

6. East Berlin: Rutten and Loening, 1951.

7. Frederick C. Barghoorn, *Soviet Foreign Propaganda* (Princeton: Princeton University Press, 1964), 36.

8. "Truman's Statement on Fundamentals of American Foreign Policy," *Department of State Bulletin* 13 (27 Oct. 1945): 653ff.

9. For an interesting discussion of the thesis of universalism versus sphere of influence, see Arthur Schlesinger, Jr., "Origins of the Cold War," *Foreign Affairs*, Oct. 1967, 22–52.

10. Rouhollah K. Ramazani, *Iran's Foreign Policy, 1941–1973: A Study of Foreign Policy in Modernizing Nations* (Charlottesville, Univ. Press of Virginia, 1975), 96–101; Department of State, *Foreign Relations of the United States, 1947: The Near East and Africa*, vol. 5 (Washington, D.C.: U.S. Government Printing Office, 1971), 963–65 (hereinafter referred to as *FRUS*).

11. J. F. C. Fuller, *Armament and History* (London: Eyre and Spottiswoode, 1946), 183 and n. 31, 185–86. Isaac Deutscher claims that sphere of influence became the basis of Soviet foreign policy (*Stalin: A Political Biography* [New York: Oxford Univ. Press, 1949], 412–13). Also see Adam B. Ulam, *Expansion of Coexistence: The History of Soviet Foreign Policy, 1917–67* (New York: Praeger, 1968), 641–42; and Anatol Rapoport, *The Big Two: Soviet-American Perception of Foreign Policy* (New York: Bobbs-Merrill, 1971), 80–81.

12. Adam B. Ulam, *The Rivals: America and Russia since World War II* (New York: Viking, 1971), 119.

13. *FRUS, 1948: The Near East, South Asia and Africa*, vol. 5, p. 1 (Washington, D.C.: U.S. Government Printing Office, 1975), 4–68; Ramazani, *Iran's Foreign Policy*, 96–108; Robert J. Donovan, *Conflict and Crisis: The Presidency of Harry S. Truman, 1945–1948* (New York: Norton, 1977), 157–58; George Lenczowski, *Soviet Advances in the Middle East* (Washington, D.C.: American Enterprise for Public Policy Research, 1971), 24–27.

14. *FRUS, 1947* 5:969–70, 982–83.

15. Ibid., 981–82. For a discussion of the Iranian problem immediately following the war, see Gary R. Hess, "The Iranian Crisis of 1945–46 and the Cold War," *Political Science Quarterly*, Mar. 1974, 117–46.

16. See John Lewis Gaddis, *The United States and the Origins of the Cold War, 1941–1947* (New York: Columbia Univ. Press, 1972), 282–315.

17. Harry S. Truman, *Years of Trial and Hope, 1946–1952* (Garden City: Doubleday, 1956), 93–95. Also see George F. Kennan, *Memoirs, 1925–1950* (Boston: Little, Brown, 1967), 547–99; and W. Averell Harriman and Elie Abel, *Special Envoy to Churchill and Stalin, 1941–1946* (New York: Random House, 1975), 547–48.

18. Thomas G. Paterson, J. Garry Clifford, and Kenneth J. Hagan, *American Foreign Policy: A History* (Lexington, Mass.: D. C. Heath, 1977), 445. The text is somewhat misleading in that it states that Grow advised the Iranian forces in their move against Azerbaijan.

19. *FRUS, 1946: General: The United Nations*, vol. 1 (Washington, D.C.: U.S. Government Printing Office, 1972), 1156–57; Robert W. Grow, "The U.S. Military Mission with the Iranian Army," *Cavalry*, Mar.–Apr. 1949, pp. 24–26. For an excellent overview of strategies for containment in Iran see Bruce R. Kuniholm, *The Origins of the Cold War in the Near East: Great Power Conflict and Diplomacy in Iran, Turkey, and Greece* (Princeton: Princeton Univ. Press, 1980), 342–50, 383–99; and Terry L. Deibel and John Lewis Gaddis, eds., *Containment: Concept and Policy*, vol. 2 (Washington, D.C.: National Defense Univ. Press, 1986), 424–26.

20. *FRUS, 1947* 5:966. Also see Ramazani, *Iran's Foreign Policy*, 159–62.

21. *FRUS, 1947* 5:978–79.

22. Ibid., 984–85, 997.

23. *FRUS, 1948* 5:88–90. This volume lists numerous correspondence between the Soviet and Iranian governments.

24. Ibid., 94.

25. Ibid., 99–101; Grow Diary, 10 Apr. 1947.

26. *FRUS, 1948* 1:154, 169–70, 174.

27. Ibid., 194.

28. Col. Jay R. Bogue, "Sworn Statement," 13 May 1952, *Record of Trial*, Adjutant General's Records Management Division and the Criminal Law Division, Office of the Judge Advocate General, Pentagon, HF (hereafter cited as RT). Col. Bogue was the assistant commandant of the Strategic Intelligence School.

29. Alfred Vagts, *The Military Attaché* (Princeton: Princeton Univ. Press, 1967), ix–xiv.

30. For a discussion of the operation of Soviet state security see William R. Carson and Robert Crowley, "The Beria Era (1938–1953)," in *The New KGB* (New York: Morrow, 1985), 187–243.

31. Maj. Gen. Alexander Bolling, "Sworn Statement," 16 May 1952, RT, p. 3; and Sergy Iranovich Tsybov and Nikolay Fedorovich Chistyakov, *Front Taynoy Voyny* (*The secret war front*) (Moscow: Ministerstva Oborony SSSR, 1965), Central Intelligence Agency, Washington, D.C. (hereafter cited as CIA), pp. 89–90. This is an edited translation prepared by the Translation Division, Foreign Technology Division, Wright-Patterson Air Force Base, Ohio.

32. Intelligence Report, Grow to Bolling, 26 Jan. 1952, Records of the Army Staff, RG 319, NA.

33. The Ambassador in the Soviet Union (Kennan) to the Deputy Under Secretary of State (Matthews), *FRUS, 1952–1954: Eastern Europe, Soviet Union, Eastern Mediterranean*, vol. 8 (Washington, D.C.: U.S. Government Printing Office, 1988), 1004–10. Also see ibid., 973, 1007, 1011–12, and Joseph C. Grew, *Turbulent Era: A Diplomatic Record of Forty Years, 1904–1945* (Boston: Houghton Mifflin, 1952), 1443–73; and George F. Kennan, *Memoirs, 1950–1963* (Boston: Little, Brown, 1972), 135.

34. Thomas Whiteside, *An Agent in Place: The Wennerström Affair* (New York: Viking, 1966), 45–46. The Central Intelligence Agency called Whiteside's book a "vivid account." See Report, *Agent in Place*, Central Intelligence Agency, Document No. 8, in "AFFIDAVIT," *George F. Hofmann* v. *United States Central Intelligence Agency, et al.*, Civil Action, No. 80-1792. Also see Subcommittee to Investigate the Administration of the Internal Security Act and Other Internal Security Laws, Committee on the Judiciary, Senate, *The Wennerström Spy Case: Excerpts from the Testimony of Stig Eric Constans Wennerström, A Noted Soviet Agent*, 88th Cong., 2d sess. (1964), pp. 164–65, and Memorandum for: Chief, Research Branch, 8 Jan. 1974, CIA, p. 3.

2. THE BOOK AND THE DIARY

1. Excerpts from Grow's Diary Broadcast, "USSR Overseas and Far East Service," 12 Mar. 1952, CIA, pp. 1–2.

2. Richard Squires, *Auf dem Kriegspfad. Aufzeichnungen eines englischen Offiziers* (East Berlin: Rutten and Loening, 1951), 209–10.

3. Ibid. The following translations from German are from chapter 6, pp. 209–34.

4. Robert W. Grow, "Outline of Facts and Circumstances Connected with the Diary and Court-Martial of Major General Robert W. Grow, with Comments," 18 Feb.

1954, Grow Files, HF; Elmer Cox, "Deposition," in "Review of the Staff Judge Advocate," 15 Aug. 1952, in RT, p. 20.

5. Agent Report, 66th CIC (Counter Intelligence Corps) Detachment, File No. D310346, 3 Mar. 1952, Office of the Director of Intelligence, EUCOM (IACSF), p. 0087.

6. Top Secret Telegram: From Moscow to Secretary of State, No. 1172, Central Files: 120.32161/1.1452, 14 Jan. 1952, United States Department of State.

7. Top Secret Telegram: From Berlin to Secretary of State. No. 920, Central Files: 120.32161/1.1452, 14 Jan. 1952, U.S. State Department.

8. George A. Henri, "Affidavit re: 'Auf Dem Kriegspfad,' " 27 May 1952, and "Review of the Staff Judge Advocate," 15 Aug. 1952, in RT, pp. 15–16.

9. Grow Diary, 18 Jan. 1952; Grow, "Memorandum for Whom It May Concern," 18 Feb. 1954, Grow Files, HF, p. 3.

10. The Central Intelligence Agency was established under the National Security Act of 1947 to collect and coordinate foreign intelligence, analyze it, and make it available to the president, National Security Council, and other United States intelligence agencies.

11. "Compromise of Classified Information," AC. of S, G-2, OCS 380.01 (26 Jan. 1952), Records of the Army Staff, RG 319, NA.

12. Brig. Gen. Fay B. Prickett, Col. Edward J. Maloney, and Col. John E. Ray, "Sworn Statements," 13 May 1952, and "Statement of BG F. B. Prickett, Deputy to the Inspector General," 1 May 1952, RT, pp. 1–3.

13. Ibid.

14. Col. John E. Ray, "Trial Statement," in "Review of the Staff Judge Advocate," RT, p. 9.

15. Memo: The Inspector General. Subject: Investigation, 28 Jan. 1952, RT, p. 1.

16. Grow Diary, 29 Jan. 1952.

17. Col. Harold R. Booth, "Sworn Statement," 14 May 1952, RT, p. 7.

18. The following testimony of General Grow was taken stenographically and transcribed by Robert I. Henderson, Reporter, Office of the Inspector General, and entitled "Testimony of Maj. Gen. Robert W. Grow, USA, 0-4621, Office of the Assistant Chief of Staff, G-2, US Army, Pentagon, Washington, D.C., taken at the Pentagon, Washington, D.C., at 1420 to 1540 hours on 30 January 1952, by Col. Harold R. Booth, IG," RT, pp. 1–10, 27–30.

19. Grow Diary, 30 Jan. 1952.

20. "Compromise of Classified Information," AG T/S 87T-52, 31 Jan. 1952, RT.

21. "Report of investigation of alleged compromise of classified security information," AG T/S 87T-52, 4 Feb. 1952, RT, pp. 1–5.

22. Ibid., 3–5.

23. "Court-martial Action against Major General Robert Grow," Office of the Assistant Chief of Staff, G-2, Intelligence, 5 Feb. 1952, RT, pp. 1–2.

24. Ibid., 2.

25. Bolling to Graling, G-2 Attaché Branch, American Embassy, Ottawa, Canada, 6 Feb. 1952, Records of the Army Staff, RG 319, NA.

26. Grow Diary, 20, 22, 25 Feb. 1952.

3. MEDIA REACTION

1. *Current Digest of the Soviet Press,* 2d Qtr, Nos. 14–26, 1952, passim.

2. Agent's Daily Log, 5, 6 Mar. 1952, CIA; Maj. Gen. Alexander R. Bolling, "Sworn Statement," 16 May 1952, RT, p. 7.

3. John G. Norris, "Agents Reveal U.S. General's Diary," *Washington Post,* 6 Mar. 1952.

4. "Compromise of Classified Information," 26 Jan. 1952, and "Court-martial Action against Robert Grow," 5 Feb. 1952, Office of G-2, Records of the Army Staff, RG 319, NA.

5. Agent's Daily Log, 6 Mar. 1952, CIA; Grow Diary, 6 Mar. 1952.

6. Agent's Daily Log, 6 Mar. 1952, CIA; Grow Diary, 6 Mar. 1952.

7. Grow Diary, 6 Mar. 1952.

8. "Dere Diary," *Washington Post,* 7 Mar. 1952.

9. Grow Diary, 1951, passim.

10. Norris, "U.S. Warns Attachés Not to Keep Diaries," *Washington Post,* 7 Mar. 1952.

11. "Reds Quote General's Stolen Diary to 'Prove' U.S. Plots World War," *New York Times,* 7 Mar. 1952.

12. Rob F. Hall, "U.S. General in USSR Picked Targets for A-Bomb Attack," and Joseph Clark, "Gen. Grow Gambles on War—and on War Stocks," *Daily Worker,* 7 Mar. 1952; "Washington Jittery Over Grow Exposure of Plans for War," ibid., 9 Mar. 1952.

13. "Stolen Diary of US Attaché, Excerpts Circulated in Russia," *London Times,* 7 Mar. 1952.

14. Grow Diary, 7 Mar. 1952.

15. "Stolen Diary's Views Repudiated by 'Voice'," *New York Times,* 9 Mar. 1952.

16. "Top Secrets Feared Stolen in Grow Case," ibid., 8 Mar. 1952.

17. See the report of CIC agent Schroeder in chapter 4.

18. See note 15. Also see "Washington Jittery Over Grow Exposure of Plans for War," *Daily Worker,* 9 Mar. 1952.

19. "Attached Court-marital Charges," Memorandum, Taylor to Collins, 24 Apr. 1952 (CS 201, Grow, Robert W., 1952), RG 319, NA.

20. "What Gen. Grow Revealed," 10 Mar. 1952, and Rob F. Hall, "Gen. Grow Holds Up a Mirror to America," *Daily Worker,* 11 Mar. 1952.

21. Agent's Daily Log, 10 Mar. 1952, CIA.

22. Ya. Semenov, "Instigators of War Without a Mask," *Bolshevik* no. 6; (Mar. 1952): 75–80.

23. "Excerpts from Grow's Diary Broadcast," Moscow, in English, to North America, 12 and 14 Mar. 1952, USSR: Overseas and Far East Service, CIA Files, 14 Mar. 1952, CC1-3.

24. "Grow's Diary Proves U.S. Aims at War," Moscow, in English, to the United Kingdom, 14 Mar. 1952, USSR: European and Near East Service, CIA Files, 17 Mar. 1952, BB1-4.

25. "Gen. Grow Pinpointed Targets in USSR" and "Grow Diary Bares Policy of War Maniacs," Moscow, in English, to North America, 17 Mar. 1952, USSR: Overseas and Far East Service, CIA Files, 18C19, CC13,1.

26. "Course of Action in the Case of Major General Grow," Memorandum, Bolling to Taylor, 17 Apr. 1952, (CS 201, Grow, Robert W., 1952), p. 1, RG 319, NA.

27. Memorandum of Conversation by the Ambassador to the Soviet Union (Kirk), 26 Oct. 1951, *FRUS, 1951: Europe: Political and Economic Development,* vol. 4, pt. 2 (Washington, D.C.: U.S. Government Printing Office, 1985), 1665; Ambassador in the Soviet Union (Kennan) to the Department of State, 22 May 1952, *FRUS, 1952–1954: Eastern Europe; Soviet Union; Eastern Mediterranean,* vol. 8 (Washington, D.C.: U.S. Government Printing Office, 1988), 971–72; Kennan, *Memoirs, 1950–1963,* 122; Department of State, *Contemporary Soviet Propaganda and Disinformation: A Conference Report,* 9536, 25–27 June 1985 (Washington, D.C.: U.S. Government Printing Office, 1987) xiii–xix, 47. Also see Jacques Ellul, *Propaganda: The Formation of Men's Attitudes* (New York: Knopf, 1965), 31–32. Ellul, a French professor of law and social history, argued that the Soviets employ conditioned reflexes such as words to mold attitudes. The United States, by contrast, creates myths designed to characterize that which is good and just to mold attitudes.

28. "Washington Jittery over Exposé of Gen. Grow Diary," *Daily Worker,* 16 Mar. 1952. The Pennsylvania and Michigan edition of the *Daily Worker,* the *Worker,* used the Grow incident to increase its sinking circulation. The *Daily Worker* claimed to have seventeen hundred subscriptions, including the various editions of the *Worker.* The Grow exposé was used as a last effort to increase subscriptions and circulation of communist papers in the United States. See "Soon to End Sub Drive on Press Parley Date," *Worker,* 16 Mar. 1952.

29. "Moscow Diary," *Newsweek,* 17 Mar. 1952, 25, "Dear Diary," *Time,* 17 Mar. 1952, 18.

30. "Memorandum for Whom It May Concern," 18 Feb. 1954, Grow Files, HF, p. 3.

31. Memorandum for G-2, Grow to Bolling, 17 Mar. 1952, RT, pp. 1–2.

32. "General Grow's Diary," Memorandum for General Bolling, 18 Mar. 1952, RT, p. 1.

33. Bolling, "Sworn Statement," RT, p. 6.

34. "Pentagon Bans Diaries but Keeps General Grow," *Daily Worker,* 19 Mar. 1952.

35. Plainville Council of Churches to Harry S. Truman, President and Commander in Chief, 20 Mar. 1952 (CS 201, Grow, Robert W., 1952), RG 319, NA; "Grow's Dismissal Urged," *New York Times,* 25 Mar. 1952. Also see "800 Connecticut Churches Demand Truman Fire Gen. Grow, Disavow War Aims," *Daily Worker,* 25 Mar. 1952.

36. Memorandum for General Vaughn from Assistant Secretary of the General Staff, 5 Apr. 1952, and Vaughan to Rev. Fred Treverrow, 7 Apr. 1952 (CS 201, Grow, Robert W., 1952), RG 319, NA.

37. Great Neck Peace Forum to Honorable Harry S. Truman, 7 Apr. 1952; Memorandum for General Vaughan from Assistant Secretary of the General Staff, 10 Apr.

1952; Vaughan to Edgar J. Moore, Sec'y., 11 Apr. 1952 (CS 201, Grow, Robert W., 1952), RG 319, NA.

38. "The Strange Case of General Grow," *Nation*, 22 Mar. 1952, 264–65.

39. Editorial, "The Case of the Careless General's Diary," *Christian Century*, 26 Mar. 1952, 355–56.

40. Grow Diary, 22, 28 Mar., 4 Apr. 1952; Grow, interview with author, 18, 19 Mar. 1979.

41. "Russians Link Grow to Germ Warfare," *New York Times*, 25 Mar. 1952.

42. "The Ideas of Grow, the Spy in the Uniform of a General," Moscow, in German, to Germany, 28 Mar. 1952, USSR: European and Near East Service, CIA, 31 Mar. 1952, BB1-2.

43. U.S. Department of State, *Documents on Germany, 1944–1985*, 4th ed. (Washington, D.C.: U.S. Government Printing Office, 1985), 273–314, 344, 347.

44. Grow Diary, 31 Mar. 1952.

45. Hanson W. Baldwin, "Army Intelligence—I. Grow's Diary Incident Brings to Light Misassignments of Military Attachés," *New York Times*, 13 Apr. 1952.

46. Hanson W. Baldwin, "Army Intelligence—II. Army Policy Shortcomings Held Factor in G-2, Miscasting of Officers Like Grow," ibid., 14 Apr. 1952.

47. Hanson W. Baldwin, "Army G-2 Is Defended. Intelligence Head Says Grow Incident Led to No Shifts—Others Join Criticism," ibid., 6 May 1952.

48. C. Wright Mills, *The Power Elite* (New York: Oxford Univ. Press, 1956), 209–10.

49. Vagts, *Military Attaché*, 98, 256, 332; Sanche de Gramont, *The Secret War: The Story of International Espionage since World War II* (New York: G. P. Putnam's Sons, 1962), 445–49. Apparently Gramont was not aware of Billy Mitchell's court-martial in 1925. General Mitchell was found guilty of conduct prejudicial to good order and military discipline for his outspoken views of the strategic use of air power. Shortly before his court-martial, he reverted to his permanent rank of colonel.

50. G. Korothevich, "Yet Another Exposure of Warmongers," *For a Lasting Peace, for a People's Democracy*, 4 Apr. 1952; B. Leontyev, "Facts Exposing the Warmongers," *Pravda*, 19 Apr. 1952, 3–6; Moscow Home Service broadcast, 19 Apr. 1952, CIA Files, 20 Apr. 1952; D. Melnikov, "Notes of a British Officer," 16 Apr. 1952, *New Times*, 29–31, and "Confirmation from the Pentagon," 7 May 1952, ibid., 15.

51. "A Kind Word for General Grow," *American Mercury*, May 1952, 9–11.

52. Barghoorn, *Soviet Foreign Propaganda*, 36.

53. Chalmers M. Roberts, *The Washington Post: The First 100 Years* (Boston: Houghton Mifflin, 1977), 256–312.

4. THE VICTORY GUEST HOUSE

1. "Chronology of Events" (CS 201, Grow, Robert W., 1952), Records of the Army Staff, RG 319, NA. Also see Maxwell D. Taylor, "Sworn Statement," 21 May 1952, RT, p. 1.

2. The following interviews were taken by the 66th CIC Detachment and are listed as Agents' Reports and First Interim Report, 21 Feb. 1952, and Second Interim

Report, 29 Feb. 1952, Re: "Compromise of General Grow's Diary," HQ, EUCOM, Office of the Director of Intelligence, U.S. Army Intelligence and Security Command (IACSF), Fort George Meade, Maryland, pp. 0001–0020, 0068–0086, 0157–0172.

3. Grow Diary, 7, 12, 20, 22 Feb., 5 Mar. 1952.

4. The following interviews were taken by the 66th CIC Detachment and are listed as Agents' Report and Fourth Interim Report, 7 Apr. 1952; Fifth Interim Report, 1 May 1952; Sixth Interim Report, 15 May 1952; Seventh Interim Report, 21 May 1952; Re: "Compromise of General Grow's Diary," HQ, EUCOM (IACSF), pp. 0026–0033, 0036–0067, 0147–0175.

5. Collonia to Grow, Re: "Large-scale Communist political and military espionage activities from 1946 through 1951 at the Victory Guest House near Frankfurt/Main (Germany), former Official Residence of OMGUS (USFET/EUCOM) and HICOG," 20 and 26 July 1975; Grow to Collonia, 1 Nov. 1975, Grow Files, HF.

6. 66th CIC Det. to Director, Intelligence Division, EUCOM, "Grow, Robert W., Major General, 0-4621," 3 Apr. 1952 (IACSF), pp. 0034–0035.

7. "Der fall Grow," *Frankfurter Allgemeine,* 13 Mar. 1952.

8. "Agenten photokopierten US-Generals Tagebuch," *Ludwigsburger Kreiszeitung,* 14 Mar. 1952.

9. "Propaganda: Bob Grows intimes Tagebuch," *Der Spiegel,* 19 Mar. 1952.

10. See Earl Latham, *The Communist Controversy in Washington* (New York: Atheneum, 1969), 63, 103–4, 196, 229–30; and Peter Grothe, *To Win the Minds of Men: The Story of the Communist Propaganda War in East Germany* (Palo Alto, Calif.: Pacific Books, 1958), 60–63.

11. "Tagebuchblätter an der Kreml-Mauer," *Die Tat,* 19 Mar. 1952.

12. McClure to Assistant Chief of Staff, "Compromise of General Grow's Diary," 1 Apr. 1952, and McClure to Bolling, 21 May 1952 (IACSF), p. 1.

13. Adams (Deputy Director G-2, EUCOM) to Assistant Chief of Staff G-2, "Compromise of General Grow's Diary," 7 Apr. 1952 (IACSF), p. 1.

14. "Sixth Interim Report," pp. 0036–0067.

15. Cryptomessage from: Co HQ 66th CIC Det. EUCOM, 8, 10, 11 Apr. 1952 (IACSF), pp. 0135–0140.

16. Agent Report, 66th CIC Det., 22 Apr. 1952 (IACSF), pp. 0150–0151.

17. "Sixth Interim Report," p. 0066; CIC to Assistant Chief of Staff, G-2, Intelligence, Re. Gerhard Poss, 10 Feb. 1953, CIA.

18. "Court-marital Action against Major General Robert Grow," Office of the Assistant Chief of Staff, G-2, Intelligence, 5 Feb. 1952, and Bolling to Deputy Chief of Staff for Operations and Administration, "Course of Action in the Case of Major General Grow," 17 Apr. 1952, RT, p. 1.

5. COMMAND INFLUENCE

1. Telegram: Cumming to Secretary of State, 14 Jan. 1952, Central File 120.32161/1-1452, State Department. The chargé in Moscow, Cumming, reported that the excerpts appeared in the *Taegliche Rudnschau,* published by the Soviet army. Later the paper was correctly identified as the *Berliner Zeitung.*

2. Maj. Gen. Alexander R. Bolling, "Sworn Statement," 16 May 1952, RT, p. 1.

3. Foreign Service Dispatch, "Book by Richard Squires, *Auf dem Kriegspfad,*" 14 Mar. 1952, Central File 120.3216/3-1452, State Department.

4. Agent's Daily Log, 5, 6, 18 Mar. 1952, CIA. Also see Rhodri Jeffreys-Jones, *The CIA and American Democracy* (New Haven: Yale Univ. Press, 1989), 66. The author maintains that the CIA has probably become the world's best intelligence organization, but its advice has seldom been taken seriously enough by American policy makers.

5. "Papers re Propaganda Approach to the Soviet Union," 9 Apr. 1952, Central File 511.61/4-953, State Department.

6. Phillips to Fritchey, 9 Apr. 1952 (CS 201 Grow, Robert W., 1952), Records of the Army Staff, RG 319, NA; Deposition: Frank Pace, Jr., 1 July 1952, RT, p. 5.

7. Memorandum for General Dorn, 10 Apr. 1952, and Memorandum for General Bolling, 10 Apr. 1952, RG 319, NA.

8. Col. Gordon E. Dawson, "Sworn Statement," 14 May 1952, RT, pp. 1, 7.

9. Grow Diary, 15 Apr. 1952.

10. "Memo for Col. Dawson," RG 319, NA, pp. 1–8.

11. Dawson, "Sworn Statement," RT, p. 7.

12. "Course of Action in the Case of Major General Grow," 17 Apr. 1952, RG 319, NA. An extensive check of State Department records failed to turn up the final execution of Phillips's request.

13. Grow Diary, 17 Apr. 1952.

14. "Course of Action in the Case of Major General Grow," RG 319, NA.

15. Ibid.

16. Ibid.

17. "Report of Investigation of alleged compromise of classified security information" (IG 333.9-Squires, Richard), 18 Apr. 1952, RG 319, NA.

18. "Court-martial Action against Major General Robert Grow," 5 Feb. 1952, Office of the Assistant Chief of Staff, G-2, Intelligence, RG 319, NA.

19. Agent's Daily Log, 18, 22 Apr. 1952, CIA.

20. Morris Janowitz, *The Professional Soldier: A Social and Political Portrait* (New York: Free Press, 1971), 154, 297–98; Maxwell D. Taylor, *Swords and Plowshares* (New York: Norton, 1972), 30, 38, 71; J. Lawton Collins, *Lightning Joe: An Autobiography* (Baton Rouge: Louisiana State Univ. Press, 1979), 95, 347; Lawrence J. Korb, *The Joint Chiefs of Staff: The First Twenty-five Years* (Bloomington: Indiana Univ. Press, 1976), 46–54.

21. "Chronology of Events" (CS 201 Grow, Robert W., 1952), p. 2, RG 319, NA; handwritten note from Col. Bard to Col. Godwin, 19 Apr. 1952, RT, p. 1. The note was a report on the meeting in Taylor's office at 0900 by Colonel C. Robert Bard from the Judge Advocate General's Office. Also Taylor Diary, 19 Apr. 1952, Special Collections, Archives and History, National Defense University Library, Fort Lesley McNair, Washington. Taylor's diary is more of a handwritten appointment book and lacks the commentary found in Grow's diary.

22. "Action Relative to Major General Robert W. Grow," Bolling to Collins, 21 Apr. 1952, RG 319, NA.

23. First draft, "Action Relative to Major General Robert W. Grow," memo, Collins to Pace, undated, RT, p. 1.

24. See violation of the Uniform Code of Military Justice, Article 92, RG 319, NA. Also see *Manual for Court-Martial United States, 1951* (Washington, D.C.: U.S. Government Printing Office, 1951), 442.

25. Second draft, Collins to Pace, 21 Apr. 1952, RG 319, NA; Interrogatories and Deposition of Frank Pace, Jr., *United States* v. *Major General Robert Walker Grow*, 21 July 1952, RT, pp. 1–5.

26. Col. Robert Bard, "Sworn Statement," 13 May 1952, RT, p. 9, and Maj. Gen. Ernest M. Brannon, "Sworn Statement," 21 May 1952, RT, p. 9; "Compromise of Classified Information," 5 Feb. 1952, RT, and "Statement of Colonel Gordon E. Dawson, GS, OAC of S, G-2," May 1952, RT. Also see "Chronology of Events," p. 2, RG 319, NA.

27. See penciled notes re: specifications by phone from Gen. Brannon, 0930, 24 Apr. 1952, RT, p. 1.

28. "Court-Martial Charges," Harbaugh, Jr., to Hass, 24 Apr. 1952, RT, p. 1.

29. Attached Court-Martial Charges, Taylor to Collins, 24 Apr. 1952, RG 319, NA.

30. First Charge Sheet, DD 458, 22 Apr. 1952, RT, pp. 1–4; Penciled notes re: List of Prospective Members, 24 Apr. 1952, RT, p. 1.

31. "Review of the Staff Judge Advocate," 15 Aug. 1952, Second Army, pp. 2, 4, and Second Charge Sheet, 25 Apr. 1952, RT, pp. 1–4.

32. Third Charge Sheet, 25 Apr. 1952, RT, pp. 1–4.

33. Deposition: Pace, RT, pp. 1–5; "Chronology of Events," p. 2, RG 319, NA; "Review of the Staff Judge Advocate," RT, p. 2.

34. "Chronology of Events," p. 2, RG 319, NA.

35. Bard, "Sworn Statement," RT, pp. 5, 9.

36. "Review of the Staff Judge Advocate," RT, p. 5.

37. *Manual for Courts-Martial, United States, 1951*, pp. 44–45, 424.

38. "Memorandum for Colonel Belieu," 1 Aug. 1955, Grow Files, HF; Grow Diary, 28–30 Apr. 1952; Judge Advocate General's Corps, *The Army Lawyer: A History of the Judge Advocate General's Corps, 1775–1975* (Washington, D.C.: U.S. Government Printing Office, 1975), 205–6; Grow, interview with author, 18 July 1980.

39. John G. Norris, "Gen. Grow Is Charged in 'War!' Diary Case," *Washington Post*, 29 Apr. 1952; Austin Stevens, "Gen. Grow Faces Army Charges for Letting Reds Obtain His Diary," *New York Times*, 29 Apr. 1952. Also see "Court-Martial Charges," *Army-Navy-Air-Force Journal*, 3 May 1952.

40. "Confirmation from the Pentagon," *New Times*, 7 May 1952.

41. Draft: Press release, undated, RG 319, NA.

42. Memorandum for Director, Office of Public Information, Department of Defense, 25 Apr. 1952; "State Department Request for Information from Diary of General Grow, Bolling to Collins," 28 Apr. 1952, RG 319, NA; Department of State— FOI to author, 2 Mar. 1976.

43. In his memoirs, *Swords and Plowshares*, Taylor virtually ignored his experience as Deputy Chief of Staff for Operations and Administration. Even though the Grow

case had occupied a considerable amount of his time since early 1952, and especially April to August, he did not mention the episode (131–34). Likewise, Collins in his autobiography, *Lightning Joe,* did not mention the Grow affair (347–77).

44. James F. Schnabel, *Policy and Direction: The First Year* (Washington, D.C.: U.S. Government Printing Office, 1972), 61–65.

45. Comptroller General of the United States, *Military Jury System Needs Safeguards Found in Civilian Courts* (Washington, D.C.: U.S. Government Printing Office, 1977), 3–5.

6. PRETRIAL INVESTIGATION

1. Edward M. Byrne, *Military Law,* 3d ed. (Annapolis: Naval Institute Press, 1981), 92–94.

2. "Investigation of Charges," 6 May 1952, RT, p. 1.

3. As prosecution witnesses, the final charge sheet listed Maj. Gen. A. B. Bolling, OAC of S, G-2, Washington, D.C.; Col. G. E. Dawson, OAC of S, G-2, Washington, D.C.; Brig. Gen. John Weckerling, OAC of S, G-2, Washington, D.C.; Col. Charles Ott, OAC of S, G-2, Washington, D.C.; Maj. Gen. Fay Prickett, OIG, Washington, D.C.; Col. J. E. Ray, OIG, Washington, D.C.; W. O. George Henri (Hq, EUCOM), 66th CIC Det., Berlin; W. O. Gustav Bard, 66th CIC Det., Berlin; Maj. Edward S. Robbins, OAC of S, G-3, Washington, D.C.; and Col. Harold R. Booth, OIG, Washington, D.C. Five documents were listed on the charge sheet: *Auf dem Kriegspfad* (On the Path to War) by Richard Squires, OAC of S, G-2; Date Book 1951 (Diary of Major General Robert Walker Grow), OTIG; Statement of Major General Robert Walker Grow, OAC of S, G-2; Statement of Major General Robert Walker Grow, OTIG; and Conference report, OAC of S, G-2.

4. "Chronology of Events" (CS 201 Grow, Robert W., 1952), Records of the Army Staff, pp. 1–2, RG 319, NA.

5. Taylor, *Swords and Plowshares,* 123–30, 132–33.

6. Ibid., 123–30. For comment and comparison of Taylor's management style see Clay Blair, *Ridgway's Paratroopers: The American Airborne in World War II* (New York: Dial Press, 1985), 50–54.

7. "Request for Declassification of Charge Sheet," 9 May 1952, and "Reply," 14 May 1952, RT, p. 1.

8. "Request for TDY Orders to EUCOM," 12 May 1952, and replies, 14 May 1952, RT, p. 1.

9. "Investigation of the Charges in the Case of Major General Robert W. Grow, held Fort George G. Meade, Maryland at 0900 hours," 13 May 1952, RT, pp. 1–3.

10. Joseph based his argument on *Boyd v. United States,* 116 U.S. (1886), pp. 616, 633. Also see 29 *Law Edition* 746. This case dealt with unreasonable searches and seizures and the nature of compelling an individual to give evidence against himself.

11. "Statement of Brigadier General F. B. Prickett, Deputy The Inspector General," 1 May 1952, and Prickett, "Sworn Statement," 13 May 1952, RT, pp. 1–7.

12. Col. Edward J. Maloney, "Sworn Statement," 13 May 1952, RT, pp. 1–7.

13. Col. John E. Ray, "Sworn Statement," 13 May 1952, RT, pp. 1–6.

14. Col. C. Robert Bard, "Sworn Statement," 13 May 1952, RT, pp. 1–12.

15. Ibid.

16. "Court-martial Action against Major General Robert Grow," 5 Feb. 1952, Office of the AC of S, G-2 (Intelligence), RG 319, NA.

17. Bard, "Sworn Statement," RT, pp. 1–2.

18. Col. Jay R. Bogue, "Sworn Statement," 13 May 1952, RT, pp. 1–4.

19. "Investigation," 380.01, Case 209, 28 Jan. 1952, Records of the Army Staff, RG 319, NA. This memorandum for the IG was signed by Colonel M. F. Hass, secretary of the General Staff. The memorandum was accompanied by Squires's book and the East German newspaper articles with translations. No mention was made regarding the authenticity of Squires's exposé.

20. Col. Harold R. Booth, "Sworn Statement," 14 May 1952, RT, pp. 1–8. Also see "Testimony of MG Robert W. Grow, OAC of S, G-2," 30 Jan. 1952, Records of the Army Staff, pp. 1–10, RG 319, NA. For a recent article on why Article 31b was a debatable issue and historically why there was no consensus over its interpretation see Manuel E. F. Supervielle, "Article 31(b): Who Should Be Required to Give Warnings?" *Military Law Review* 123 (1989): 151–214.

21. Booth, "Sworn Statement," 14 May 1952, RT, pp. 1–8; "Testimony of MG Robert W. Grow, OAC of S, G-2," 30 Jan. 1952, Records of the Army Staff, pp. 1–10, RG 319, NA.

22. Grow Diary, 14 May 1952.

23. Robert I. Henderson, "Sworn Statement," 14 May 1952, RT, pp. 1–4.

24. Col. Gordon E. Dawson, "Compromise of Classified Information," 1 May 1952, RT.

25. Col. Gordon E. Dawson, "Sworn Statement," 14 May 1952, RT, pp. 1–10.

26. Grow Diary, 14 May 1952.

27. Col. Charles H. Ott, "Sworn Statement," 14 May 1952, RT, pp. 1–4.

28. Maj. Edward S. Robbins, "Sworn Statement," 14 May 1952, RT, pp. 1–7; "Statement of Major Edward S. Robbins, OAC of S, G-3, Department of the Army," 2 May 1952, RT, p. 1; Grow Diary, 13 July and 27 Sept. 1951.

29. "Request for Documents Pertaining to Case of United States v. Major General Robert W. Grow," 14 May 1952, and reply, "Headquarters Second Army, Fort George G. Meade, Maryland, 15 May 1952," RT, p. 1.

30. Dwight D. Eisenhower, *Crusade in Europe* (New York: Doubleday, 1952). Eisenhower's book was based on wartime notes, memoranda, and memories. A diary was maintained on instructions from Eisenhower by his naval aide Harry C. Butcher. Entitled "Diary, Office of the Commander-in-Chief," it was the substance of Butcher's book, *My Three Years with Eisenhower: The Personal Diary of Captain Harry C. Butcher, USNR* (New York: Simon and Schuster, 1946). Omar N. Bradley, *A Soldier's Story* (New York: Henry Holt, 1951), was based on a personal diary kept by Chester B. Hensen, who served as an aide to Bradley. Also see Mark C. Clark, *Calculated Risk* (New York: Harper and Brothers, 1950).

31. "Motion to Dismiss and Consolidate against Major General Robert W. Grow," 14 May 1952, RT, p. 11; Brief, "In the Matter of Court-Martial Charges

against Major General Robert W. Grow, USA: Memorandum in Support of Motion to Dismiss and Consolidate Charges against Major General Robert W. Grow," 14 May 1952, RT, pp. 1–11.

32. "Basic: Ltr. fr. Ind. Defense Counsel, Subj: Motion to Dismiss and Consolidate Charges against Major General Robert W. Grow, dtd. 14 May 1952," RT, p. 1.

33. "Motion to Suppress and Return Diary of Major General Robert W. Grow," 15 May 1952, RT, pp. 1–2; Brief, "In the Matter of Court-Martial Charges against Major General Robert W. Grow, USA," RT, pp. 1–11; Memorandum in Support of Motion to Suppress and Return Diary of Major General Robert Grow, 15 May 1952, RT, pp. 1–11.

34. CM 345745, Sherwood, 11 BR-JC 239, 249, 251, and cases cited; MCM, 1951, par. 152, pp. 287–89; Boyd v. United States, 116 U.S. 616 (1886); Weeks v. United States, 232 U.S. (1914), as referred to in Brief, RT.

35. UCMJ, Art. 31; MCM, 1951, supar. 150b, pp. 283–84.

36. In Boyd v. United States, 116 U.S. 616 (1886), the Supreme Court held that the compulsory production of a man's private papers, pursuant to a court order, to be used in evidence against him in a quasi-criminal proceeding is both the equivalent of an unreasonable search and seizure within the meaning of the Fourth Amendment and compelling the man to be a witness against himself within the meaning of the Fifth Amendment. In Gouled v. United States, 255 U.S. 298 (1921), the Court held that the admission of private papers, obtained through an unreasonable search and seizure and leading to a situation in which such an act compels the defendant to be a witness against himself was in violation of the Fifth Amendment. The Court emphasized the importance of these constitutional protections "as the very essence of constitutional liberty." In Weeks v. United States, 232 U.S. 383 (1914), the Supreme Court held that the order refusing the accused's application for the return of letters seized in his house in his absence and without his authority was a denial of his constitutional rights. The question of surrendering the diary because of what was induced by an official order or compulsion was referred to in United States v. Abrams et al., 230 Fed. 313 (DC, Vt., 1916). A customs agent entered the defendant's place of business and stated it would be better for him if he gave the agent what he wanted. A number of private papers were taken with a promise to return them at a later date. None of the papers were returned, and eventually they were used before a grand jury to obtain the indictment against the defendant and retained to be used against him at the trial. The court held that the delivery of the papers was "involuntary in the eye of the law." Cited in reference was the Supreme Court decision in Bram v. United States, 168 U.S. 532 (1897). In the Bram case, the Supreme Court pointed out that an involuntary confession such as one obtained "by the exertion of any improper influence" could not be received in evidence because of the prohibition in the Fifth Amendment.

37. "Customs of the Service," The Officer's Guide (Washington, D.C.: U.S. Government Printing Office, 1951), 236.

38. "Reply, Lt. Col. Robert E. Joseph, JAGC, Individual Counsel for General Grow, Headquarters Second Army, Fort George G. Meade, Maryland," 16 May 1952, RT, p. 1.

39. Brig. Gen. John Weckerling, "Sworn Statement," 16 May 1952, RT, pp. 1–2; Grow Diary, 16 May 1952.
40. Brig. Gen. James H. Phillips, "Sworn Statement," 16 May 1952, RT, pp. 1–5; Grow Diary, 16 May 1952.
41. Maj. Gen. Alexander R. Bolling, "Sworn Statement," 16 May 1952, RT, pp. 1–8.
42. "Report of investigation of classified security information," IG, 4 Feb. 1952, RT, p. 4; Grow Diary, 7 Feb. 1952; Bolling, "Sworn Statement," 16 May 1952, RT, p. 3.
43. "Court-martial Action against Major General Robert Grow," RG 319, NA.
44. AC of S, G-2, "Secret to McClure from Bolling," 22 Apr. 1952, and G-2, EUCOM, "Secret Bolling from McClure," 25 Apr. 1952, Office of the AC of S, G-2, (Intelligence), RT, p. 1.
45. Bolling, "Sworn Statement," 16 May 1952, RT, p. 2.
46. Memorandum for G-2, Grow to Bolling, 17 Mar. 1952, RT, pp. 1–2.
47. Agent's Daily Log, 6 Mar. 1952, CIA.
48. Lloyd Norman, "The Love-Hate Affair between the Pentagon and the Press," *Army*, Feb. 1980, 14–20.
49. Bolling, "Sworn Statement," 16 May 1952, RT, pp. 3–4.
50. Grow Diary, 16 May 1952.
51. Maj. Gen. Ernest M. Brannon, "Sworn Statement," 21 May 1952, RT, pp. 1–4.
52. Maj. Gen. Reuben E. Jenkins, "Sworn Statement," 21 May 1952, RT, pp. 1–4.
53. Lt. Gen. Maxwell D. Taylor, "Sworn Statement," 21 May 1952, RT, pp. 1–2; "Chronology of Events" (CS 201 Grow, Robert W., 1952), RG 319, NA, and Taylor Diary, Special Collections, Archives and History, National Defense University Library, 19 Apr. 1952.
54. Matthews's disposal, 22 May 1952, RT, pp. 1–4. Shortly after Bard signed the charge sheet, he requested that Henri return to the United States as a prosecution witness. On 15 May, Commander in Chief, Europe (CINCEUR), Heidelberg, advised the Pentagon that George Henri was himself under investigation, AR 600-443 (Separation of Homosexuals), and would not be released to Zone of Interior until the European investigation was completed. On 20 June the Pentagon was notified that Henri had tendered his resignation for the good of the service (AR 605-275) as a result of charges under AR 600-443. See Bard, "Return of Witness to the United States," 1952/274; Message: CINCEUR, Heidelberg, Germany, 1 May 1952; Message: DEPTAR WASH DC FOR AGPA-OS, 15 May 1952; Memorandum for General Brannon, 16 May 1952; Message: DEPTAR WASH DC FOR AGPA-OS, 20 June 1952, Department of the Army, Staff Communication Office.
55. "Request for TDY Orders to EUCOM," 23 May 1952, RT, p. 1.
56. *Manual for Courts-Martial, United States, 1951 (Effective 31 May 1951)*, (Washington, D.C.: U.S. Government Printing Office, 1951), 44–47.
57. 1 USCMA 342, 3 CMR 76, and 1 USCMA 255, 2 CMR 161 (1952). In *United States* v. *LaGrange et al.* and *United States* vs. *Clay,* the court stated that the Uniform

Code provided that when an officer was the accuser, the special court-martial must be convened by superior competent authority. This holding, according to Joseph and Stevens, applied equally to the similar provision in Article 22b of the Uniform Code, requiring that competent authority superior to the accuser must convene a general court-martial. As stated in both the *LaGrange* (1952) and *Clay* (1952) cases: "It was . . . necessary to provide a procedure whereby the accused could be brought to trial in an atmosphere free from coercion by one who could, directly or indirectly, influence the court." Grow's counsel, citing *United States* v. *Gordon*, 2 CMR 161, 1 USCMA 255 (1952), noted that Congress intended when it modernized the military judicial system to "narrow the commander's influence on the court by insulating members from any type of control by the commander's expressed direction or by his moral suasion or persuasion."

58. "Power of Commanding General, Second Army, to Appoint Court-Martial for Trial of Major General Robert W. Grow," 27 May 1952, RT, pp. 1–4.

59. IO and IDC/AIDC discussion, "Fort George G. Meade, Maryland, 29 May 1952, 1320 hours," RT, pp. 1–3.

60. Additional Charge Sheet, DD 458, 26 May 1952, RT, pp. 1–4.

61. G-2, "Compromise of Classified Information," 5 Feb. 1952; Dawson, "Sworn Statement," 14 May 1952, RT, pp. 1–10.

62. Col. Gordon E. Dawson, "Sworn Statement," 29 May 1952, RT, pp. 1–4; Major Nicholas A. Povendo, "Statement of Major Nicholas A. Povendo," and "Sworn Statement," 29 May 1952, RT, pp. 1–3.

63. Preliminary brief, "Memorandum in Support of Motion to Dismiss Charge and Specification against Major General Robert W. Grow, Re: In the Matter of Court-Martial Charges against Major General Robert W. Grow, USA," 29 May 1952, RT, pp. 1–2.

64. Investigation Officer's Report, DD 457, 31 May 1952, RT, pp. 1–2.

7. THE GENERAL COURT-MARTIAL

1. They were Lieutenant General John R. Hodge, Lieutenant General Thomas B. Larkin, Lieutenant General Harold R. Bull, Lieutenant General Joseph M. Swing, Lieutenant General William M. Hoge, Major General Clift Andrus, Major General Edwin P. Parker, Major General Orlando Ward, Major General James A. Lester, Major General Paul J. Mueller, Major General Leland Hobbs, and Major General Roscoe B. Woodruff.

2. The eight generals named were Lieutenant General John R. Hodge, Chief, Army Field Forces; Lieutenant General Harold R. Bull, Commandant, National War College; Lieutenant General William M. Hoge, CG, Fourth Army; Major General Orlando Ward, Chief, Military History; Major General James A. Lester, CG, San Francisco Port of Embarkation; Major General Clift Andrus, Deputy CG, Second Army; Major General Leland Hobbs, Deputy CG, First Army; and Major General Roscoe B. Woodruff, CG, XV Corps.

3. "Members for General Court-Martial," Office of the Chief of Staff, 5 June 1952 (CS 201 Grow, Robert W., 1952), Records of the Army Staff, RG 319, NA. Also

see "Army to Put General Grow on Trial on Diary That Fell to Communists," *New York Times*, 6 June 1952.

4. Demaree Bess, "Tomorrow They'll Be Famous," *Saturday Evening Post*, 14 June 1952, 25, 107, 111; "Court-Martial of Grow Opens Wednesday," *Washington Post*, 19 July 1952.

5. "Board of Officers," 18 June 1952, Office of the Adjutant General, RG 319, NA; "Retirement and Recall of Lieutenant General Harold R. Bull," 8 July 1952, Chief, Military Justice Division, RT; Memorandum for General Collins, 9 July 1952, Office of the Chief of Staff, RG 319, NA; "Members of General Court Martial," 14 July 1952, p. 1, Office Assistant Chief of Staff, G-1 Personnel, RG 319, NA.

6. Memorandum to Judge Advocate General, Department of the Army, Washington, D.C., from the Board of Governors, 6th Armored Division Association, 13 June 1952, RT, pp. 1–18.

7. Christopher M. Maher, "The Right to a Fair Trial in Criminal Cases Involving the Introduction of Classified Information," *Military Law Review* 120 (1988): 135–36.

8. Uniform Code of Military Justice, Article 46, *MCM, 1951*, paragraph 115, p. 188; Byrne, *Military Law*, 311–17.

9. "Request for Witnesses at the Trial of the Case of the United States v. Major General Robert W. Grow, USA," 2 July 1952, Hq, Second Army, RT; Verbatim Record of Trial, CM 355736, 23–29 July 1952, Grow Files, HF, p. 27.

10. "Request for Postponement of General Court-Martial Trial of Major General Robert W. Grow, United States Army," 22 July 1952, and "Request for Attendance of Witness at General Court-Martial Trial of Major General Robert W. Grow, United States Army," 22 July 1952, Hq, Second Army, RT, p. 1.

11. "Deposition in Grow Case," Office of the Department Counselor, Department of the Army, 21 July 1952 (CS 201 Grow, Robert W., 1952), pp. 1–2, Records of the Office of the Secretary of the Army, RG 335, NA.

12. Interrogatories and Deposition of Frank Pace, Jr., *United States* v. *Major General Robert Walker Grow*, 21 July 1952, RT, pp. 1–5.

13. Lt. Gen. Maxwell D. Taylor, "Stipulation," *United States* v. *Grow*, 21 July 1952, pp. 1–3, Office of the Chief of Staff, RG 319, NA; Taylor Diary, Special Collections, Archives and History, National Defense University, 18 and 21 July 1952.

14. "Basic: Ltr. Hq, 2nd Army, Subj: Request for Attendance of Witness at General Court-Martial Trial of Major General Robert W. Grow, United States Army, dtd 22 July 1952," 23 July 1952, Hq, Second Army, RT, p. 1.

15. Byrne, *Military Law*, 315.

16. The following notes of the general court-martial are taken from three sources unless otherwise noted: Verbatim Record of Trial, Prosecution Exhibits, Defense Exhibits and Appellate Exhibits, CM 355736; "Review of the Judge Advocate," 15 Aug. 1952, RT; Board of Review, *United States* v. *Grow*, 11 CMR 77, Grow Files, HF.

17. *United States* v. *LaGrange et al.* (CMA No. 313), 3 CMR 76 (1952), and *US Army 1954 Cumulative Pocket Part, MCM, 1951*, p. 28–33.

18. Memorandum C of S, "General Grow's Court-martial," 24 July 1952 (CS 201 Grow, Robert W., 1952), Records of Army Staff, RG 319, NA.

19. See *Cantrell v. United States,* 15 Fed (2d Series), and *Schroyer* 28 BR 75 (1944); *Kremerer,* 28 BR 393 (1944); *Davis* v. *United States,* 328 U.S. (1946), in Verbatim Record of Trial, pp. 93-94.

20. Brig. Gen. Fay B. Prickett, interview with author, 5 Apr. 1979. General Prickett also stated, "Even today my conscience bothers me." On 24 April 1979, however, I received a letter from Prickett changing his statement given on 5 April. He wrote: "Gen. Taylor *asked* me if I could obtain the Diary." Whereas on 5 April Prickett had very good recall regarding the Grow episode, he now pleaded no recall, as he had in July 1952.

21. Demaree Bess, "Tomorrow They'll Be Famous," *Saturday Evening Post,* 14 June 1952, and "The Truth about General Grow's Moscow Diary," ibid., 27 Sept. 1952. Also see Verbatim Record of Trial, pp. 205-6.

22. Verbatim Record of Trial, 28 July 1952, pp. 204-5; MG Alexander R. Bolling, "Sworn Statement," 16 May 1952, RT; Agent's Daily Log, 6 Mar. 1952, CIA; Secret, Bolling from McClure, 25 Apr. 1952, AG T/587T-5, RG 319, NA.

23. U.S. Army Board of Review, CM 355736, p. 51; RT, pp. 241-53.

24. "Reds Propagandize Excerpts. Secrecy Is Clamped on Trial of Grow in Stolen Diary Case," 24 July 1952, and "Grow Diary Classified 'Top Secret'," 25 July 1952, *Washington Post;* "Grow Court-Martial Is Started in Secret," *New York Times,* 24 July 1952; Harold B. Hinton, "Army Convicts Gen. Grow for Misusing Secret Data," ibid., 30 July 1952.

25. Austin Stevens, "Grow Diary Held Falsified by Reds. Army Releases Excerpts to Show Distortions—Denies He Advocated War Now," *New York Times,* 31 July 1952.

26. "Subject: Request for Witnesses at the Trial of the Case of the United States v. Major General Robert W. Grow, Hq, Second Army," 2 July 1952, RT, p. 1.

CONCLUSION

1. 61 U.S. (20 How.) 65 (1858) in Edward S. Corwin, ed., *The Constitution of the United States of America: Analysis and Interpretation* (Washington, D.C.: U.S. Government Printing Office, 1964), 333. For a short recent excellent history of the role the military plays in the U.S. constitutional system see Walter T. Cox III, "The Army, the Courts, and the Constitution: The Evolution of Military Justice," *Military Law Review* 118 (1987): 1-30.

2. The most ambitious, critical work, though biased, on the history of the agency theory of separatism and command control is Luther C. West, *They Call It Justice: Command Influence and the Court-Martial System* (New York: Viking, 1977), and West, "A History of Command Influence on the Military Judicial System," *UCLA Law Review* 18 (1970): 1-156. West condemns the military legal system and the efforts of military commanders to persist in controlling every aspect of the court-martial process. In addition, see Edward F. Sherman, "The Civilianization of Military Law," *Maine Law Review* 22 (1970): 1-103. Sherman, though more restrained than West, deals with the dichotomy of civilian versus military law. Like West, he finds fault— nurtured in historical tradition—with American military law and its lack of limitation

on command control. Moreover, Sherman argues, the movement for civilianization (bringing military law under the scope of judicial article III) has achieved limited success only in the twentieth century. Also see Sherman, "Military Justice without Military Control," *Yale Law Review* 22 (1973): 1398–1425. Here he refers to the system as an inferior form of criminal justice. Both authors wrote their indictments of the military justice system during the Vietnam era, when legal and moral issues were heightened by the passions and recriminations arising out of America's involvement in an unpopular conflict. One of the most passionate articles condemning the system during the Vietnam era is "U.S. Military Justice on Trial," *Newsweek,* 31 Aug. 1970, 18–23. For contrasting opinions see Homer E. Moyer, Jr., "Procedural Rights of the Military Accused: Advantages over a Civilian Defendant," *Maine Law Review* 22 (1970): 105–40, and Joseph Bishop, Jr., *Justice under Fire: A Study of Military Law* (New York: Charterhouse, 1974). A lengthy rebuttal of West's book is Brian R. Price's review in *Military Law Review* 78 (1978): 184–95. Other interesting articles on command influence are Arthur E. Farmer and Richard H. Wels, "Command Control—or Military Justice?" *New York University Law Quarterly Review* 24 (1949): 263–82, and Frank E. Barker, "Military Law—A Separate System of Jurisprudence," *University of Cincinnati Law Review* 36 (1967): 223–37. Barker maintained that separate constitutional jurisdiction is not an ideal state of total justice in a democracy. A more recent look at command influence is Jonathan P. Tomes, "Illegal Command Influence: The Unnecessary Evil," *Army,* Apr. 1987, 26–29. For an excellent but short chronological account see Robert O. Rollman, "Of Crimes, Courts-Martial and Punishment—A Short History of Military Justice," *USAF JAG Law Review* 11 (1969): 212–22.

3. Samuel T. Ansell, "Some Reforms in Our System of Military Justice," *Yale Law Journal* 32 (1922): 146.

4. For an excellent legal discussion of the dispute, see Terry W. Brown, "The Crowder-Ansell Dispute: The Emergence of General Samuel T. Ansell," *Military Law Review* 35 (1967): 1–45. Brown asserted that Ansell's reforms, as proposed to Congress in 1919 as the Chamberlain Bill, if passed, would have closely paralleled, if not exceeded, the 1950 Uniform Code of Military Justice. An apologist for Crowder is David A. Lockmiller, *Enoch H. Crowder: Soldier, Lawyer and Statesman* (Columbia: Univ. of Missouri Studies, 1955), 199–216. For a recent discussion on the Ansell-Crowder controversy see Frederick Bernays Wiener, "The Seamy Side of the World War I Court-Martial Controversy," *Military Law Review* 123 (1989): 109–28. Wiener argues that the debate had not been thoroughly examined and recounted. He defends Crowder's position.

5. As quoted in Sherman, "Civilization of Military Law," 18–19.

6. George Gleason Bogert, "Courts-Martial: Criticism and Proposed Reforms," *Cornell Law Quarterly* 5 (1919): 15.

7. Samuel T. Ansell, "Military Justice," *Cornell Law Quarterly* 5 (1919): 1–17. This article is one of the most succinct denunciations of military justice published in U.S. military and legal literature.

8. Bogert, "Courts-Martial," 18–47.

9. John H. Wigmore, "Address," *Maryland State Bar Association Transactions* 24 (1919): 183, 188.

10. Howard Thayer Kingsbury, "Courts-Martial and Military Justice," *National Service with the International Military Digest* 5 (1919): 280–81. Other authors who supported Crowder and the agency theory are Frederic Gilbert Bauer, "The Court-Martial Controversy and the New Articles of War," *Massachusetts Law Quarterly* 6 (1920–21): 61–85; Bogert, "Courts-Martial," 18–47; Harvey C. Carbaugh, "Separateness of Military and Civil Jurisdiction," *Journal of Criminal Law and Criminology* 9 (1918–19): 571–88; Ridby McLean, "A Historical Sketch of Military Law," *Journal of Criminal Law and Criminology* 8 (1917–19): 27–32; William C. Rigby, "Military Penal Law: A Brief Survey of the 1920 Revision of the Articles of War," *Journal of Criminal Law and Criminology* 12 (1921–22): 84–90; Max Schoetz, Jr., "Military Law," *Marquette Law Review* 3 (1918–19): 26–31; John Henry Wigmore, "Lessons from Military Justice," *Journal of the American Judicature Society* 4 (1921): 151–80.

11. Edmund M. Morgan, "The Existing Court-Martial System and the Ansell Army Articles," *Yale Law Journal* 29 (1919–20): 53–67.

12. West, "History of Command Influence," p. 40.

13. The dichotomy that developed between civilian and military law has been and still is the subject of controversy. Gordon D. Henderson, "Court-Martial and the Constitution: The Original Understanding," *Harvard Law Review* 71 (1957): 293–324, argued that the Bill of Rights was intended by the Framers to apply to the military. The opposite view appears in Frederick Bernays Wiener, "Courts-Martial and the Bill of Rights: The Original Practice I and II," *Harvard Law Review* 72 (1958): 1–49, 266–304. Wiener argued that the Framers did not intend the military to be subjected to constitutional protection but to be governed exclusively by the legislative and executive branches. The Virginia Bill of Rights (1776), which had a considerable impact on the Constitution and its first ten amendments, outlined in Section 8, in part, "that in all cases the military should be under strict subordination to, and governed by, the civil power." No doubt the Antifederalists did not expect military law to develop and exist as an instrument to augment military power, which in turn could be used to support coercion. James Madison in support of the Constitution commented: "A standing force . . . is dangerous, at the same time that it may be a necessary provision." He goes on to say, "a wise nation . . . will exert all its prudence in diminishing both the necessity and the danger of resorting to one [standing force], which may be inauspicious to its liberties." See Alexander Hamilton, James Madison, and John Jay, *The Federalist Papers* (New York: Mentor Books, 1961), 257–58. Neither the Antifederalists nor the Federalists solved the dichotomy of civilian and military law, thus resulting in future conflict, vagueness, and much conjecture. In 1962, Chief Justice Earl Warren, speaking off the bench and taking note of the size of the armed forces, stated: "Military law has such a sweeping capacity for affecting the lives of our citizens, the wisdom of treating the military establishment as an enclave beyond the reach of the civilian courts almost inevitably is drawn into question" ("The Bill of Rights and the Military," *New York University Law Review* 37 [1962]: 187–88). In *Justice under Fire*, Bishop maintained that soldiers have constitutional rights but that it would be precarious to exact the precise extent of those rights (113–73, esp. 122).

14. Robert J. White, "The Uniform Code of Military Justice—Its Promise and Performance: The Background and the Problem," *St. John's Law Review* 35 (1961):

200–201. White's article was part of a symposium entitled "The Uniform Code of Military Justice—Its Promise and Performance (The First Decade: 1951–1961)."

15. "Army to Overhaul Its Courts-Martial," *New York Times*, 26 Mar. 1946. Also see Leonard M. Wallstein, Jr., "The Revision of the Army Court-Martial System," *Columbia Law Review* 48 (1948): 219–36.

16. Samuel Morgan, "Army Courts-Martial: The Double Standard," *Atlantic Monthly* 178 (Dec. 1946): 97–102. Morgan, a Chicago attorney who served in the Judge Advocate General's Department during the war, believed the American public was not aware of the defects in the administration of military justice.

17. Felix E. Larkin, "Professor Edmund M. Morgan and the Drafting of the Uniform Code," *Military Law Review* 28 (1965): 12–13. The papers of Professor Morgan on the Uniform Code of Military Justice are located in the Treasure Room, Harvard Law School.

18. Sherman, "Civilianization of Military Law," 36.

19. Eisenhower speech, quoted ibid., 35. Also see White, "Uniform Code of Military Justice," 208, and Armed Service Committee, Senate, *Hearings before a Subcommittee . . . on S.857 and H.R. 4080*, 81st Cong., 1st sess. (1949).

20. West, "History of Command Influence," 80–81, 84–85.

21. See Farmer and Wels, "Command Control," 263–82. For a criticism of the military court by Keeffe, see "Universal Military Training with or without Reform of Courts-Martial?" *Cornell Law Quarterly* 33 (1948), and "Drumhead Justice: A Look at Our Military Courts," *Reader's Digest*, Aug. 1951, 39–44. "Armed Services Code," *New York Times*, 8 May 1950, 22; "Can Military Trials Be Fair? Command Influence Over Courts-Martial," editorial, *Stanford Law Review* 2 (1950): 547–58. Also see Notes, "The Proposed Uniform Code of Military Justice," *Harvard Law Review* 62 (1949): 1377–87.

22. Other changes or reforms were in statements of crimes and punishments, membership and selection of the court, judicial functions, right to be represented by a lawyer, and the nature of the trial. The latter provided a more judicial proceeding for a general court-martial by requiring the law officer and counsel to be lawyers. See Sherman, "Civilianization of Military Law," 38–46.

23. For a discussion of Article 32, see William A. Murphy, "The Formal Pretrial Investigation," *Military Law Review* 11–12 (1961): 1–47. The noted defense counsel F. Lee Bailey commented that the pretrial investigation was the most notable inclusion in the Uniform Code (*For the Defense* [New York: Atheneum, 1975], 35). For criticism of Article 32 as being redundant, expensive, and cumbersome see James W. Swanson, "The Article 32 Right of an Accused to Pre-trial Cross-examination of the Witness Against Him 'if they are available'," *Air Force Review* 24 (1984): 246–59.

24. Chester Ward, "UCMJ—Does It Work?" *Vanderbilt Law Review* 6 (1953): 224; Moyer, "Procedural Rights of the Military Accused." For a contemporary assessment of the impact of the new statute see Ernest L. Langley, "Military Justice and the Constitution—Improvements Offered by the New Uniform Code of Military Justice," *Texas Law Review* 29 (1951): 71–92. An article designed to provide the civilian attorney with an insight into the new military code is Joseph B. Kelly, "Uniform Code and the Evolution of Military Law," *University of Cincinnati Law Review* 22 (1953):

343–69. Kelly saw considerable improvement in the 1951 *MCM* and the new code as compared to the 1921 and 1949 *MCM* and the Articles of War. A more recent defense of the military justice system is Jack B. Zimmermann, "Civilian v. Military Justice: A Comparison of Defendants' Rights," *Trial,* Oct. 1981, 34–40, 81–83. Also see Bishop's excellent *Justice under Fire.* He argues that U.S. military justice is a good system designed to meet the needs of the military; however, he recommends a direct path of appeal from the civilian Court of Military Appeals to the U.S. Supreme Court, thus bringing military law and justice under Article III of the Constitution. This was very similar to Sherman's argument in "The Civilianization of Military Law."

25. In April 1775 the Massachusetts Articles of War were adopted. These articles were influenced by the military code of Gustavus Adolphus, which with some modifications eventually became the British Articles of War in 1765. On 30 June 1775, a five-man committee, which included George Washington, adopted the existing British articles. See Rollman, "Of Crimes, Courts-Martial and Punishment," 215, and William Winthrop, *Military Law and Precedents,* 2d ed. (Washington, D.C.: U.S. Government Printing Office, 1920), 21–22, App. VIII, 947–52. Winthrop's work, first published late in the nineteenth century, was the standard text on military law and justice and a major source on precedents. See William C. Mott, John E. Hartnett, Jr., and Kenneth B. Morton, "A Survey of the Literature of Military Law: A Selective Bibliography," *Vanderbilt Law Review* 6 (1953): 337. Also see George S. Prugh, Jr., "Colonel William Winthrop: The Tradition of the Military Lawyer," *American Bar Association Journal* 42 (1956): 126–29, 188–91; Eugene R. Fidell, "The Culture of Change in Military Law," *Military Law Review* 126 (1989): 125–32.

26. Mandeville Mullally, Jr., "Military Justice: The Uniform Code in Action," *Columbia Law Review* 53 (1953): 5. An article questioning "equal justice under the law" and the unrestrained judicial power given to commanding officers is Delmar Karlen, "The Personal Factors in Military Justice," *Wisconsin Law Review* (1946).

27. Grow to Gerald D. Morgan (Special Counsel for the President), 12 July 1957, Grow Files, HF.

28. "Review of the Staff Judge Advocate," Hq, Second Army, 15 Aug. 1952, RT, p. 40.

29. Sherman, "Civilianization of Military Law," 48.

30. *United States* v. *Grow* (CM 355736), 11 CMR 77, p. 4.

31. Bess, "The Truth about General Grow's Moscow Diary," 22–23, 47–48, 52–59. Also see Bess, "Tomorrow They'll Be Famous," 111.

32. Gramont, *Secret War,* 445–49; Book review, *New York Herald Tribune,* 20 May 1962, and Tsybov and Chistyakov, *Front Taynoy Voyny,* CIA, pp. 89–90. See the edited translation, *The Secret War Front,* prepared by the Translation Division, Foreign Technology Division, Wright-Patterson Air Force Base, Dayton, Ohio.

33. Douglas Kinnard, *The War Managers* (Wayne, N.J.: Avery Publishing Group, 1985), 17, 19, 21, 88, 92. Also see Richard A. Gabriel and Paul L. Savage, *Crisis in Command: Mismanagement in the Army* (New York: Hill and Wang, 1978); and William L. Hauser, *America's Army in Crisis: A Study in Civil-Military Relations* (Baltimore: Johns Hopkins Univ. Press, 1973). Gabriel and Savage argue that since World War II the officer corps has evolved into a society of individual entrepreneurs, rather than

adhering to the traditional military corporate society based on honor, duty, cohesion, and selflessness. Their Bibliographical Essay provides an excellent list of useful sources. Hauser argues that the army was having difficulties in adjusting to the economic, social, political, and intellectual changes brought about by modern America and its industrial society of mass production and consumption. Hauser also criticizes the military justice system. He briefly discusses the vices of command influence which came under significant attack in 1971 (104–12). Like Gabriel and Savage, Hauser chides the notion of careerism (173–86). Both books provide ample examples of the problem of careerism.

34. Taylor to author, 14 Jan. 1977 and 21 Mar. 1979; Interview by author with Taylor, 5 Apr. 1979; Blair, *Ridgway's Paratroopers*, 52–53. Other assessments of Taylor can be found in Mark Perry, *Four Stars: The Inside Story of the Forty-Year Battle between the Joint Chiefs of Staff and America's Civilian Leaders* (Boston: Houghton Mifflin, 1989), 111–16, 118. Perry cites an interesting comment made by one of Taylor's antagonists, the distinguished diplomat and businessman W. Averell Harriman, who claimed that Taylor had not executed a right decision since World War II when he wanted to send an airborne division into Rome (196 n). Also see David Halberstam, *The Best and the Brightest* (New York: Random House, 1972), 162–64, 179–80, 200, 204–5, 489, 566–67. For a tribute to Taylor see John M. Taylor, *General Maxwell Taylor: The Sword and the Pen* (New York: Doubleday, 1989). This eulogy by his son contains no reference to Taylor's seven-month involvement in the Grow case. Only a few pages deal with Taylor's role as a deputy chief of staff for operations and administration (167–71).

35. Collins to author, 9 Mar. 1976, and 12 Mar. 1979; Collins, interview with author, 5 Apr. 1979.

36. One function of the appellate court is to review "all cases in which the sentence, as affirmed by a Court of Military Review, affects a general or flag officer."

37. William T. Generous, Jr., *Sword and Scales: The Development of the Uniform Code of Military Justice* (Port Washington, N.Y.: Kennikat Press, 1973), 60–63, 213; Robert Emmett Quinn, "The United States Court of Military Appeals and Military Due Process," *St. John's Law Review* 35 (1961): 227, and West, "History of Command Influence," 92–94.

38. For a discussion of military due process see Seymour W. Wurfel, " 'Military Due Process': What is It?" *Vanderbilt Law Review* 6 (1953): 251–87.

39. *United States* v. *Marsh*, 11 CMR 48, 3 USCMA 48 (1953); Frank Fedele, "The Evolution of the Court-Martial System and the Role of the United States Court of Military Appeals in Military Law" (J.S.D. dissertation, George Washington Univ. Law School, 1954), 493. See especially the section "As Applied to Command Control," 245–59; *United States* v. *Du Bay*, 37 CMR 411, 17 USCMA 147 (1967). For an interesting article on the Court of Military Appeals see Roger M. Currier and Irvin M. Kent, "The Boards of Review of the Armed Services," *Vanderbilt Law Review* 6 (1953): 241–50.

40. The analysis of the appeal is based on *Decision of the United States Court of Military Appeals*, vol. 3, Oct. Term 1952–53 (Rochester: Lawyers Co-operative Publishing Company) and *Digest of Opinions: The Judge Advocates General of the Armed Forces,*

vol. 3, no. 1, July, Sept. 1953 (Rochester: Lawyers Co-operative Publishing Company), Re: *United States* v. *Grow,* 3 USCMA 77, 11 CMR 77. Also see "Grow's Conviction in Diary Case Upheld by Military Appeals Court," *New York Times,* 18 July 1953.

41. Article of War 96 was referred to as a reference because in it the failure to classify military information, as noted in the additional charge, occurred before the effective date of the Uniform Code. This caused some confusion during the pretrial investigation, and defense counsel would argue that the charge was improperly designated.

42. Maj. Gen. Robert W. Grow, "Basis for new trial—Maj. Gen. R. W. Grow," 18 July 1953, Grow Files, HF.

43. Maj. Gen. Robert W. Grow, "Memorandum for Colonel Belieu," 1 Aug. 1955, Grow Files; interview by author with Grow 18, 19 Mar. 1979, and with Forrest Herbert, 14 May 1980. The latter was a past president of the 6th Armored Division Association and a close confidant of General Grow.

44. Grow to Eisenhower, 12 July 1957, Grow Files, HF.

45. Jones to Grow, 30 July 1957, Grow to Eisenhower, 2 July 1958; Morgan to Grow, 17 July 1958, Grow Files, HF.

46. Ansell, "Military Justice," 1–17; Morgan, "The Existing Court-Martial System," 65–66.

47. Tomes, "Illegal Command Influence," 26–29.

48. Gabriel and Savage, *Crisis in Command,* 18, 212 n. 4. For a role model for the military adoption of modern procedures and structure for war management see Forrest C. Pogue, *George C. Marshall: Organizer of Victory, 1943–1945* (New York: Viking, 1973), passim, and James E. Hewes, Jr., *From Root to McNamara: Army Organization and Administration, 1900–1963* (Washington, D.C.: U.S. Government Printing Office, 1975), 300.

49. Hewes, *From Root to McNamara,* 126–28. Hewes noted in his bibliography the influence of Alfred Dupont Chandler, Jr., whose pioneering studies on the development of modern industrial management provided the framework for his study on army organization and administration. Also see H. Struve Hensel, "Changes Inside the Pentagon," *Harvard Business Review,* Jan.–Feb. 1954, 98–108, and Alice C. Cole, Alfred Goldberg, Samuel A. Tucker, and Rudolph A. Winnacker, eds., *The Department of Defense: Documents on Establishment and Organization, 1944–1978* (Washington, D.C.: U.S. Government Printing Office, 1978), esp. 3:3, "The Rockefeller Committee—11 Feb.–11 Apr. 53," 126–49.

50. J. Lawton Collins, "Answers to Questions by the Rockefeller Committee," 27 Mar. 1952, Records of the Army Staff, RG 319, NA; B. H. Liddell Hart, *Why Don't We Learn from History?* (New York: Hawthorn Books, 1971), 30–31; Leonard M. Wallstein, Jr., "The Revision of the Army Court-Martial System," *Columbia Law Review* 48 (1948): 223–24, n. 23.

51. Taylor, *Swords and Plowshares,* 132–34.

52. Comptroller General of the United States, *Military Jury System Needs Safeguards Found in Civilian Federal Courts* (Washington, D.C.: U.S. Government Printing Office, 1977), 3–5; Tomes, "Illegal Command Influence," 26–29.

53. Joseph B. Kelly, "Uniform Code and the Evolution of Military Law," *University of Cincinnati Law Review* 22 (1953): 369; Cox, "The Army, the Courts, and the Constitution," 30.

54. See Art. 67(h) (1–2) (Review by the Court of Military Appeals), *Uniform Code of Military Justice, 1984*, pp. A2–22. The Military Justice Act of 1983, Public Law 98-209, was a landmark statute (1393) because it permitted for the first time direct petitions to the Supreme Court.

ESSAY ON SOURCES

B ECAUSE THE MAJORITY of primary sources associated with the Grow case were not in archives, it was necessary to go to the various agencies involved. Under the Freedom of Information Act, I was able to solicit varying degrees of action from the concerned agencies. Otherwise the task could have become a demonstration in futility. Most helpful were "How to Take the New 1974 Freedom of Information Act," *AHA Newsletter,* Oct. 1975, and 5 U.S.C. 552 et seq., the Freedom of Information Act. For a follow-up on the American Historical Association recommendations see "Kirkendall Testifies before Senate," *AHA Newsletter,* May 1980. This testimony dealt with provisions of the Freedom of Information Act that would exempt the CIA. In addition, the U.S. Department of Justice, *Attorney General's Memorandum on the 1974 Amendments to the Freedom of Information Act* (Feb. 1975), and the Bureau of Public Affairs, Department of State, *Gist: Freedom of Information* (Nov. 1978), were most valuable. Finally, the Department of the Army, *Program for Unofficial Historical Research in Classified Army Records,* Memorandum No. 340-3 (26 July 1976), was helpful in prescribing policies and procedures for the army's program enabling American citizens to engage in unofficial historical research in classified army records. The problems of using the Freedom of Information Act and possible solutions are discussed by Paul L. Luedtke, "Open Government and Military Justice," *Military Law Review* 87 (1980): 7–72.

Beginning late in 1975, over a six-year period, hundreds of documents were declassified. By far the most cooperative and accommodating was the Department of the Army, especially the Intelligence and Security Command, the Office of the Adjutant General and the Adjutant General Center, and the Office of the Judge Advocate General. The Intelligence and Security Command (IACSF), located at Fort George G. Meade, Maryland, provided numerous documents dealing with the 66th CIC Detachment investigation in EUCOM and the seven interim reports submitted to the Office of the Assistant Chief of Staff, G-2 (Intelligence). The Adjutant General's Records Management Division and the Criminal Law Division, Office of the Judge Advocate General, located in the Pentagon, furnished the Record of the Trial (RT) (mainly composed of documents leading up to the pretrial investigation), and the "Review of the Staff Judge Advocate," Second Army. Though the Record of Trial (RT) contained an abundance of documents, they were not all seen by Grow or his defense counsel. The numerous sworn statements were also located in the RT. There was very little documentation on the general court-martial, and noticeably missing were the trial transcripts. The clerk of court, United States Army Judiciary, is the official custodian of all general court-martial records. As of January 1980, however, there was no record of Grow's trial transcripts; the clerk of court had been unable to locate them. Even a search at the Washington National Records Center met with negative results. Apparently later, the U.S. Army Judiciary was finally able to locate and consolidate approximately fifteen hundred pages of material relating to the Grow court-martial. These documents are now available for review by appointment at the NASSIF Building, Falls Church, Virginia. The Judge Advocate General's School in Charlottesville, Virginia, and the editor of the *Army Lawyer* provided information on various army regulations applicable to the Grow episode. Other army agencies that provided helpful information and direction were the Office of the Secretary of the Army, Office of the Chief of Public Information, Office of the Deputy Chief of Staff of Operations and Plans, Office of the Assistant Chief of Staff for Intelligence (Security Division), the Chief of Military History and the Center of Military History, and the United States Audiovisual Center.

The trial transcripts, Verbatim Record of Trial: *United States* v. *Grow* (CM 355736), 11 CMR 77, and CMA No. 2050, were furnished by General Grow. Included were Defense Exhibits, Prosecution Exhibits, and Appellate Exhibits. In addition, he permitted complete examination of his diaries for the years 1946 through 1952 and all correspondence and documents associated with the court-martial and subsequent efforts at appeal. At no time did he attempt to interpret or interfere in the research efforts. Furthermore, Grow turned over correspondence he later received from Paul Collonia, an employee of the Victory Guest House at the time the diary was compromised. All the above documents are located in the Grow Files, which are in the possession of the author, except the diaries, which are now held by General Grow's grandson, Thomas, at Fort Bragg, North Carolina.

The Reference Branch, General Archives Division, National Archives and Record Service, Washington, D.C., was helpful and provided some documentation. Of importance were the Records of the Army Staff (CS 201

Grow, Robert W., 1952) and "Answers to Questions by Rockefeller Committee," Record Group 319. The most valuable document was "Chronology of Events" prepared by the army staff in 1952. In addition, the records of the Office of the Secretary of the Army, Record Group 335, were most helpful. Also, Historical Section, Army Ground Forces, 1946, Record Group 407, provided supportive material on Grow's reputation as a combat commander.

General Maxwell D. Taylor's diary–appointment book for 1952 is located in the Special Collections, Archives and History, National Defense University Library, Fort Lesley McNair, Washington. Only four entries mention the Grow case, but other entries identify meetings with his management group. The bulk of General Taylor's collection begins when he became army chief of staff.

The Bureau of Administration, Department of State, provided a few documents pertaining to diplomatic involvement in the Grow case, including a copy of Richard Squires's *Auf dem Kriegspfad*. Unfortunately, hours searching the Central Foreign Policy Files, the retired files of the legal adviser, the Bureau of European Affairs, and the post files of Berlin, Bonn, and Frankfurt failed to turn up information on Gerhard Poss and Soviet penetration of the U.S. High Commissioner for Germany (HICOG). Further examination of the Office of Security George Wolfe file (retired FSO) and a file in the name of HICOG, Berlin, Attempted Penetration of Political Affairs Division, failed to disclose any references to Margaret and Gerhard Poss and Glenn C. Wolfe (executive director of HICOG). Apparently, the Department of State was kept in the dark regarding the army's CIC investigation in Europe. It appeared that the managers of the Grow case wished to keep the episode in-house. *Foreign Relations of the United States, 1946 to 1949*, were valuable in assessing Grow's activities in Iran and the Soviet government's reaction.

The most difficult to obtain access to was the Central Intelligence Agency. Its action, though initially responsive, was the most time-consuming and raised serious doubts about its ability accurately to summarize the substance of various documents requested. For example, the important draft copy "Plan for Propaganda Counter-Offensive re: the Diary of General Grow" was not located. The reason why this document was not used was never fully explained. The documents that were released after the initial Freedom of Information Act request were so sanitized and full of cryptonyms that an appeal was made on 20 August 1976. The result of this appeal was not satisfactory, and late in 1980 Civil Action, *George F. Hofmann* v. *United States Central Agency, et al.* (No. 80-1792), was prepared and shortly filed in the U.S. District Court for the District of Columbia. On 10 September 1981, the court filed a Memorandum Opinion and Order granting the government's motion for summary judgment and dismissing the case. Though the CIA identified and explained the reasons for sanitizing the documents that were challenged during the arguments, material issues of fact raised earlier were never resolved. Thus the bureaucratic intrigues between the CIA and the army staff were never completely resolved. At no time did I knowingly attempt to acquire information that would compromise the security of the United States or its agents. For an interesting article on this problem see Arnold H. Lubasch, "Federal Judge Doubts Good Faith of Agencies in Disclosure Dispute," *New York Times,* 20 Oct. 1981. The CIA documents released included excerpts from the Agent's Daily Log, 5 March through April 1952 (released with concurrence of the Department of the Army); Foreign Broadcast Information Service releases, 14 March through 21 April 1952; a few interoffice memorandums; and an excerpt and comments from Thomas Whiteside's *Agent in Place.*

Interviews and correspondence with the participants in the Grow episode were rewarding and at the same time disappointing. Many refused to respond, and those who did offered a convenient "no recall." The most adamant were those who formed around the Taylor-Bolling clique. The following contributed in some way: Honorable Frank Pace, Jr., General Maxwell D. Taylor (Ret.), General J. Lawton Collins (Ret.), Major General Ernest M. Brannon (Ret.), and Brig. General Fay B. Prickett (Ret.).

Finally, the most important reference sources were Donald G. Nieman, "Military Law, Martial Law, and Military Government," in Robin Higham and Donald J. Mrozek, eds., *A Guide to the Sources of United States Military History: Supplement I* (Hamden, Conn.: Archon Books, 1981); the bibliography in William T. Generous, Jr., *Swords and Scales: The Development of the Uniform Code of Military Justice* (Port Washington, N.Y.: Kennikat Press, 1973); and William C. Mott, John E. Harnett, Jr., and Kenneth B. Morton, "A Survey of the Literature of Military Law: A Selective Bibliography," *Vanderbilt Law Review* 6 (1953): 333–69. Edward M. Byrne, *Military Law,* 3d ed. (Annapolis: Naval Institute Press, 1981), provides an excellent overview of military law and justice, not only for attorneys but also for civilians who need a basic reference work. Finally, the source that provides a wealth of excellent information on U.S. courts-martial and the appeals process is Frank Fedele's outstanding study "The Evolution of the Court-Martial System and the Role of the United States Court of Military Appeals in Military Law" (J.S.D. dissertation, George Washington University Law School, 1954).

BIBLIOGRAPHY

ARTICLES—LEGAL AND MAGAZINE

Ansell, Samuel T. "Military Justice." *Cornell Law Quarterly* 5 (1919): 1–17.
———— . "Some Reforms in Our System of Military Justice." *Yale Law Journal* 32 (1922): 146–55.
Antieau, Chester J. "Courts-Martial and the Constitution." *Marquette Law Review* 33 (1949): 25–36.
Armstrong, Walter P., Jr. "Protection of the Accused's Rights in Courts-Martial." *Mississippi Law Journal* 16 (1944): 175–80.
Aycock, William B. "The Court of Military Appeals—the First Year." *North Carolina Law Review* 31 (1952): 1–45.
———— . "Professor Morgan and the Drafting of the Manual for Courts-Martial." *Military Law Review* 23 (Apr. 1965): 14–15.
Barker, Frank E. "Military Law—A Separate System of Jurisprudence." *University of Cincinnati Law Review* 36 (1967): 223–37.
Bauer, Frederic Gilbert. "The Court-Martial Controversy and the New Articles of War." *Massachusetts Law Quarterly* 6 (1920–21): 61–86.
Bess, Demaree. "Tomorrow They'll Be Famous." *Saturday Evening Post,* 14 June 1952, 24–25, 107, 111.
———— . "The Truth about General Grow's Moscow Diary." *Saturday Evening Post,* 27 Sept. 1952, 22–23, 47–48, 52, 55, 57–58.
Bishop, Joseph W., Jr. "Perspective: The Case for Military Justice." *Military Law Review* 62 (Fall 1973): 215–24.
Bogert, George Gleason. "Courts-Martial: Criticisms and Proposed Reforms." *Cornell Law Quarterly* 5 (1919): 18–47.
Bower, Joseph L. "Business and Battles: Lessons from Defeat." *Harvard Business Review* (July–Aug. 1990): 48–53.
Bower, Martha Huntley. "Unlawful Command Influence: Preserving the Delicate Balance." *Air Force Law Review* 28 (1988): 65–96.
Brosman, Paul W. "The Court: Freer Than Most." *Vanderbilt Law Review* 6 (1953): 48–53.

————. "The Uniform Code of Military Justice: Some Problems and Opportunities." *Oklahoma Bar Association Journal* 25 (1954): 1605–10.

Brown, Terry W. "The Crowder-Ansell Dispute: The Emergence of General Samuel T. Ansell." *Military Law Review* 35 (Jan. 1967): 1–45.

Bruce, Andrew A. "Double Jeopardy and the Power of Review in Court-Martial Proceedings." *Minnesota Law Review* 3 (1918–19): 484–509.

Butts, A. B. "The Uniform Code of Military Justice." *Mississippi Law Journal* 22 (1951): 203–11.

"Can Military Trials Be Fair? Command Influence over Courts-Martial." Editorial, *Stanford Law Review* 2 (1950): 547–58.

Carbaugh, Harvey C. "Separateness of Military and Civil Jurisdiction—A Brief." *Journal of Criminal Law and Criminology* 9 (1918–19): 571–88.

Cardozo, Benjamin N. "A Ministry of Justice." *Harvard Law Review* 35 (1921): 113–26.

"The Case of the Careless General's Diary." Editorial, *The Christian Century*, 26 Mar. 1952, 355–56.

Chaze, William L., with Harold Kennedy. "The Great Propaganda War." *U.S. News and World Report*, 11 Jan. 1982, 27–30.

Clark, Howard. "A Comparison of Civil and Court-Martial Procedure." *Indiana Law Journal* 4 (1929): 589–99.

Clervi, Ferdinand C. "Military Rule of Evidence and the Available Witness." *Army Lawyer* 51 (Nov. 1986): 51–55.

"Court-Martial Charges." *Army-Navy-Air-Force Journal*, 3 May 1952, 1072.

Cox, Walter T., III. "The Army, the Courts, and the Constitution: The Evolution of Military Justice." *Military Law Review* 118 (Fall 1987): 1–30.

Crump, G. F. "History of the Structure of Military Justice in the U.S., 1775–1966." Parts 1 and 2. *Air Force Law Review* 16 and 17 (Winter 1974 and Spring 1975): 41–68, 55–72.

Currier, Roger M., and Irvin M. Kent. "The Boards of Review of the Armed Services." *Vanderbilt Law Review* 6 (1953): 241–50.

"Dear Diary." *Time*, 17 Mar. 1952, 8.

Dixon, Frederick R., and Rudolph S. Zadnik. "Military Justice—A Uniform Code for the Armed Services." *Western Reserve Law Review* 2 (1950): 147–61.

Duke, Robert D., and Howard S. Vogel. "The Constitution and the Standing Army: Another Problem of Court-Martial Jurisdiction." *Vanderbilt Law Review* 13 (1960): 435–60.

Farmer, Arthur E., and Richard H. Wels. "Command Control—or Military Justice?" *New York University Law Quarterly Review* 24 (1949): 263–82.

Fedele, Frank. "Appellate Review in the Military Justice System." *Federal Bar Journal* 15 (1955): 399–435.

Feld, Benjamin. "Courts-Martial Practice: Some Phases of Pretrial Procedure." *Brooklyn Law Review* 23 (1956): 25–37.

Fidell, Eugene R. "The Culture of Change in Military Law." *Military Law Review* 126 (Fall 1989): 125–32.

Fratcher, William F. "Appellate Review in American Military Law," *Missouri Law Review* 14 (1949): 15–75.

————. "History of the Judge Advocate General's Corps: United States Army." *Military Law Review* 4 (Mar. 1959): 89–111.

————. "Presidential Power to Regulate Military Justice: A Critical Study of Decisions of the Court of Military Appeals." *New York University Law Review* 34 (1959): 861–90.

Garland, Albert N. "Military Justice before the Bar." *Army,* Jan. 1972, 27–29.

Goulet, Lionel J. "The United States Court of Military Appeals and Sufficiency of the Evidence." *Georgetown Law Journal* 42 (1953): 109–25.

Grow, Robert W. "The Ten Lean Years: From the Mechanized Force (1930) to the Armored Force (1940)." *Armor,* Jan.–Feb., Mar.–Apr., May–June, July–Aug. 1987.

————. "The U.S. Military Mission with the Iranian Army." *Cavalry,* Mar.–Apr. 1949: 24–26.

Hamilton, William C., Jr. "Military Law: Drumhead Justice Is Dead!" *American Bar Association Journal* 43 (1957): 797–800, 849–53.

Harmon, Reginald C. "Progress under the Uniform Code." *Judge Advocate Journal* (Oct. 1954): 10–14.

Henderson, Gordon D. "Courts-Martial and the Constitution: The Original Understanding." *Harvard Law Review* 71 (1957): 293–324.

Hensel, H. Struve. "Changes Inside the Pentagon." *Harvard Business Review,* Jan.–Feb. 1954, 98–108.

Hess, Gary R. "The Iranian Crisis of 1945–46 and the Cold War." *Political Science Quarterly* (Mar. 1974): 117–46.

Hodson, Kenneth J. "Perspective: The Manual for Courts-Martial–1984." *Military Law Review* 57 (Summer 1972): 1–16.

Hofmann, George F. "Tactics vs. Technology: The U.S. Cavalry Experience." *Armor,* Sept.–Oct. 1973, 10–14.

Holtzoff, Alexander. "Administration of Justice in the United States Army." *New York University Law Quarterly Review* 22 (1947): 1–18.

"The Injustice of Military Justice." *Literary Digest,* 19 Apr. 1919, 13.

Jaffe, Louis L. "The Right to Judicial Review." Parts 1 and 2. *Harvard Law Review* 71 (1958): 401–37, 769–814.

Johnson, Richard C. "Unlawful Command Influence: A Question of Balance." *JAG Journal (Navy),* Mar.–Apr. 1965, 87–94, 110–16.

"Judicial Checks on Command Influence under the Uniform Code of Military Justice." *Yale Law Journal* 63 (1954): 880–88.

Karlen, Delmar. "Civilianization of Military Justice: Good or Bad." *Military Law Review* 60 (Spring 1973): 113–22.

————. "Lawyers and Courts-Martial." *Wisconsin Law Review* (1946): 240–56.

————. "Personal Factors in Military Justice." *Wisconsin Law Review* (1946): 394–409.

Karlen, Delmar, and Louis H. Pepper. "The Scope of Military Justice." *Journal of Criminal Law, Criminology, and Political Science* 43 (1952): 285–98.

Keeffe, Arthur John. "Drumhead Justice: A Look at Our Military Courts." *Reader's Digest,* Aug. 1951, 39–44.

————. "University Military Training with or without Reform of Courts-Martial?" *Cornell Law Quarterly* 33 (1948): 465–87.

"Keeping the Company's Secrets: The Censors Turn on a Former CIA Director." *Time,* 30 May 1983, 19.

Kelly, Joseph B. "Uniform Code and the Evolution of Military Law." *University of Cincinnati Law Review* 22 (1953): 343–69.

"A Kind Word for General Grow." *American Mercury,* May 1952, 9–11.

King, Archibald. "The Army Court-Martial System." *Wisconsin Law Review* (1941): 311–42.

Kingsbury, Howard Thayer. "Courts-Martial and Military Justice." *National Service with the International Military Digest* 5 (1919): 280–81.

Kiser, Jackson L. "Command Control of Courts-Martial." *American Bar Association Journal* 42 (1956): 969.

"The Korean War: Mystery? Maybe the Chinese Can't Take It." *Newsweek,* 5 Feb. 1951, 29.

"The Korean War: Reds on Run—But They're Not Routed." *Newsweek,* 26 Mar. 1951, 27–30.

"The Korean War: Ringing in the Year of the Rabbit." *Newsweek,* 19 Feb. 1951, 27–28.

"The Korean War: Time of Decision and Death Dealing." *Newsweek,* 19 Mar. 1951, 30.

Korothevich, G. "Yet Another Exposure of Warmongers," *For a Lasting Peace, for a Peoples' Democracy,* 4 Apr. 1952, 1595.

Krueger-Sprengel, Friedhelm. "The German Military Legal System." *Military Law Review* 57 (Winter 1972): 17–26.

Kuhfeld, Albert M. "Prejudicial Error—The Measurement of Reversal by Boards of Review and the U.S. Court of Military Appeals." *St. John's Law Review* 35 (1961): 255–63.

Landman, Bernard, Jr. "One Year of the Uniform Code of Military Justice: A Report of Progress." *Stanford Law Review* 4 (1952): 491–508.

Langley, Ernest L. "Military Justice and the Constitution—Improvements Offered by the New Uniform Code of Military Justice." *Texas Law Review* 29 (1951): 651–71.

Larkin, Felix E. "Professor Edmund M. Morgan and the Drafting of the Uniform Code." *Military Law Review* 28 (April 1965): 7–11.

Latimer, George W. "Military Justice." *Law Library Journal* 45 (1952): 148–59.

McBratney, William H. "Reform of Military Justice Is Not Complete." *Journal of the American Judicature Society* 35 (1951): 81–83.

McLean, Ridby. "A Historical Sketch of Military Law." *Journal of Criminal Law and Criminology* 8 (1917–19): 27–32.

McNiece, Harold F., and John V. Thornton. "Military Law from Pearl Harbor to Korea." *Fordham Law Review* 22 (1953): 155–82.

Maher, Christopher M. "The Right to a Fair Trial in Criminal Cases Involving the Introduction of Classified Information." *Military Law Review* 120 (Spring 1988): 83–137.

Malone, D. M. "You Can't Run an Army Like a Corporation." *Army,* Feb. 1980, 39–41.

Margulies, Herbert F. "The Articles of War, 1920: The History of a Forgotten Reform." *Military Affairs,* Apr. 1979, 85–89.

Matthews, Lloyd J. "Is Ambition Unprofessional?" *Army*, July 1988, 28–37.

Melnikov, D. "Confirmation from the Pentagon." *New Times*, 7 May 1952, 15.

———. "Notes of a British Officer." *New Times*, 16 Apr. 1952, 29–31.

"Military Law." *Washington Law Reporter* 87 (1959): 553–55.

"Military Law Review: A Symposium on Military Justice. The Uniform Code of Military Justice, 1951–61." *Military Law Review* 11–12 (1961): 1–267.

Morgan, Edmund M. "The Background of the Uniform Code of Military Justice." *Vanderbilt Law Review* 6 (1953): 169–85.

———. "The Existing Court-Martial System and the Ansell Army Articles." *Yale Law Journal* 29 (1919–20): 52–74.

Morgan, Samuel. "Army Courts-Martial: The Double Standard." *Atlantic Monthly*, 178, no. 6 (1946): 97–102.

"Moscow Diary." *Newsweek*, 17 Mar. 1952, 25–26.

Mott, William C. "An Appraisal of Proposed Changes in the Uniform Code of Military Justice." *St. John's Law Review* 35 (1961): 300–305.

Mott, William C., John E. Hartnett, Jr., and Kenneth B. Morton. "A Survey of the Literature of Military Law: A Selective Bibliography." *Vanderbilt Law Review* 6 (1953): 333–69.

Moyer, Homer E., Jr. "Procedural Rights of the Military Accused: Advantages over a Civilian Defendant." *Maine Law Review* 22 (1970): 105–40.

Mullally, Mandeville, Jr. "Military Justice: The Uniform Code in Action." *Columbia Law Review* 53 (1953): 1–27.

Murphy, Arthur A. "The Army Defense Counsel: Unusual Ethics for an Unusual Advocate." *Columbia Law Review* 61 (1961): 233–53.

Murphy, William A. "The Formal Pretrial Investigation." *Military Law Review* 11–12 (1961): 1–47.

NSC-68. "A Report to the National Security Council, 14 Apr. 1950." *Naval War College Review*, May–June 1975, 51–108.

Newman, A. S. "Are Morals and Espirit Alike?" *Army*, Dec. 1975, 51–52.

———. "Harsh Discipline: Balance Justice with Judgment." *Army*, Jan. 1973, 45–46.

Norman, Lloyd. "The Love-Hate Affair between the Pentagon and the Press." *Army*, Feb. 1980, 14–20.

O'Connell, D. P. "The Nature of British Military Law." *Military Law Review* 19 (Jan. 1963): 141–55.

Page, William Herbert. "Military Law: A Study in Comparative Law." *Harvard Law Review* 32 (1919): 349–73.

Pasley, Robert S., Jr. "A Comparative Study of Military Justice Reforms in Britain and America." *Vanderbilt Law Review* 6 (1953): 305–31.

———. "The Federal Courts Look at the Court-Martial." *University of Pittsburgh Law Review* 12 (1950): 7–34.

Peterson, Fred H. "A Review of Gen. Crowder's Letter on Military Justice." *Central Law Journal* 89 (1919): 44–48.

Philpott, Tom. "Congress Caught in Crossfire; Top CMA Judge, Military at 'War.'" *Army Times*, 30 Apr. 1979, 4.

Price, Arthur L. "Growth in Military Jurisprudence since World War II." *Illinois Bar Journal* 41 (1952): 56–61.

"Propaganda: Bob Grows intimes Tagebuch." *Der Spiegel,* 19 Mar. 1952, 16–17.

"The Proposed Uniform Code of Military Justice." *Harvard Law Review* 62 (1949): 1377–87.

Prosser, John R. "Three Views: Reforming Military Justice." *Army,* Apr. 1973, 38–40.

Prugh, George S., Jr. "Colonel William Winthrop: The Tradition of the Military Lawyer." *American Bar Association Journal* 42 (1956): 126–29, 188–91.

Quinn, Robert Emmett. "Military Law: A Twenty-Year Metamorphosis." *Cornell Law Forum* 22 (1969): 1–2.

———. "The Role of Criticism in the Development of Law." *Military Law Review* 35 (Jan. 1967): 47–58.

———. "Some Comparisons between Courts-Martial and Civilian Practice." *Military Law Review* 46 (Oct. 1969): 77–87.

———. "The United States Court of Military Appeals and Military Due Process." *St. John's Law Review* 35 (1961): 225–54.

Re, Edward D. "The Uniform Code of Military Justice." *St. John's Law Review* 25 (1951): 155–87.

Rheinstein, Max. "Comparative Military Justice." *Federal Bar Journal* 15 (1955): 276–85.

Rigby, William C. "Military Penal Law: A Brief Survey of the 1920 Revision of the Articles of War." *Journal of Criminal Law and Criminology* 12 (1921–22): 84–90.

Rollman, Robert O. "Of Crimes, Courts-Martial, and Punishment—A Short History of Military Justice." *USAF JAG Law Review* 11 (1969): 212–22.

Royall, Kenneth C. "Revision of the Military Justice Process as Proposed by the War Department." *Virginia Law Review* 33 (1947): 269–88.

Russell, G. L. "The Uniform Code of Military Justice." *George Washington Law Review* 19 (1951): 233–74.

Schlesinger, Arthur M., Jr. "Origins of the Cold War." *Foreign Affairs,* Oct. 1967, 22–52.

Schlueter, David A. "The Court-Martial: A Historical Survey." *Military Law Review* 87 (Winter 1980): 129–66.

Schoetz, Max, Jr. "Military Law." *Marquette Law Review* 3 (1918–19): 26–31.

Semenov, Ya. "Instigators of War without a Mask." *Bolshevik* 6 (Mar. 1952): 75–80.

"Sen. Bayh's Proposal to Civilianize the UCMJ." *Army,* Apr. 1973, 41–42.

Sherman, Edward F. "The Civilianization of Military Law." *Maine Law Review* 22 (1970): 1–103.

———. "Military Justice without Military Control." *Yale Law Review* 82 (1973): 1398–425.

Sherrill, Robert. "Justice, Military Style." *Playboy,* Feb. 1970, 120–22, 214–28.

Shoup, David M. "The New American Militarism." *Atlantic Monthly,* Apr. 1969, 51–56.

Snedeker, James. "The Uniform Code of Military Justice." *Georgetown Law Journal* 38 (1949–50): 521–73.

Spiegelberg, George A., and Milton Ackman. "Court-Martial Vacuum." *Nation*, 24 Dec. 1960, 499–502.

"Strange Case of General Grow." *Nation*, 22 Mar. 1952, 264–65.

Stuart-Smith, James. "Military Law: Its History, Administration and Practice." *Law Quarterly Review* 85 (1969): 478–504.

Supervielle, Manuel E. F. "Article 31(b): Who Should Be Required to Give Warnings?" *Military Law Review* 123 (Winter 1989): 151–214.

Sutherland, Arthur E., Jr. "The Constitution, the Civilian, and Military Justice." *St. John's Law Review* 35 (1961): 215–24.

Swanson, James W. "The Article 32 Right of an Accused to Pre-trial Cross-examination of the Witness against Him 'if they are available.' " *Air Force Law Review* 24 (1984): 246–59.

"A Symposium on Military Justice." *Vanderbilt Law Review* 6 (Feb. 1953): 161–369.

Taylor, Frank E. "Military Courts-Martial Procedure under the Revised Articles of War." *Virginia Law Review* 12 (1926): 463–94.

Taylor, Maxwell D. "A Do-It-Yourself Professional Code for the Military." *Parameters*, Dec. 1980, 10–15.

Thode, Wayne E. "The Ethical Standard for the Advocate." *Texas Law Review* 39 (1961): 575–600.

Thornton, John V. "Military Law." *Annual Survey of American Law* (1954): 112.

Tomes, Jonathan P. "Illegal Command Influence: The Unnecessary Evil." *Army*, Apr. 1987, 26–29.

"The Uniform Code of Military Justice—Its Promise and Performance (The First Decade: 1951–1961): A Symposium." *St. John's Law Review* 35 (1961): 197–322.

"U.S. Military Justice on Trial." *Newsweek*, 31 Aug. 1970, 18–23.

Walker, Daniel. "An Evaluation of the United States Court of Military Appeals." *Northwestern University Law Review* 48 (1954): 714–33.

———. "The United States Court of Military Appeals: A Long Overdue Addition to the Judiciary." *American Bar Association Journal* 38 (1952): 567–70.

Walker, Daniel, and C. George Niebank. "The Court of Military Appeals—Its History, Organization and Operation." *Vanderbilt Law Review* 6 (1953): 228–40.

Wallstein, Leonard M., Jr. "Justice in the Army." *Nation*, 19 July 1947, 71–73.

———. "The Revision of the Army Court-Martial System." *Columbia Law Review* 48 (1948): 219–36.

Walsh, William F. "Military Law: Return to Drumhead Justice?" *American Bar Association Journal* 42 (1956): 521–25.

Ward, Chester. "UCMJ—Does It Work?" *Vanderbilt Law Review* 6 (1953): 186–227.

Warren, Earl. "The Bill of Rights and the Military." *New York University Law Review* 37 (1962): 181–203.

West, Luther C. "A History of Command Influence on the Military Judicial System." *UCLA Law Review* 18 (1970): 1–156.

White, Robert J. "Has the Uniform Code of Military Justice Improved the Courts-Martial System?" *St. John's Law Review* 28 (1953): 19–29.

———. "The Uniform Code of Military Justice—Its Promise and Performance: The Background and the Problem." *St. John's Law Review* 35 (1961): 197–214.

Wiener, Frederick Bernays. "Courts-Martial and the Bill of Rights: The Original Practice I and II." *Harvard Law Review* 72 (1958): 1–49, 266–304.

——— . "History Vindicates the Supreme Court's Ruling on Military Justice." *American Bar Association Journal* 51 (1965): 1127–30.

——— . "The Perils of Tinkering with Military Justice." *Army,* Nov. 1970, 22–25.

——— . "The Seamy Side of the World War I Court-Martial Controversy." *Military Law Review* 123 (Winter 1989): 109–28.

Wigmore, John Henry. "Address." *Maryland State Bar Association Transactions* 24 (1919): 183–95.

——— . "Lessons from Military Justice." *Journal of the American Judicature Society* 4 (1920): 151–54.

Williams, D. M., Jr. "Admissibility of Polygraph Results under the Military Rules of Evidence." *Army Lawyer* 45 (June 1980): 1–6.

Willis, John T. "The United States Court of Military Appeals: Its Origin, Operation and Future." *Military Law Review* 55 (Winter 1972): 39–93.

Wright, Ben C. "Mr. X and Containment." *Slavic Review,* Mar. 1976, 1–36.

Wurfel, Seymour W. " 'Military Due Process': What Is It?" *Vanderbilt Law Review* 6 (1953): 251–87.

——— . "Military Habeas Corpus." *Michigan Law Review* 49 (1951): 493–528, 699–722.

Zimmerman, Jack B. "Civilian v. Military Justice: A Comparison of Defendants' Rights." *Trial,* Oct. 1981, 34–40, 81–83.

BOOKS

Acheson, Dean. *Present at the Creation: My Years in the State Department.* New York: Norton, 1969.

Adams, Charles Francis. *The Works of John Adams.* 3 vols. Boston: Charles C. Little and James Brown, 1851.

Adenauer, Konrad. *Memoirs, 1945–53.* Chicago: Henry Regnery, 1965.

American Bar Association Committee on Military Law. *Report of Majority and Report of Minority.* American Bar Association, 1919.

Aycock, William B., and Seymour W. Wurfel. *Military Law under the Uniform Code of Military Justice.* Chapel Hill: Univ. of North Carolina Press, 1955.

Bailey, F. Lee. *For the Defense.* New York: Atheneum, 1975.

Barghoorn, Frederick C. *Soviet Foreign Propaganda.* Princeton: Princeton Univ. Press, 1964.

——— . *The Soviet Image of the United States. A Study in Distortion.* New York: Harcourt, Brace and World, 1950.

Bishop, Joseph W., Jr. *Justice under Fire: A Study of Military Law.* New York: Chaterhouse, 1974.

Blackstone, Sir William. "Of the Military and Maritime States." In *The Rights,* Book I. London, 1778.

Blair, Clay. *Ridgway's Paratroopers: The American Airborne in World War II.* Garden City: Dial Press, 1985.

Blumenson, Martin. *The Patton Papers, 1940–1945*. Boston: Houghton Mifflin, 1974.

Borden, Morton, ed. *The Antifederalist Papers*. Lansing: Michigan State Univ. Press, 1965.

Bradley, Omar N. *A Soldier's Story*. New York: Henry Holt, 1951.

Brand, C. E. *Roman Military Law*. Austin: Univ. of Texas Press, 1968.

Bredin, Jean-Dennis. *The Affair: The Case of Alfred Dreyfus*. New York: George Braziller, 1986.

Butcher, Harry C. *My Three Years with Eisenhower: The Personal Diary of Captain Harry C. Butcher, USNR*. New York: Simon and Schuster, 1946.

Byrne, Edward M. *Military Law*. 3d ed. Annapolis: Naval Institute Press, 1981.

Campbell, Thomas M., and George C. Herring, eds. *The Diaries of Edward R. Stettinius*. New York: New Viewpoints, 1975.

Clark, Mark C. *Calculated Risk*. New York: Harper and Brothers, 1950.

Coffman, Edward M. *The Hilt of the Sword: The Career of Payton C. March*. Madison: Univ. of Wisconsin Press, 1966.

———. *The Old Army: A Portrait of the American Army in Peacetime, 1784–1898*. New York: Oxford Univ. Press, 1986.

Cohen, Bernard C. *The Press and Foreign Policy*. Princeton: Princeton Univ. Press, 1963.

Cole, Hugh M. *The Ardennes: Battle of the Bulge*. Washington, D.C.: U.S. Government Printing Office, 1965.

Collins, J. Lawton. *Lightning Joe: An Autobiography*. Baton Rouge: Louisiana State Univ. Press, 1979.

Condit, Dorris M. *The Test of War, 1950–1953*. Washington, D.C.: U.S. Government Printing Office, 1988.

Corson, William R. *The Armies of Ignorance: The Rise of the American Empire*. New York: Dial Press, 1977.

Corson, William R., and Robert T. Crowley. *The New KGB*. New York: William Morrow, 1985.

Corwin, Edward S., ed. *The Constitution of the United States of America: Analysis and Interpretation*. Washington, D.C.: U.S. Government Printing Office, 1964.

Crowder, Enoch H. *Military Justice during the War*. Washington, D.C.: U.S. Government Printing Office, 1919.

Davis, George B. *A Treatise on the Military Law of the United States*. 3d ed. New York: John Wiley and Sons, 1915.

Decision of the United States Court of Military Appeals. Vol. 3. Oct. Term 1952–53. Rochester: Lawyers Co-operative Publishing Co., n.d.

Deibel, Terry L., and John Lewis Gaddis, eds. *Containment: Concept and Policy*. 2 vols. Washington, D.C.: National Defense Univ. Press, 1986.

Deutscher, Isaac. *Stalin: A Political Biography*. New York: Oxford Univ. Press, 1949.

Digest of Opinions. The Judge Advocates General of the Armed Forces. Vol. 3, no. 1. July–Sept. 1953. Rochester: Lawyers Co-operative Publishing Co., n.d.

Dixon, Norman F. *On the Psychology of Military Incompetence*. London: Jonathan Cape, 1976.

Donovan, James A. *Militarism, U.S.A.* New York: Charles Scribner's Sons, 1970.

Donovan, Robert J. *Conflict and Crisis: The Presidency of Harry S. Truman, 1945–1948.* New York: Norton, 1977.

———. *Tumultuous Years: The Presidency of Harry S. Truman, 1949–1953.* New York: Norton, 1982.

Downs, Anthony. *Inside Bureaucracy.* Boston: Little, Brown, 1966.

Eisenhower, Dwight D. *Crusade in Europe.* New York: Doubleday, 1952.

Ellul, Jacques. *Propaganda: The Formation of Men's Attitudes.* New York: Knopf, 1965.

Everett, Robinson O. *Military Justice in the Armed Forces of the United States.* Westport, Conn.: Greenwood Press, 1956.

Farrand, Max, ed. *Federal Convention of 1787.* 2 vols. New Haven: Yale Univ. Press, 1911.

Freeland, Richard M. *The Truman Doctrine and the Origins of McCarthyism: Foreign Policy, Domestic Politics, and Internal Security, 1946–1948.* New York: Knopf, 1972.

Fuller, J. F. C. *Armament and History.* London: Eyre and Spottiswoode, 1946.

Gabriel, Richard A. *To Serve with Honor: A Treatise on Military Ethics and the Way of the Soldier.* Westport, Conn.: Greenwood Press, 1982.

Gabriel, Richard A., and Paul L. Savage. *Crisis in Command: Mismanagement in the Army.* New York: Hill and Wang, 1978.

Gaddis, John Lewis. *Russia: The Soviet Union and the United States, An Interpretive History.* New York: John Wiley and Sons, 1978.

———. *The United States and the Origins of the Cold War, 1941–1947.* New York: Columbia Univ. Press, 1972.

Generous, William T., Jr. *Sword and Scales: The Development of the Uniform Code of Military Justice.* Port Washington, N.Y.: Kennikat Press, 1973.

Gramont, Sanche de. *The Secret War: The Story of International Espionage since World War II.* New York: G. P. Putnam's Sons, 1962.

Grew, Joseph C. *Turbulent Era: A Diplomatic Record of Forty Years, 1904–1945.* 2 vols. Boston: Houghton Mifflin, 1952.

Grothe, Peter. *To Win the Minds of Men: The Story of the Communist Propaganda War in East Germany.* Palo Alto, Calif.: Pacific Books, 1958.

Halberstam, David. *The Best and the Brightest.* New York: Random House, 1972.

Hamilton, Alexander, James Madison, John Jay. *The Federalist.* Chicago: Univ. of Chicago Press, 1952.

———. *The Federalist.* New York: Mentor Books, 1961.

Harriman, W. Averell, and Elie Abel. *Special Envoy to Churchill and Stalin, 1941–1946.* New York: Random House, 1975.

Hauser, William L. *America's Army in Crisis: A Study in Civil-Military Relations.* Baltimore: Johns Hopkins Univ. Press, 1973.

Herring, George C. *Aid to Russia, 1941–1946: Strategy, Diplomacy, the Origins of the Cold War.* New York: Columbia Univ. Press, 1973.

Hewes, James E., Jr. *From Root to McNamara: Army Organization and Administration, 1900–1963.* Washington, D.C.: U.S. Government Printing Office, 1975.

Higham, Robin, and Donald J. Mrozek, eds. *A Guide to the Sources of United States Military History: Supplement I.* Hamden, Conn.: Archon Books, 1981.

Hofmann, George F. *The Super Sixth: History of the 6th Armored Division in World War II and Its Post-war Association*. Louisville: 6th Armored Division Association, 1975.

Hunt, Gaillard, and James B. Scott. *Debates in the Federal Convention of 1787*. New York: Oxford Univ. Press, 1920.

Huntington, Samuel P. *The Common Defense: Strategic Programs in National Politics*. New York: Columbia Univ. Press, 1961.

———. *The Soldier and the State: The Theory and Politics of the Civil-Military Relations*. New York: Random House, 1957.

Janowitz, Morris. *The Professional Soldier: A Social and Political Portrait*. New York: Free Press, 1971.

Jeffreys-Jones, Rhodri. *The CIA and American Democracy*. New Haven: Yale Univ. Press, 1989.

Judge Advocate General's Corp. *The Army Lawyer: A History of the Judge Advocate General's Corps, 1775–1975*. Washington, D.C.: U.S. Government Printing Office, 1975.

Kennan, George F. *Memoirs, 1925–1950*. Boston: Little, Brown, 1967.

———. *Memoirs, 1950–1963*. Boston: Little, Brown, 1972.

———. Pseud X. "The Sources of Soviet Conduct." In Hamilton Fish Armstrong, ed., *Fifty Years of Foreign Affairs*. New York: Praeger, 1972.

Kinnard, Douglas. *The Secretary of Defense*. Lexington: Univ. Press of Kentucky, 1980.

———. *The War Managers*. Wayne, N.J.: Avery Publishing Group, 1985.

Kohn, Richard H. ed. *The United States Military under the Constitution of the United States, 1789–1989*. New York: New York Univ. Press, 1991.

Korb, Lawrence J. *The Joint Chiefs of Staff: The First Twenty-five Years*. Bloomington: Indiana Univ. Press, 1976.

Kuniholm, Bruce R. *The Origins of the Cold War in the Near East: Great Power Conflict and Diplomacy in Iran, Turkey and Greece*. Princeton: Princeton Univ. Press, 1980.

Latham, Earl. *The Communist Controversy in Washington: From the New Deal to McCarthyism*. New York: Atheneum, 1969.

Lenczowski, George. *Russia and the West in Iran*. New York: Cornell Univ. Press, 1949.

———. *Soviet Advances in the Middle East*. Washington, D.C.: American Enterprise for Public Policy Research, 1971.

Levy, Leonard W. *Original Intent and the Framers' Constitution*. New York: Macmillan, 1988.

Liddell, Hart, B. H. *Why Don't We Learn from History?* New York: Hawthorn Books, 1971.

Lindley, John M. *"A Soldier Is Also a Citizen": The Controversy over Military Justice, 1917–1920*. New York: Garland, 1990.

Lippmann, Walter. *Liberty and the News*. New York: Harcourt, Brace, 1920.

Lockmiller, David A. *Enoch H. Crowder: Soldier, Lawyer and Statesman*. Columbia: University of Missouri Studies, 1955.

Lurie, Jonathan. *Arming Military Justice: The Origins of the United States Court of Military Appeals, 1775–1950*. Princeton: Princeton University Press, 1992.

Military Law Review Bicentennial Issue. Washington, D.C.: U.S. Government Printing Office, 1975.

Mills, C. Wright. *The Power Elite.* New York: Oxford Univ. Press, 1956.

Morgan, Roger. *A Study in Alliance Politics, 1945–73.* London: Oxford Univ. Press, 1974.

Motter, T. H. Vail. *The Persian Corridor and Aid to Russia.* Washington, D.C.: U.S. Government Printing Office, 1952.

Perry, Mark. *Four Stars: The Inside Story of the Forty-Year Battle between the Joint Chiefs of Staff and America's Civilian Leaders.* Boston: Houghton Mifflin, 1989.

Paterson, Thomas G. *On Every Front: The Making of the Cold War.* New York: Norton, 1979.

Paterson, Thomas G., J. Garry Clifford, and Kenneth J. Hagan. *American Foreign Policy: A History.* Lexington, Mass.: D. C. Heath, 1977.

Pogue, Forrest C. *George C. Marshall: Organizer of Victory, 1943–1945.* New York: Viking, 1973.

———. *George C. Marshall: Statesman, 1945–1959.* New York: Viking Penguin, 1987.

Ramazani, Rouhollah K. *The Foreign Policy of Iran, 1500–1941: A Developing Nation in World Affairs.* Charlottesville: Univ. Press of Virginia, 1966.

———. *Iran's Foreign Policy, 1941–1973: A Study of Foreign Policy in Modernizing Nations.* Charlottesville: Univ. Press of Virginia, 1975.

Rapoport, Anatol. *The Big Two: Soviet-American Perceptions of Foreign Policy.* New York: Bobbs-Merrill, 1971.

Rearden, Steven L. *The Formative Years, 1947–1950.* Washington, D.C.: U.S. Government Printing Office, 1984.

Reeves, Thomas C. *The Life and Times of Joe McCarthy.* New York: Stein and Day, 1982.

Roberts, Chalmers M. *The Washington Post: The First 100 Years.* Boston: Houghton Mifflin, 1977.

Rutland, Robert A., ed. *The Papers of James Madison, 1787–1788.* 10 vols. Chicago: Univ. of Chicago Press, 1977.

Schlueter, David A. *Military Criminal Justice: Practice and Procedure.* Charlottesville, Va.: The Michie Company, 1982.

Schnabel, James F. *Policy and Direction: The First Year.* Washington, D.C.: U.S. Government Printing Office, 1972.

Sherrill, Robert. *Military Justice Is to Justice as Military Music Is to Music.* New York: Harper & Row, 1969.

Sims, Robert B. *The Pentagon Reporters.* Washington, D.C.: National Defense Univ. Press, 1983.

Sivachev, Nikolia V., and Nikolia N. Yakovlev. *Russia and the United States.* Chicago: Univ. of Chicago Press, 1979.

Snedeker, James. *Military Justice under the Uniform Code.* Boston: Little, Brown, 1953.

Smythe, Donald. *Pershing: General of the Armies.* Bloomington: Indiana Univ. Press, 1986.

Squires, Richard. *Auf Dem Kriegspfad, Aufzeichnungen eines englishen Offiziers.* East Berlin: Rutten and Loening, 1951.

Steele, Ronald. *Walter Lippmann and the American Century.* Boston: Little, Brown, 1980.

Taylor, John M. *General Maxwell Taylor: The Sword and the Pen.* New York: Doubleday, 1989.

Taylor, Maxwell D. *Swords and Plowshares.* New York: Norton, 1972.

———. *The Uncertain Trumpet.* New York: Harper & Row, 1960.

Theoharis, Athan G. *Seeds of Repression: Harry S. Truman and the Origins of McCarthyism.* Chicago: Quadrangle Books, 1971.

———. *Spying on Americans: Political Surveillance from Hoover to the Huston Plan.* Philadelphia: Temple Univ. Press, 1978.

Truman, Harry S. *Years of Trial and Hope, 1946–1952.* Garden City: Doubleday, 1956.

Tsybov, Sergy Ivanovich, and Nikolay Fedorovich Chistyabov. *Front Taynoy Voyny.* Moscow: Ministerstva Oborony, SSSR, 1965.

Tytler, Alexander Fraser. *Essays on the Military Law and in Practice of Courts-Martial.* London, 1799.

———. *Treatis on the Law of Courts-Martial.* London, 1790.

Ulam, Adam B. *Expansion and Coexistence: The History of Soviet Foreign Policy, 1917–67.* New York: Praeger, 1968.

———. *The Rivals: America and Russia since World War II.* New York: Viking, 1971.

Ulmer, S. Sidney. *Military Justice and the Right to Counsel.* Lexington: Univ. Press of Kentucky, 1970.

Uniform Code of Military Justice. Index of Legislative History. Washington, D.C.: U.S. Government Printing Office, 1950.

Vagts, Alfred. *The Military Attaché.* Princeton: Princeton Univ. Press, 1967.

Vandiver, Frank E. *Black Jack: The Life and Times of John T. Pershing.* 2 vols. College Station: Texas A&M Univ. Press, 1977.

Weigley, Russell. *History of the United States Army.* New York: Macmillan, 1967.

West, Luther C. *They Call It Justice: Command Influence and the Court-Martial System.* New York: Viking, 1977.

Whiteside, Thomas. *An Agent in Place: The Wennerström Affair.* New York: Viking, 1966.

Winthrop, William. *Military Law and Precedents.* 2d ed. Washington, D.C.: U.S. Government Printing Office, 1920.

Yarmolinsky, Adam. *The Military Establishment: Its Impact on America.* New York: Harper & Row, 1971.

COURT DECISIONS

Boyd v. United States, 116 U.S. (1886).

Bram v. United States, 168 U.S. (1897).

Davis v. United States, 328 U.S. (1946).

Dynes v. Hoover, 61 U.S. (20 How.) (1858).

Ex parte Milligan, 71 U.S. (4 Wall.) (1866).

Ex parte Reed, 100 U.S. (1879).

Ex parte Vallandingham, 68 U.S. (1 Wall.) (1864).
Gouled v. United States, 255 U.S. 298 (1921).
Hiatt v. Brown, 339 U.S. (1950).
Hofmann v. United States Central Intelligence Agency et al., Civil Action, No. 80-1792.
Olmstead v. United States, 277 U.S. (1928).
United States v. Abrams et al., 230 Fed (DC, Vt. 1916).
United States v. Berry (No. 69) 2CMR 141 (1952).
United States v. Clay (CM 349653) 1 CMR 74 (1952).
United States v. Du Bay, 37 CMR 411, 17 USCMA 147 (1967).
United States v. Gordon, 2 CMR 161, 1 USCMA 255 (1952).
United States v. Grow (CM 355736) 11 CMR 77, 3 USCMA 77 (1953).
United States v. LaGrange et al., 3 CMR 76, 1 USCMA 342 (1952).
United States v. Littrice, 3 CMR 487, 13 CMR, (1953).
United States v. Marsh, 11 CMR 48, 3 USCMA 48 (1953).
United States v. Rosser, 6 MJ 267 (CMA 1979).
United States v. Snyder, 4 CMR 15, 1 USCMA 409 (1952).
United States v. Thomas, 12 MJ 388 (CMA 1986).
Weeks v. United States, 232 U.S. (1914).

GOVERNMENT DOCUMENTS

Armed Services Committee, House of Representatives. *Full Committee Hearings on H.R. 774 and H.R. 2575.* 80th Cong., 1st sess. (1947).
———. *Hearings Before a Subcommittee . . . on S. 857 and H.R. 4080.* 81st Cong., 1st sess. (1949).
———. *Hearings Before a Subcommittee . . . on H.R. 2498: A Bill to Unify, Consolidate, and Codify the Articles of War . . . Establish a Uniform Code of Military Justice.* 81st Cong., 1st sess. (1949).
———. *Subcommittee Hearings on H.R. 2575, to Amend the Articles of War.* 80th Cong., 1st sess. (1947).
Army Ground Forces. *The Armored Force Command and Center.* Study No. 27 (1946).
A Citizen's Guide on Using the Freedom of Information Act and Privacy Act of 1974 to Request Government Records. Washington, D.C.: U.S. Government Printing Office, 1989.
Committee on Foreign Affairs, House of Representatives. *Soviet Diplomacy and Negotiating Behavior: Emerging New Context for U.S. Diplomacy.* 96th Cong., 1st sess., House Document No. 96-238. Washington, D.C.: U.S. Government Printing Office, 1979.
Committee on the Judiciary, Senate. *The Wennerström Spy Case: Excerpts from the Testimony of Stig Eric Constans Wennerström, A Noted Soviet Agent,* 88th Cong., 2d sess. (1964).
Comptroller General of the United States. *Military Jury System Needs Safeguards Found in Civilian Federal Courts.* Washington, D.C.: General Accounting Office, 1977.
Department of the Army. *Military Security: Safeguarding Military Information.* AR 380-5 (15 Nov. 1949), AR 380-5 (28 June 1951), and AR 380-5 (6 June 1952).

——— . *Officers: Resignation.* AR 605-275 (12 Feb. 1951).

——— . *Personnel: Separation of Homosexuals,* AR 600-443 (14 June 1951).

——— . *United States Army Register Active and Retired List.* 1 Jan. 1952 to 1 Jan. 1958. Washington, D.C.: U.S. Government Printing Office, 1958.

Department of Defense. *Documents on Establishment and Organization, 1944–1978.* Washington, D.C.: U.S. Government Printing Office, 1978.

——— . *Report of the Task Force on the Administration of Military Justice in the Armed Forces.* 2 vols. Washington, D.C.: U.S. Government Printing Office, 1972.

Department of State. *Contemporary Soviet Propaganda and Disinformation: A Conference Report.* 9536, 25–27 June 1985 Washington, D.C.: U.S. Government Printing Office, 1987.

——— . *Documents on German Unity.* 4th ed. Frankfurt: U.S. High Commissioner for Germany, 1951–53.

——— . *Documents on Germany, 1944–1985.* Washington, D.C.: U.S. Government Printing Office, 1985.

——— . *Foreign Relations of the United States, 1944: The Near East, South Asia and Africa.* Vol. 5. Washington, D.C.: U.S. Government Printing Office, 1965.

——— . *Foreign Relations of the United States, 1945: The Near East and Africa.* Vol. 8. Washington, D.C.: U.S. Government Printing Office, 1969.

——— . *Foreign Relations of the United States, 1946: General: The United Nations.* Vol. 1. Washington, D.C.: U.S. Government Printing Office, 1972.

——— . *Foreign Relations of the United States, 1947: The Near East and Africa.* Vols. 5, 8. Washington, D.C.: U.S. Government Printing Office, 1971.

——— . *Foreign Relations of the United States, 1948: The Near East, South Asia and Africa.* Vol. 5, pt. 1. Washington, D.C.: U.S. Government Printing Office, 1975.

——— . *Foreign Relations of the United States, 1950: Western Europe.* Vol. 3. Washington, D.C.: U.S. Government Printing Office, 1977.

——— . *Foreign Relations of the United States, 1951: Europe, Political and Economic Developments.* Vol. 4, pt. 2. Washington, D.C.: U.S. Government Printing Office, 1985.

——— . *Foreign Relations of the United States, 1952–1954: Eastern Europe, Soviet Union, Eastern Mediterranean.* Vol. 8. Washington, D.C.: U.S. Government Printing Office, 1988.

Manual for Courts-Martial, United States, 1984. Washington, D.C.: U.S. Government Printing Office, 1984.

Manual for Courts-Martial, United States, 1951 (Effective 31 May 1951). Washington, D.C.: U.S. Government Printing Office, 1951.

Manual for Courts-Martial, United States Army, 1949. Washington, D.C.: U.S. Government Printing Office, 1949.

Manual for Courts-Martial, United States Army, 1928. (Corrected to April 20, 1943). Washington, D.C.: U.S. Government Printing Office, 1943.

Military Affairs Committee, Senate. *Hearing on S. 64 on the Establishment of Military Justice before a Subcommittee.* 66th Cong., 1st sess. (1919).

Senate. *Document 196* ("Doolittle Report"). 79th Cong., 2d sess. (1946).

Senate. *Report 486.* 81st Cong., 1st sess. (1949).

"Truman's Statement on Fundamentals of American Foreign Policy." *Department of State Bulletin* (27 Oct. 1945).

U.S. War Department, *Proceedings and Report of the Special War Department Board on Courts-Martial and Their Procedures*. Kernan Board. Washington, D.C.: U.S. Government Printing Office, 1919.

NEWSPAPER ARTICLES

Berliner Zeitung. "USA-Diplomat auf dunklen Wegen. Wofür sich Generalmajor Grow interessierte/Aufzeichnungen des englishen Offiziers Squires," 3 Jan. 1952.

Cincinnati Enquirer. Blake, George. "Work of Fiction Dishonors Pulitzer Profession," 19 Apr. 1981.

"General Grow Is Convicted of Recording Army Secrets in Diary Stolen by Soviets," 30 July 1952.

Cincinnati Post. "Court-Martial Is Demanded in Diary Case. Rep. Sutton Asks Stiff Penalty for War-Minded General," 7 Mar. 1952.

"General's Diary Stolen Used as Red Propaganda," 6 Mar. 1952.

Goldenberg, Gene. "Study Questions Rights of GIs at Military Trials," 11 June 1977.

Graham, Michael. "Cronkite Attacks Judicial 'Construction' of News," 23 Apr. 1979.

Lecky, George. "It's No Lie: Polygraph Tests Can Help Prove Truthfulness," 6 May 1980.

Maxey, Alexander. "Bad News for the Press: Public Doesn't Trust It," 7 Jan. 1982.

Will, George. "A Great Champion of Conventional Forces," 27 Apr. 1987.

Current Digest of the Soviet Press. 2d quarter, 1952.

Daily Worker. Clark, Joseph. "Gen. Grow Gambles on War—and on War Stocks," 7 Mar. 1952.

Editorial. "What Gen. Grow Revealed," 10 Mar. 1952.

"800 Conn. Churches Demand Truman Fire Gen. Grow, Disavow War Aims," 25 Mar. 1952.

"4 Foreign Offices Linked by Grow's Diary to Spy Ring," 21 Mar. 1952.

Hall, Rob F. "Gen. Grow Holds up a Mirror to America," 11 Mar. 1952.

———. "U.S. General in USSR Picked Targets for A-Bomb Attack," 7 Mar. 1952.

"Pentagon Bans Diaries but Keeps General Grow," 19 Mar. 1952.

"Washington Jittery over Exposé of Gen. Grow Diary," 16 Mar. 1952.

"Washington Jittery over Grow Exposure of Plans for War," 9 Mar. 1952.

Frankfurter Allgemeine. "Der fall Grow," 13 Mar. 1952.

London Times. "General Grow's Diary," 31 July 1952.

"Stolen Diary of US. Attaché, Excerpts Circulated in Russia," 7 Mar. 1952.

"US General's Trial Charge of Failing to Safeguard Secrets," 24 July 1952.

Ludwigsburger Kreiszeitung. "Agenten photokopierten US-Generals Tagebuch," 14 Mar. 1952.

Neues Deutschland. "Die Aufzeichnungen des britischen Majors Squires. Zu seinum Buch *Auf dem Kriegspfad,*" 6 Jan. 1952.

New York Herald Tribune. Book review, 20 May 1962.

New York Times. "Armed Services Code," 8 May 1950.

    "Army to Overhaul Its Courts-Martial," 26 Mar. 1946.

    "Army to Put General Grow on Trial on Diary That Fell to Communists," 6 June 1952.

    Baldwin, Hanson W. "Army G-2 Is Defended. Intelligence Head Says Grow Incident Led to No Shifts—Others Join Criticism," 6 May 1952.

    ――――. "Army Intelligence—I. Grow's Diary Incident Brings to Light Misassignments of Military Attachés," 13 Apr. 1952.

    ――――. "Army Intelligence—II. Army Police Shortcomings Held Factor in G-2 Miscasting of Officers Like Grow," 14 Apr. 1952.

    ――――. "Military Justice Code," 24 Mar. 1955.

    ――――. "New Military Justice," 25 Mar. 1955.

    Editorial. "For Military Justice," 12 Mar. 1948.

    "Grow Appeals Court-Martial," 8 Apr. 1953.

    "Grow Court-Martial Is Started in Secret," 24 July 1952.

    "Grow's Conviction in Diary Case Upheld by Military Appeals Court," 18 July 1953.

    "Grow's Dismissal Urged," 25 Mar. 1952.

    Hinton, Harold B. "Army Convicts Gen. Grow for Misusing Secret Data," 30 July 1952.

    "New Grow Trial Dropped," 19 Dec. 1953.

    "No Decision Yet on Gen. Grow," 26 Mar. 1952.

    "Reds Quote General's Stolen Diary to 'Prove' U.S. Plots World War," 7 Mar. 1952.

    "Russians Link Grow to Germ Warfare," 25 Mar. 1952.

    "2nd Army Head Backs Punishment of Grow," 20 Aug. 1952.

    Stevens, Austin. "Gen. Grow Faces Army Charges for Letting Reds Obtain His Diary," 29 Apr. 1952.

    ――――. "Grow Diary Held Falsified by Reds. Army Releases Excerpts to Show Distortions—Denies He Advocated War Now," 31 July 1952.

    "Stolen Diary's Views Repudiated by 'Voice,' " 9 Mar. 1952.

    "Top Secrets Feared Stolen in Grow Case," 8 Mar. 1952

New York World. Thomas, Rowland. "The Thing That Is Called Military Justice!" 19 Jan. 1919.

Pravda. Leontyev, B. "Facts Exposing the Warmongers," 19 Mar. 1952.

Die Tat. "Tagebuchblätter an der Kreml-Mauer," 19 Mar. 1952.

Washington Post. "Court-Martial of Grow Opens Wednesday," 19 July 1952.

    Editorial. "Dere Diary," 7 Mar. 1952.

    "Gen. Grow Held Guilty, Suspended Six Months," 30 July 1952.

    "General Support Court Findings in Grow Diary Case," 20 Aug. 1952.

    "Grow Dairy Classified 'Top Secret,' " 25 July 1952.

    Norris, John G. "Agents Reveal U.S. General's Diary," 6 Mar. 1952.

——— . "Army Says Reds Fabricated 'Quotes' from Grow's Diary," 31 July 1952.

——— . "Gen. Grow Is Charged in 'War!' Diary Case," 29 Apr. 1952.

——— . "Grow Stolen Diary Incident Gives Support to Advocates of Separate G-2 Career Service," 17 May 1952.

——— . "U.S. Warns Attachés Not to Keep Diaries," 7 Mar. 1952.

"Prosecution Rests Case in Grow Trial," 23 July 1952.

"Reds Propagandized Excerpts. Secrecy Is Clamped on Trial of Grow in Stolen Diary Case," 24 July 1952.

Winchell, Walter. " . . . of New York. Man about Town," 17 Mar. 1952.

Worker. "Soon to End Sub Drive on Press Parley Date." 16 Mar. 1952.

DISSERTATION

Fedele, Frank. "The Evolution of the Court-Martial System and the Role of the United States Court of Military Appeals in Military Law." J.S.D. dissertation, George Washington Univ. Law School, 1954.

INDEX

Abrams, Creighton, 103
Acheson, Dean, 26, 27
Alexander, John, 74
Allen, George V., 15, 16, 57
American Mercury, 59
America's Army in Crisis: A Study in Civil-Military Relations. See Hauser, William L.
Anderson, John B., 142, 150
Andrus, Clift, 152, 166
Ansell, Samuel T., 173–74, 177, 180, 192
Appeals of verdict in court-martial of Grow, 182–91
Army, 4, 196
Army-Navy-Air Force Journal, 163
Atlantic, 4
Atlantic Monthly, 176
Auf dem Kriegspfad, 7, 11, 21–39, 92, 99; authenticity of, challenged by Grow, 55; authenticity of, implied by U.S. Army, 40–44, 60, 79, 100, 104, 114, 151, 184; evidence in court-martial, 108; review of, 58; sales of, 63–64, 164; in Soviet press, 100; in U.S. press, 40–41, 81, 100, 104, 131; translated into Russian, 48

Baldwin, Hanson W., 56–58, 60
Barbour, Walworth, 38
Bard, C. Robert, 63, 97, 103, 142, 145, 150; nominal accuser of Grow,

107–10, 117, 121–22, 135, 137, 146, 147, 148–49; testimony of, in pretrial investigation of Grow, 121–22, 132, 144
Bard, Gustav, 63, 109
Barr, David G., 154
Berliner Zeitung, 11, 25, 30, 34
Bess, Demaree, 142, 163, 184–85
Board of Governors of the 6th Armored Division Association, 142
Board of Military Review, 183
Bogert, George Gleason, 173–74
Boggs, J. Caleb, 154
Bogue, Joy R., 122
Bolling, Alexander R., 95, 125, 133, 148, 156, 188; career of, 114–15, 186; conferences in office of, regarding charges against Grow, 62–63, 127; Counter Intelligence Corps report on theft of diary received by, 85, 89–91, 183; evaluation of Grow, 18–19, 26, 56–57, 130; failure to counter diary propaganda, 45–46; failure to testify at court-martial of Grow, 143–44, 146–47, 149, 150–51, 169, 181, 190–91; management of charges against Grow, 47, 51–53, 62, 108–12, 116–20, 153, 185; reaction to diary publicity in German press, 27, 28–30, 92; recommendation against court-martial of Grow, 37–38, 69–70; recommendation to prefer charges against Grow, 145;

244

COLD WAR CASUALTY
was composed in 10½/13 Bembo
on a Xyvision system with Linotronic output
by BookMasters, Inc.;
printed by sheet-fed offset on 60-pound acid-free
Glatfelter Natural Smooth stock,
Smyth sewn and bound over binder's boards
in Holliston Kingston Natural cloth,
wrapped with dustjackets printed in two colors
on 80-pound enamel stock finished with film lamination
by Braun-Brumfield, Inc.;
designed by Diana Gordy;
and published by
The Kent State University Press
KENT, OHIO 44242